University Life in
Eighteenth-Century
Oxford

University Life in Eighteenth-Century Oxford

Graham Midgley

Yale University Press
New Haven and London

Set in Goudy by Fakenham Photosetting, Norfolk.
Printed and bound in Great Britain by Biddles Ltd, Guildford and Kings Lynn.

Library of Congress Cataloging-in-Publication Data
Midgley, Graham.
    University life in eighteenth-century Oxford/Graham Midgley.
    Includes bibliographical references (pp. 160–72) and index.
    ISBN 0–300–06813–1 (c: alk. paper)
    1. University of Oxford – Students – History – 18th century.
  2. College students – England – Oxford – Conduct of life – History – 18th century. I. Title.
  LF516.M53   1996   96–19288
  378.42'57 – dc20   CIP

A catalogue record for this book is available from the British Library.

10 9 8 7 6 5 4 3 2 1

For
Rebecca, Alex and Katie

Beneath those domes in Gothic grandeur grey
Where rears that spire its old fantastic crest,
Snug in their mouldy cells from day to day
Like bottled wasps the Sons of Science rest

Contents

Illustration Acknowledgements

The Ashmolean Museum, Oxford, Dept. of Prints and Drawings: plates 6, 8, 17, 18, 22, 24, 30 (964 (53), Almanack 1807, Almanack 1767, 919 (8), Almanack 1779, Almanack 1798, Almanack 1773, 960)

The Bodleian Library, Oxford, Dept. of Western Manuscripts: plates 2, 3, 4, 5, 36 (Ms Top. Oxon c. 16. Nos 21–4, 45, Fol. 65); Dept. of Western Books: plates 1 (170. n. 176. p. 216), 9, 14, 15, 16 (GA. Oxon 4° 312 pp. 193, 30, 45, 15), 10 (GA. Oxon. h. 109. b. p. 76), 20 (GA. Oxon. a. 64. p. 98), 21 (GA. Oxon. h. 109. b. p. 241), 23 (GA. Oxon. a. 64. p. 78), 25, 26 (GA. fol. B33. pp. 55, 24), 27 (GA. Oxon. 4° 312. p. 133), 28 (170. n. 177. p. 213), 29 (2/1355. p. 156), 31 (Don. c. 27. p. 123), 37 (GA. Oxon. b. 109(a)), 38 (GA. Oxon. a. 64. p. 26), 39 (GA. Oxon. a. 73 p. 11. no. 20)

The British Museum, London, Dept. of Prints and Drawings: plates 7, 32, 33, 34, 40, 41 (D. George: *Catalogue of Political and Social Satirical Prints*, nos 4727, 7447, 4250, 5802, 6857, 6856)

Private collection, photographs from the Courtauld Institute of Art, London: plates 11, 12, 13, 19, 35

Foreword

Professor Lawrence Stone, looking at many periods in the history of the University of Oxford, named the eighteenth century 'The Great Depression'.[1] He found the story of the university in this period 'an uninspiring one, even if a few learned dons were making important advances in pure scholarship, and even if a few colleges were maintaining respectable standards of teaching'.[2] Even as early as 1685 Anthony à Wood found the town 'very dead for want of scholars'[3] and a French visitor some forty years later recorded that the Oxford dons 's'endorment dans l'abondance ... il y a tres-peu qui s'appliquent a l'étude. Les bons livres qui viennent d'Angleterre sortent rarement d'Oxford.'[4]

There were, of course, those exceptions which Professor Stone admits, and recent historians of the university have tended to stress more their number and importance. L.G. Mitchell asserts that 'Oxford was therefore not the moribund institution that its critics depicted, even if it fell short of the high standards claimed by its apologists. Then, as always, the reformer and the traditionalist, the conscientious and the less than conscientious, the religiously inclined and the secular-minded all jostled one another in the High and the Broad.'[5]

Learned and industrious scholars, too, lived and jostled alongside their more idle and sleepy colleagues, producing throughout the century many notable works of research and scholarship. The beginning of the century saw George Hickes's *Linguarum veterum septrionalium thesaurus grammatico-criticus et archaeologicus* in 1703–5. Literary scholarship established itself alongside classical study in such works as Joseph Warton's *Essay on the Writings and Genius of Pope* in 1756, in Thomas Warton's *Observations on the Faerie Queene of Spenser* in 1754 and his magisterial *History of English Poetry* in three volumes which appeared from 1774 to 1781. Robert Lowth's lectures of 1753, 'De Sacra Poesi Hebraeorum' were translated and published as *Lectures on the Sacred Poetry of the Hebrews*, to become one of the influences on the changing emphases of the poetry of the closing decades of the century. Anglo-Saxon studies were flourishing at the beginning of the century, while

Humfrey Wanley studied and catalogued the Anglo-Saxon manuscripts in the Bodleian Library, and Thomas Hearne indefatigably studied and preserved antiquities and produced many learned editions of texts of chronicles and ancient writings.[6]

The other great part of the university, the undergraduate body, could from some points of view be seen as part of Stone's 'Great Depression'. It was numerically in decline. In 1759 only 182 freshmen were admitted, undergraduate numbers then reaching their lowest in the four hundred years from 1500 to 1900. Many colleges were, at times, half empty, with the notable exception of Christ Church where the noble and gentlemen commoners tended to gather, so avoiding any dangerous effect on their manners which close social contact with the lower orders in other colleges might occasion. It was a socially diverse society, despite the falling numbers of the nobility and members of the upper reaches of the affluent and landed gentry at one end of the scale, and the diminishing numbers of the sons of the poor whose chance of a servitor's place to work their way through college was lessened by rising costs and the increased employment of full-time college servants. It was a young society – the average age at matriculation being just over eighteen – and regionally diverse. Every quarter of the land sent its quota of young students. For a good part of the century men from Wales represented 15 per cent of the student body, forming 75 per cent of the undergraduates of Jesus College. Other colleges had other regional preferences or connections, 70 per cent of Exeter College men coming from Devon and Cornwall, some 50 per cent at Queen's College from the north, Cumberland, Westmorland and Yorkshire, and 30 per cent of Wadham men from Dorset and Somerset.[7]

This undergraduate body, as that of its elders and rulers, found its severe critics in the world outside. As the censorious eye found only idleness and sloth in the unproductive dons, it condemned the life of the undergraduates as a squalid mixture of laziness, waste and vice. 'In no places of education,' wrote Vicesimus Knox in 1781, 'are men more extravagant; in none do they learn to drink sooner; in none do they more effectively shake off the firm sensibilities of shame and learn to glory in debauchery; in none do they learn more extravagantly to dissipate their fortunes.'[8]

It is not, however, the purpose of this book to adjudicate between Professor Stone's 'Great Depression' and the defendants of the university's far from moribund state. Rather its interest is in the details of the rich social life which was enjoyed not only by those unproductive drones who 's'endorment dans l'abondance' but was shared by their scholarly and industrious colleagues when they left their libraries and closed the books in their studies. The following chapters attempt, without passing judgment or censure, to build up a picture of this social life of the old as well as the young, finding there much to watch with interest, surprise and amusement, and even perhaps a little envy, a life which was full of zest, variety and sometimes violence, but seldom solemn or dull.

CHAPTER ONE

Hierarchy and Rank: the Social Structure

This small and varied community, a powerful, rich and influential city within a city, was organized and governed as an hierarchical state, a hierarchy which ordained privileges and freedoms, disciplines and inhibitions, even social intercourse and the making of friendships, and at its worst spawned a sub-society of flatterers seeking to climb the social ladder, or of privileged louts secure in their idleness and dissipation.

At the very top of the pyramid, with the Vice-Chancellor chosen from among their number, were the Heads of Houses, privileged not only to rule their colleges, but to have a wife who might or might not bear children and enjoy a powerful rule behind the scenes. Gathered in Council, jocularly referred to as Golgotha, they issued edicts for the discipline and order of the university – and sometimes the city – and, separately in their own colleges, led the Fellows, all Masters of Arts and mostly ordained clerics of the Church of England, in decisions concerning the wealth, buildings, discipline and the disposition of the clerical livings in their gift. Their social life, the life of high table and senior common room, their involvement in the wider social life of the town and the countryside, was no less varied and rich than that of the lower degrees of the hierarchy, though possibly lacking in the excitement and danger of the youngsters below the proctor-protecting degree of Master of Arts.

On the top rung of this ladder stood the noblemen, a comparatively small group in the university. Their privileges were many and their obligations few. They dined at high table with the dons and were admitted to the senior common room. They were excused any supervision by a tutor and the work or examination he might have set them, nor did they need to take a degree or present themselves for the university exercises which qualified a man for his degree, formal and scandalously lax as those exercises were. Their days could be filled with the pursuits they loved, dinner parties in their superior sets of rooms, drinking, and – as they were exempted in the *Statutum de reprimendis sumptibus non Academicis* from the prohibition against keeping

I

servants, horses and dogs – riding and hunting.[1] Such lack of work and discipline often led these privileged youngsters into excess and debauchery, a danger lamented by a correspondent to the *Gentleman's Magazine* in 1758:

> The higher a young man's rank is, the more he is suffered to be idle and vicious in our universities, an evil which arises partly from the fondness and vanity of parents ... partly from the conduct of tutors who make their court to idle sons and weak mothers, in proportion as they suffer their wealthy pupils to live and return laden with ignorance and vice. ...[2]

Thomas Hearne, outraged at the association of the young Duke of Beaufort of University College with his drunken tutor, 'that vicious loose Fellow, Mr. Ward'[3] put the blame on those same tutors, believing that 'so much Atheism, Deism, Debauchery and all kinds of Immorality for which the young men are blamed, whereas the Fault lyes in the Govenours & Tutors'.[4] But these young noblemen, with too much money and leisure, were by no means alone in their misuse of privilege and freedom.

One step below them in the hierarchy came the gentlemen commoners, almost equally privileged and more notorious for misbehaviour and wildness than their noble and less numerous superiors. The sons of country gentlemen or successful merchants and professional men, they arrived with full purses and ample allowance, able to sustain in their new surroundings a style of living to which they believed themselves entitled, hunting, shooting, fishing, drinking and gambling. A gentleman commoner of Merton recalled that in his day 'they were under no restraint, and never called upon to attend either lectures, or chapel, or hall'.[5] Gibbon, on his matriculation as a gentleman commoner at Magdalen, settled into his elegant set of rooms, on a generous allowance and unlimited credit, and was admitted to the senior common room – which he found irredeemably stagnant and boring – for, as he remembered, 'our velvet cap was the cap of liberty'.[6] That velvet cap and silken gown inspire a later satirist who

> Points to the *Velvet Cap*, whose Power
> Exempts from Care the frolic Hour – ...
> There gives, as TRIUMPH lights her Face,
> The *Silken Gown* its *Fringed Grace*,
> And bids it rustle in the Breeze
> A Sanction to the Sons of Ease!
> And still, with supercilious Air,
> The *tufted* Cap of FOLLY wear.[7]

Brasenose College, sensitive to the especial threat of this liberty and privilege, attempted to curb both, expelling the gentlemen commoners from their special seats in chapel – no doubt infrequently filled, abolishing their right to be members of the senior common room, and no longer allowing them to house their private servants in the college garrets.[8] The general picture, however, remains very much that described by a correspondent in the *Gentleman's Magazine* in a fierce attack particularly on this rank of the hierarchy, and in general on the ruinous effect of 'the irresistible influx of commercial wealth' on the nation and its youth:

> Universities may rue the contagion. They were soon irrecoverably infected . . . the emulation of literature was gradually superseded by the emulation of profligate extravagance; till a *third* order of pupils appeared; a pert and pampered race, too froward for control, too headstrong for persuasion, too independent for chastisement; privileged prodigals. These are the *gentlemen commoners* of Oxford. They are perfectly their own masters, and they take the lead in every disgraceful frolic of juvenile debauchery.[9]

Below these miscreants came the large body of commoners and, at their head, the scholars of their colleges. These young men, though in no way innocent of frolic and juvenile high spirits, were undoubtedly under discipline and tutorial supervision. Each had his assigned tutor and was required to attend his lectures or classes; to write impositions for absence; to attend chapel regularly or receive similar punishment; to eat his dinners in Hall; to be in college at the time laid down; not to leave Oxford without his tutor's permission. And every edict and regulation forbidding the possession of certain objects, attending at various places or wearing certain clothing, applied to them without exception or privilege. In college their tutors and the Dean were their fear; on the streets the Proctors were their terror, who patrolled those streets and the taverns each night to surprise and apprehend the unwary reveller in forbidden haunts or at forbidden hours:

> Ah soon – too soon – his Sight aggrieve
> The Terrors of the *Velvet Sleeve*; –
> The frown-clad Personage appears –
> Anathemas affront his Ears!
> And lo the Fury RUSTICATION
> Threatens the Loss of Reputation![10]

One other spectre haunted the commoner's life more frighteningly than that of his superiors, the spectre of debt. For, with much more slender means from much poorer parents and yet an inability to control the expense of his necessities and pleasures, he availed himself of the credit too easily offered by the tradesmen and innkeepers of the town, with the inevitable consequences of pursuit by and the avoidance of omnipresent duns:

> O *Ticking*, what a Train of Woes,
> Sudden, thy lavish Favors close;
> Yet thoughtless *Gownsmen*, by thy Care,

> Breathe freely academic Air;
> By thee display, though penniless,
> The Kick in fashionable Dress;
> And quaff the sparkling Bowl by thee,
> In all the Roar of social Glee![11]

Ticking, debt and duns come to form a notable part of the life and literature of the eighteenth-century commoner, With his money not plentiful and that little controlled by his tutor, not even college cuts by bursars or Vice-Chancellors' edicts forbidding tradesmen to grant over 5 shillings credit[12] could prevent undergraduates from obtaining their desires and promising to pay later. It was a way of life easily and quickly learned. Woodforde, as an undergraduate, had wine and punch 'upon tick being the first time' and soon 'Had two cravats from Austins upon tick'.[13] Another Oxford scholar confessed that 'As I was of a gay and lively Disposition, my Companions were of the same Cast, and I was soon installed into the social pleasures of the Bottle; and not caring at every turn to go to my Tutor for Money, I was very early showed into the Method of running in Debt.'[14] At the tavern drinks could be chalked up on the slate or door, as Thomas Warton, who ought to have known better, celebrates:

> Nor reckoning, name tremendous, me disturbs,
> Nor, call'd for, chills my breast with sudden fear;
> While on the wonted door, expressive mark,
> The frequent penny stands describ'd to view,
> In snowy characters and graceful row. –
> Hail TICKING! surest guardian of distress!
> Beneath thy shelter, pennyless I quaff
> The cheerful cup. . . . [15]

Even mundane necessities like ink and hairpowder help to increase the debts mainly grounded on drink and tobacco:

> For *Gown*, and *Cap*, for *Drink*, and Smoke,
> And so much more for *Ink*, and *Chalk*;
> Five pound a *Coat* . . . *Ink* Five more. . . . Ten,
> Six *Bottles* – *Chalk* as much again;
> A *Glass* broke, *Sixpence* . . . . So much more,
> Because 'twas put upon the *Score*.
> And at this rate the *Coxcombs* run
> Their *Dad*dis out of *House* and *Home*.[16]

Indeed, the daddies and mummies were often the first recipients of cries for commoners' help. 'You must know that I have been foolishly extravagant of late', wrote a young commoner of Christ Church. He admitted wine, a music

1 A college scene: asking Papa for a further allowance

party, piano lessons, painted glass and some prints among his excesses and acknowledged 'that wine, books, shoes and a long &c. which I owe, came to near thirty pounds'. Two years later, he had not yet learnt his lesson and had become less shamefaced. 'Twenty pounds, I am sure, will do; and if you double that sum you will be near the amount of my other debts.'[17]

For those without indulgent and wealthy parents, another fate awaited – the siege and oppression of the duns, within college and about the town. At the improvident commoner's door the debt-gatherers are vociferous:

> With Sir, *you know you owe me, for*
> Maintaining of *your Spotted Cur.*
> I'm sure, I bought him as good *Meat,*
> As any *Christian*, Sir, *could eat.* ...
> Here was his *Shoe-maker*, and *Taylor,*
> His fiery *Hostess*, Mrs Rayler;
> And *Drawers* shaking off their *Noddles*
> For losing of their *Wine* and *Bottles.*[18]

One way to deal with the difficulty was the high-handed defiance one young spark describes when 'a Dun came, told him I should have some money soon – would not be gone – offered him brandy – was sulky and would not have any – saw he was going to be *savage*, so kicked him downstairs to prevent his being impertinent'.[19] The other way was to remain locked in one's rooms during the danger period and only venture forth when one hoped the coast was clear:

> Always when once 'tis Afternoon,
> *Duns* with the *Colleges* have done;
> And Scholars *looking well about*
> With caution, venture to go out.[20]

No such circumspection or fear was needed by the young student who celebrates in verse the pleasure of being out of debt in town and college:

> The man, who not a farthing owes,
> Looks down with scornful eye on those,
>   Who rise by fraud and cunning;
> Tho' in the *Pig-market* he stand
> With aspect grave and clear-starch'd band,
>   He fears no tradesman's dunning.
>
> He pauses by each shop in town
> Nor hides his face beneath his gown,
>   No dread his heart invading;
> He quaffs the nectar of the *Tuns*
> Or on a spur-gall'd Hackney runs
>   To *London* masquerading.
>
> What joy attends a new-paid debt!
> Our *Manciple* I lately met
>   Of visage wise and prudent;
> I on the nail my *Battels* paid,
> The Monster turn'd away dismay'd.
>   Hear this, each *Oxford Student!*[21]

No such pride or fear attended the life of the lowest member at the bottom of this social pyramid – the servitor. A poor boy, often the son of poor parents or at least parents of narrow means, he was admitted to college and the privilege of studying and hearing lectures, supervised by a tutor and supported by a small termly allowance and free board and tuition, in exchange for varied college duties in Hall and in attendance on his superior undergraduates. From them he might obtain extra payments for special services and manage to work his way through college, gain his degree and move on to service in the Church or the professions. The eighteenth century saw, as we have said, a diminution in the ranks of servitors, but during that century the value or the scandal of their status was often discussed, and round them a rather romantic Cinderella-like picture of their hardships and sufferings was created by the poets, who found them in many ways a more picturesque subject matter than their superiors.

In the early years of the century George Fothergill, a poor boy from Ravonstondale, wrote home to tell his parents of his duties as a servitor at Queen's, and his pleasure at being admitted to that status 'by the intercession of my very kind tutor'.

> I cannot tell well how to give you a notion of what we Servitors do. We are seven of us, and we wait upon the Batchelors, Gent. Commoners, and Commoners at meals. We carry in their Commons out of the Kitchen into the Hall, and their bread and beer out of the Buttery. I call up one Gent. Commoner, which is ten shillings a quarter when he's in town, and three Commoners, which are five shillings each, on the same conditions. My Servitor's place saves me, I believe, about thirty shillings a quarter in battles, one quarter with another.[22]

George Whitefield was matriculated at Pembroke in 1732, as a servitor, and in his memoirs recorded his success in that station. He had been a drawer in his father's inn, the Bell at Gloucester, was used to service, and 'by my diligent and ready attendance I ingratiated myself into the gentlemen's favour so far, that many, who had it in their power, chose me to be their servitor'. The only duty he disliked was having to climb dark staircases at 10 o'clock each night to knock on his gentlemen's doors and check whether they were in college. 'I thought the devil would appear to me every stair I went up,' he confesses. It was a duty which might well have provoked a more mundane terror, for possibly an undergraduate behind some door

> to be revenged for being disturbed when he was as profitably employed as perhaps he could be, would join with others of the young men of the college in hunting, as they called it, the servitor, who was thus diligent in his duty; and this they did with the noise of pots and candlesticks, singing to the tune of Chevy-chace, the words of that old ballad, To drive the deer with hound and horn &c., not seldom to the endangering the life and limb of the unfortunate victim.[23]

Whitefield adds that he did so well on his wages and little presents from his tutor, that he almost paid his way, only asking his relatives, over the three years, for £24.[24] William Shenstone, also of Pembroke College, noted that the servitors there received from their superiors 'six-pence a week, not as an act of generosity, but as a tribute imposed on [them] by the standing rules of the society'.[25] If Dr Newton's proposals for new statutes for Hertford College had come into effect, the four servitors of that college would have had quite onerous duties – keeping the gate, waiting at table, ringing the bell for chapel and meals, lighting the candles in chapel, turning up the lessons of the day in chapel, reporting absentees, reporting the sick, and running any errands for the Principal or the tutors. For all this each would have received 1 penny a week from every member of the society present or absent.[26]

Further additions to a servitor's income came from writing out impositions for their erring gentlemen, and even doing some teaching. Dr Johnson told his friend Strahan when his son went up to University College: 'for Greek he must get some private assistance, which a servitour of the College is very well qualified, and will be willing to afford him on very easy terms.'[27] There was some truth behind the satirical character of Chum, the servitor of Brasenose in the comedy *An Act at Oxford*, when he announces that his 'Business is to wait upon Gentlemen Commoners, to dress 'em, pimp for 'em, clean their Shoes, and make their Exercises; and the difference, Sir, between Servitors and Gentlemen Commoners, is this, we are Men of Wit and no Fortune, and they are Men of Fortune and no Wit.'[28]

Opinions in the century on the value and the rightness of this inferior social rank of men of wit and no fortune varied greatly. Dr Johnson admitted the usefulness of this economic way to a university education by encouraging the minister of Cawdor to 'send their boy to him when he was ready for university, he would get him made a servitor and perhaps would do more for him. He could not promise to do more, but would undertake for the servitorship'.[29] The young Macanlay, through Johnson's interest with Dr Adams, the Master of Pembroke, later matriculated servitor, and made good the promise. On the other hand, Hawkins comments on Johnson's belief that the serving at meals was disgraceful, and 'that the scholar's, like the Christian life, levelled all distinctions of rank and worldly pre-eminence'.[30] A full-blooded attack on the rank was published in the *Gentleman's Magazine* in 1787 denouncing

> such distinctions as are certainly a disgrace to this liberal and enlightened age. I can see no advantage in degrading a young man in his own eyes because of his poverty, when in after-life he is to be regarded as a gentleman. ... It were to be wished that Oxford would ... make the situation of the *servitor* as comfortable (by changing the term &c.) or entirely abolish the order. At present it serves only to depress the mind of those who from a want of fortune are precluded those benefits which their acquirements and behaviour give them a just title to, and to inspire a contempt of, perhaps their superiors in virtue and knowledge, the fortunate sons of upstart wealth.[31]

The forbidding of social acquaintance and friendship between youngsters of different ranks must have been an additional burden to the servitor. That distinguished commoner of Pembroke, William Shenstone, 'had one ingenious and much-valued friend in Oxford, Mr. Jago, his school-fellow, whom he could only visit in private, as he wore a servitor's gown: it being then deemed a great disparagement for a commoner to appear in public with one in that situation'.[32] Dr Newton of Hertford, however, thought it quite natural to include in his proposed college statutes a clause insisting 'That no Person of a *Superior Degree* admit into his Company Those of an Inferior, unless with a View of Countenance and Improvement of them.'[33]

The picture is neither clear nor simple. Some servitors, we discover, were neither downtrodden nor depressed. We read of one young man of Jesus College, the nephew of the Principal, Dr Hoare, who was entered servitor there 'in order to render the young man more studious than he might have otherwise been, but the purpose was not answered' and the reason for that failure is far from those the earlier correspondent in the *Gentleman's Magazine* put forward: 'for Master Lewis, being more than commonly handsome and shewy, and not bookishly inclined exhibited his well-dressed person among the multitudinous sect of peripatetics, alias loungers in the streets and charming public walks, full as much as he could have done, if his cap and gown had not been plain.'[34] Nor could the lad, a servitor of Exeter College, have been entirely downtrodden, who had found funds and time to have been drinking all afternoon, and fallen on the spikes as he tried to climb out of college after 10 o'clock at night.[35]

Moreover there were not lacking servitors who succeeded, after their alleged life of subservience and degradation, in attaining rank and respectability. Whitefield himself, that servitor with 'unpowdered hair, woollen gloves, patched gown and dirty shoes',[36] became a great figure and voice in the Evangelical movement of the century; George Fothergill of Queen's was elected Fellow of his college and became Principal of St Edmund Hall; Robinson, a former ploughman, servitor of Oriel, became Bishop of Bristol and subsequently of London; Birkenhead of Oriel rose to be Sir John Birkenhead; and Samuel Wesley, servitor of Exeter, fathered two famous sons. Such a rank, however humble, could not be entirely condemned when it gave such chances of learning and promotion to the ploughman, the tapster and the clever sons of husbandmen. Its disappearance by the middle of the next century closed the doors of Oxford against many a Jude of later years.

Even so, the figure of the servitor appears in fiction and verse with only his poverty emphasized by satire, or romanticized by a sentimental sympathy for these suffering but enduring Cinderellas. The first decade of the century provides the most extensive example of the first in *The Servitour: A Poem*, which alleges that it was written by a servitor of the University of Oxford 'and Faithfully taken from his Own original'. The hero of the poem, after a good record at his free school, is sent to Oxford by his poor but ambitious father:

> By Carrier then, the lumpish Drone
> Is brought to *Oxford*, puts on Gown:

and becomes the creature who appears to the poet:

> When to my wond'ring Eye appear'd,
> Emerging from a Skittle-Yard,
> An o'er grown looby, with Arms dangling,
> And Pendant Noddle like a Changling:
> With Cap in form of Cow-Turd stinking,
> Like Cheesy-Pouch of Shon-ap-Shenking.

He stands in ragged and filthy clothes, a threadbare gown and dishevelled bands:

> A thousand like him you may see
> About the University.
> What! don't you know a Servitour?
> A Servitour, said I! I'll swear
> I took him for some Natural,
> Or Idiot, from an Hospital.[37]

He lives, half starving, in the midst of the good food he has to carry to table:

> Bout Dinner-time down comes the Lubber,
> When Belly (hungry Dog) cries Cubbord,
> To get a Mess of Broth i' th' Kitchin,
> Where he sees Dainties so bewitching,
> As Turkies, Capons, Ribs of Beef,
> No wonder if he plays the Thief ...
> Poor Scraps, and Cold, as I'm a Sinner,
> Being all that he can get for Dinner. ...

The poem reaches its climax in an Hogarthian description of the quarters in the college garrets which he and his three companions inhabit:

> A Room with Dirt, and Cobwebs lin'd
> Which here and there with Spittle shin'd;
> Inhabited, let's see – by Four;
> If I mistake not, 'twas no more.
> Two Buggy-beds had ne'er a Curtain,
> And but one Chamber-Pot to Squirt in.
> Their Dormer Windows with Brown-paper,
> Was patch'd to keep out Northern Vapour.
> The Tables broken Foot stood on
> An Old Schrevelidus Lexicon.
> Here lay together, Authors various,
> From Homer's *Iliads*, to *Cordelius*:
> And so abus'd was *Aristotle*,

> He only serv'd to stop a Bottle,
> Or light a Pipe, of which were many,
> On Chimney-piece, instead of Cheney;
> Where else stood Glass, Dark Lanthorns ancient,
> Fragments of Mirror, Pen-Knife, Trencher,
> And forty things which I can't mention.
> Old Chairs and Stools, and such-like Lumber,
> Compleatly furnish'd out the Chamber.[38]

Nearly eighty years later the servitor is still an important character in *Cursory Sketches on a University Education*, but the portrait is gentler and more sympathetic:

> Yet the poor *Servitor* whose Mind
> Droops in its narrow Cell confin'd,
> By no wild wishes taught to stray,
> Preserves the Tenor of his Way.
> How oft o'er Pots of Beer he smiles,
> The bright Reward of all his Toils,
> And cheers his Soul with golden Dreams
> Of Declamations, and of Themes:
> – Tho' Minister of Tarts and Cheese,
> With Joy he contemplates the Fees,
> And in his Purse, for all his Pains
> A *splendid Shilling* still retains:
> To his fond Hopes indulgent Heaven
> Perhaps a Chaplainship has given.[39]

Shades of Gray are falling about a forerunner of the Scholar Gypsy.

This social hierarchy had its outward and physical manifestation in the various academic dress prescribed by statute for these ranks. Gowns were a compulsory vesture in college and on the streets, and to appear ungowned or uncapped exposed the offender to proctorial arrest and punishment. It was therefore impossible to conceal by good behaviour or brilliance the lowliness of one's rank, or one's nobility and eminence by stupidity and oafishness. To the freshman these marks of rank were at first confusing but had to be learnt:

> But weak my efforts to describe
> The dress of all the motley tribe;
> Such nice distinctions one perceives
> In cut of gowns, and hoods and sleeves,
> Marking degrees, or style, or station. . . .[40]

Pre-eminent in splendour, the nobleman wore a full gown of silk of various

2   A noble graduate in full dress   3   A gentleman-commoner

colours as his taste dictated, adorned at the yoke, on the sleeves and at the hem with bands and medallions of gold lace. His velvet cap was made splendid above all caps by a gold tassel, which not only, even when he walked abroad in his darker undress gown, announced his rank, but attracted to him a race of fawners and parasites, the 'tuft-hunters' of the university, who figure frequently in the satirical comments of the time. One such effusion adores Lord Rubbish and this golden badge of distinction:

> A gay golden tuft on his cap he displays,
> Which dazzles all eyes with its ravishing rays –
> True badge of nobility, awful and grand,
> Confin'd to the essence and cream of the land ...
> How I love to adore thee with honours divine,
> To court thy bright favour, and bask in thy shine.[41]

We read much of the college Smart who 'affects great Company, and scrapes Acquaintance with *Golden Tufts* and *Brocaded Gowns*'.[42] For those affected by this social pursuit of tuft-hunting, advice on drawing the coverts is given: 'Livery-stables and Billiard rooms in the fore-noon, and Port Meadow and the High Street of an evening, are usually esteemed the likeliest places ... for game of this kind.'[43] Perhaps these noble persons were not entirely averse to the presence and possible usefulness of this flattering

4   A commoner   5   A servitor

fringe. The noble lord here is fictional, but his attributed thoughts not wholly untrue:

> His Lordship was too conscious of the intrinsick merit of his title, not to be surrounded by these vile academical parasites, call'd *tuft-hunters*: the younger ones would drink, game, intrigue, take schemes, or do anything with my Lord – at his Lordship's expence: even the old senior Fellows (who, forgetting their mushroom rise and native dunghills, lord it over their juniors) would cringe, and fawn, and stoop to the meanest offices, for the sake of a present dinner, or the prospect of future preferment.[44]

No wonder that a young man of Christ Church, the college of most of these golden tufts, wrote to his mother expressing grave doubts about the rightness of sending a younger brother to follow him: 'But with all his good sense,' he wrote, 'I fear he will be spoilt here; for 'tis scarcely in human nature to resist the foolish forms of respect to nobility which the college rules prescribe, or the crowd of flatterers which infest a golden tassel and a silk gown.'[45]

Gentlemen commoners, without the golden tuft, but with a black tuft to their velvet caps, and a silk gown adorned on the sleeves and in large panels around the hem with black tufted tassels – a rather fine creation – were conspicuously superior as they walked the town. Then came the commoners, gowned in a simple garment of black stuff, ankle-length, without sleeves but with streamers from each side of the yoke, the streamers decorated with three bands of ruched black braid, and a cap without a tassel. Young John Skinner of Trinity describes his commoner's garb:

> Behind our Gowns (black Bombazeen)
> Are sew'd two leading strings, I ween
> To teach young Students in their course
> They still have need of learning's nurse. ...'[46]

Plainest of all, the servitors wore a black stuff gown of the same pattern as the commoners', but without the distinguishing streamers, and instead of the square academic cap, they wore the round hat which Hearne describes as 'Thrum Capps or Bonnetts' but which, as we have seen, their detractors likened to cow-pats.[47]

These various garbs and the distinctions they marked were valued and considered of serious importance as part of the framework holding together the academic society in a safe and disciplined structure. No senior member of the university could have considered as anything but dangerous heresy Colley Cibber's outburst, in the character of Lampoon: 'I hate your odious gowns like so many Daggle-tail Questmen, and your filthy square Caps that serve only to teach one to squint.'[48] Violations of their use, far from being sartorial peccadilloes, were blows against the right and God-given hierarchy. As early as 1730 Hearne perceived a dangerous lack of obedience and humility in the ranks of the servitors, whom he found 'generally very haughty, and scorn to wear their proper habits, their gowns being not what properly belongs to Servitours ... and their Caps ... being what (when I came to Oxford) the Commoners wore'.[49] A worried advisor of a young gentleman just entered at the university hoped that his protégé would agree that 'In the short time you have been at college you already know enough to be shocked if a servitor should dare to be so irregular, as to put on a gentleman-commoner's cap; and never to think of putting a gold tassel on your own cap.'[50]

But unlike this young man, many others behaved like the servitors Hearne criticized, and not only servitors. Angry and prolonged debate about correct academic dress went on through the century, and came to a head in 1770 when

> the Servitors of Christ Church contrary to express statute and immemorial usage appeared in the academical habit of Foundationers. The Foundationers of several colleges, who had hitherto conformed to their statutable habit, were justly offended at this singular innovation; and having lost the distinction which the statute had given them, naturally looked out for a new one in the habit of a Bachelor.[51]

A constitutional crisis developed when Council's demand that Statute Tit.

xiv, 'De Vestitu et Habitu Scholastico' should be enforced was opposed by a minority on Council, who carried a resolution allowing these innovations, only to be opposed by members of Congregation who in turn were opposed by the Proctors. The university hummed with discussion, and Heads of Houses added to the confusion by differing in opinions and varying in the permissions they granted. By the end of the summer term, after long debate, the matter was settled, and details of dress agreed. Above all, the hated round hat of the servitor gave place to a square without a tassel, a triumph for the liberals who had insisted that 'the cap is a mark of Servility which it is illiberal to continue: the wearer does not appear like a Gentleman; Humanity pleads against the statute'.[52] The dress and headgear of the scholars and commoners were settled, and accurate drawings of the vesture of every rank were made and deposited for future reference in the university Chest.

Today it might appear strange that the time and tempers of the whole university should be concentrated on such details of costume, until we remind ourselves again that these caps and gowns were truly the outward signs of that recognized hierarchy which the conservative majority saw as necessary for the peace and stability of their society. An old member of the university put it simply in a letter to the *Gentleman's Magazine* at the end of the century:

> The Gentlemen-Commoners at Oxford, and the fellow-commoners at Cambridge, wear silk gowns; the nobility gold ones; as is surely *highly* fit; I being *no* democrat, but having myself worn a silk gown, as did my eldest son. Nothing *so* beneficial in a *wise* state as properly keeping up the distinction of different ranks in society.[53]

Hawkins, Dr Johnson's biographer, expressed the same view but less elegantly when, disapproving of Johnson's more liberal attitude to servitors, he asserted that 'long before his coming into the world [civil policy had] reduced the several classes of men to a regular subordination, and given servitude its sanction'.[54] Such men and those many worried Heads of Houses, sensing dangerous forces at work behind these quarrels over tufts and tassels and square caps, would have applauded the words of a greater conservative:

> O, when degree is shaked,
> Which is the ladder to all high designs,
> The enterprise is sick. . . .
> Take but degree away, untune that string,
> And hark what discord follows.[55]

CHAPTER TWO

Arriving and Settling In

Into this society the young freshmen arrived, apprehensive, excited, frightened, ignorant, with a new world before them and few to be their guide, once their proud fathers had left them at their college and taken the coach for home. Some perhaps, though one suspects but a few, came over the brow of Shotover, or along the roads from the north and west, with the romantic wonder at the beauty of Oxford and its scholarly ideals, which Alexander Pope felt when in the autumn of 1717 he wrote to his friends Teresa and Martha Blount of Mapledurham, describing his arrival for a short stay in Oxford:

> About a mile before I reached Oxford, all the Night bells toll'd, in different notes; the Clocks of every College answered one another; and told me in a deeper, some in a softer voice, that it was eleven a clock. All this was no ill preparation to the life I have led since; among these old walls, venerable Galleries, Stone Portico's, studious walks & solitary scenes of the University, I wanted nothing but a black Gown and a Salary, to be as meer a Bookworm as any there.[1]

But Pope, being a Papist, was excluded from the anxieties, fears and exhilaration of the young newcomers who were embarking on a residence longer than a short visit to a college friend.

Anxious fathers and relatives often accompanied them. When Jeffrey, later Lord Jeffrey and the great critic of the *Edinburgh Review*, came up, he was comforted not only by his father, but by his brother and a family friend, and when they left him, he 'felt a pang on his first entire loneliness'.[2] Samuel Johnson arrived in Oxford, and 'On that evening, his father, who had anxiously accompanied him, found means to have him introduced to Mr. Jorden, who was to be his tutor.'[3] The tutor was to be the first important acquaintance of the freshman, and in varying degrees, and for better or worse, would be the most intimate and continuing contact of the under-graduate with those who ruled above. His first visit was

6   Arriving at Oxford over Shotover Hill in floodtime

> To seek the mansion of a learned Sage,
> Y'cleped a Tutor,

who would take him to 'The mansion of a venerable Seer',[4] one of the pro-Vice-Chancellors, who would matriculate him, give him a copy of the statutes, and take his fees. From then on no rules governed the extent of the tutor's interest in or his influence over his young charge. Samuel Johnson thought that his tutor was 'a very worthy man, but a heavy man, and I did not profit much by his instructions', but he came to love and respect him for his paternal care. 'Whenever,' he said, 'a young man becomes Jorden's pupil, he becomes his son.' Recalling an occasion when he feared tutorial rebuke, he gives an account of this curious Oxford relationship:

> After dinner he sent for me to his room. I expected a sharp rebuke for my idleness, and went with a beating heart. When we were seated he told me he had sent for me to drink a glass of wine with him, and to tell me that he was *not* angry with me for missing his lecture ... some more of the boys were then sent for, and we spent a very pleasant afternoon.[5]

A Trinity father was more exercised about his son Owen's tutor's deficiencies in social propriety, for Owen had had 'an unpleasant entrée into Trinity, as

7   The hopes of the family: a university admission

his tutor did not properly introduce him. ... Poor Kett was much more attentive to Warren and myself when we entered, and invited some young men to meet us at dinner in his room, who introduced us properly to the Society.'[6]

The control of a young undergraduate's allowance was often another of the tutor's responsibilities, and as often resented as his other restrictive activities. One Oxford scholar recorded in his memoirs, 'My allowance was fixed at Eighty Pounds *per annum*, under the management of my Tutor; so that I found that what Money I was to have, was to come through his Hands. This did not please me, but I had no remedy. My Father staid 'till every Thing wanting was put in my Chamber. ...' Worse was to come. He asks his tutor leave to go to London, but he has no letter from his father to give him leave. 'Then, Sir,' says he, 'I cannot give you Leave; for I have particular Instructions from your Father not to let you lye a Night out of College, without his Orders.' But in the end frayed tempers and relationships were healed. 'When I had packed all up, I waited on my Tutor just before Supper to take my leave of him, and he very civilly, for the first Time, asked me to spend the Evening with him. Just at parting he gave me two Guineas, saying, He would examine the Buttery Book and if he found he had any Money left in his Hands, he would account with me for it at my return.'[7]

At the other extreme from this caring and on the whole sympathetic tutor is this monster, depicted by the admittedly bitter pen of *The Loiterer*, of a

newly appointed college tutor, reminiscent of many early appointed Junior
Deans:

> He enters on his office with more Zeal than Discretion, asserts his own
> opinions with arrogance and maintains them with obstinacy, calls *Contra-
> diction, Contumacy,* and *Reply, Pertness,* and deals out his *Jobations, Impositions,
> and Confinements,* to every ill-fated *Junior* who is daring enough to oppose his
> sentiments, or doubt his opinions. The consequence of this is perfectly
> natural, He treats his Pupils as Boys, and they think him a Brute.[8]

It was surely because of such abuse of responsibility that the Principal of Hart
Hall attempted, in the face of his opposing Heads of Houses, to lay down a
rational and humane scheme of tutorial duties, care and supervision. 'The
Tutor,' he wrote, 'also shall frequently Visit his Pupils in their Chambers:
shall direct them in the Proper Methods of Studying, that they may not
accustom themselves to a desultory, wandering, fruitless Application: shall
discourage them from reading light, vain, trifling, profane, and unprofitable
Books, both to the Loss of their Time, and of their innocence.' His tutors
would also oversee their pupils' financial arrangements, the traders they
should deal with, their debts, and the distribution of their quarterly
allowance from their parents.[9]

One important first demand on that quarterly allowance, unless a generous
parent had helped before he left his son, was the acquiring of the freshman's
gown, the badge of his belonging to the academic society and of his rank
therein. It was a moment of pride, both to the young man and his parent.
Jeremy Bentham's father paid out £1 12s. 6d. for his son's gown, and 7
shillings for his cap and tassel, before he left the unhappy twelve year old to
the care of his sour and gloomy tutor at Queen's. Others went shopping for
themselves. Young John James, before coming up to Queen's in 1778, hoping
to save money, bought a cap and gown in London but, when he arrived in
Oxford, he was told he would be hooted at if he wore them. 'The gown was
of a mungrel kind,' he wrote to his father. 'Neither commoners nor
gentleman commoners, strangely made and of bad stuff to boot. The cap was
too small both in crown and board.' He packed it off to his brother
demanding a refund and then, for two-thirds of the London price, equipped
himself anew, writing in triumph and pride, 'And now *eccum!* See me
strutting in my new robes, with my square cap and tassel.'[10] This was James's
first expense: for some it would be the first debt to the long-suffering tailors of
Oxford. In a little booklet of ironic advice printed for the bookseller Collicut
in Broad Street, the freshman would learn that 'Instinct will tell you not to
be guilty of such weakness as to pay the Taylor for your Cap and Gown, these
you *must* have and wear or be punished, and it is the taylor's business to
supply you with them.'[11]

For the nobleman there were other decisions to be made beyond settling
the account, for he had a wider choice to make of the silk beneath the gold

lace of his splendid gown. George Selwyn, writing to Lady Carlisle about the robing of the future Earl of Carlisle, hoped 'that you approve of my choice of what colour his gown is to be. I think a light blue *celeste*, which Lord Stafford had, would be detestable, and scarlet is too glaring. No; it must be a good deep green.'[12] Which must have rustled and glowed splendidly beneath the gold of the lace and set off his golden tassel.

This moment of assuming the gown, whether of colour and gold, black silk or plain black stuff, was always one of excitement and pride, always something of note in the first letter home. 'My appearance is much altered since I came here,' wrote Francis Jeffrey to his sister Mary. 'Do not, however be apprehensive ... while I am in the house, my appearance retains its old peculiarities. But without, a great black gown and the portentous square cap conceal the elegance of my form, and overshadow the majesty of my brow.'[13] Even the great Johnson, revisiting Oxford in 1759, took an innocent delight in flaunting himself in his newly acquired Master's gown. 'I have been in my gown ever since I came here. It was at my first coming quite new and handsome.'[14] For those whose stay was longer than Johnson's few weeks, those new and handsome gowns soon showed the wear and tear of constant use and even of deliberate 'ageing'. A poem of Mrs. D'Anvers depicts a country servant expressing his shock to his young master when he views how

> They wear their Gowns berent and tore so,
> Hanging about them all in littocks,
> That they can hardly hide their Buttocks.

His own master's gown, but a year old, is all in tatters, but he explains to his unsophisticated servant:

> Hoa laught, and cry'd, *Why, that's no fault*, John,
> Hoa tor't, to pass ye for a *Saltman*. ...
> Half *Gowns* are always *Seniours*,
> So halv'd and jag'd, if needs you'l know
> If *Seniour Soph* has Gown or no. ...[15]

For the freshman, in his new gown, there was, however, one other important and exciting thing to acquire – a room of his own, his home for the next few years. He was required by statute to live in college and in this century, with the falling number of men entering the university – Exeter College, for example, was half empty in 1767 – there was no shortage of rooms, though there was great variety of elegance and comfort. Vicesimus Knox admired the apartments of students 'for the most part handsome, and commodious, silent, retired, and in every respect fitted for a life of study'.[16] Gibbon arrived as a gentleman commoner at Magdalen to find himself genteelly accommodated, that his 'apartment consisted of three elegant and well-furnished rooms in the new building, a stately pile'.[17] Throughout the century much college income was spent on fitting out rooms more luxuriously, Brasenose panelling many rooms, and Corpus Christi and Christ Church providing three-room suites in their new buildings. At the other end of the scale the poor and plebeian students made do with less commodious accommodation, up steep staircases, in tiny rooms and in the garrets along the roofline. At Christ Church, by far the most popular college, overcrowding rather than poverty forced many into very dismal lodging. 'Christ Church was never so full as it is at present; we are as thick as three in a bed' reported one undergraduate to his father.[18] Another Christ Church man, in 1780, recalls his room's 'eight-feet square Study', and how 'This flourishing College was, at least full, if not overflowing ... for the College was so completely cramm'd, that shelving garrets, and even unwholesome cellars, were inhabited by young gentlemen.'[19] The occupier of one such room was moved to verse as he informed his sister of his plight:

> I was lucky enough to get garrets in college;
> And up a long staircase with pain did I clamber
> To reach the black door of my desolate chamber.
> Imagine, dear Jenny, a garret so small,
> That one feels like a nun in't, built up in a wall;
> With a chimney that smokes when the wind's in the south
> Like Mynheer of Holland's tobaccofied mouth;
> With a window contriv'd, as were casements of old,
> To keep out the light and to let in the cold;
> With a tatter'd settee, and a parcel of chairs
> That grievously totter and creak for repairs –
> And a poor widow'd fire-screen, without its best half,
> For Vulcan hath eaten it all but the staff.[20]

The choice of such a garret room with such decrepit furnishing could well have been on economic grounds, with an eye to a future move after an inexpensive start. A young Trinity man, himself well settled in good rooms, explained such tactics to his friend Will:

> Not but some Students also keep
> Apartments here, or soundly sleep
> In garrets overhead – few care
> At first how small their Chambers are
> Since as the older Tenants change
> They may descend to lower Range
> On paying Thirds.[21]

The same Trinity undergraduate describes his own apartments below the garrets, and the cost of living and furnishing these 'Thirds' and rent:

> For chamber, then, I occupy
> Quite neat and roomy by the bye
> Twelve pound a year must be bestowed.
> For furniture:- it is the mode
> To pay two thirds of all the sums
> The former holder of the Rooms
> Has thereon spent:- my cost I found
> Amounted just to thirty pound
> Twenty of which I may require
> When I from College walls retire.[22]

The young Christ Church man must have paid much lower thirds on the collection of rickety stuff he inherited. Dr Johnson estimated the thirds of George Strahan's son at University College at £12,[23] and a freshman at Queen's wrote home to say 'my furniture is pretty good and the thirds will run low, I believe'.[24] Room rents varied, as we have seen, according to the luxury of the rooms and their distance from the ground. At Lincoln College garrets cost £3 a year, and first floor rooms £6. Principal Newton of Hart Hall intended to fix rents at £6 for best rooms, £5 for first and second stories, and £3 for single garrets.[25] Expenditure on furniture depended on the inadequacy of the third inherited and the taste and pocket of the new tenant. Had he, for instance, taken over the furniture of David Locock, a gentleman commoner of Lincoln, he would only have need to find four guineas to inherit 'an oval table (broken), five matted-bottom chairs, two prints, two maps, a bed and bolster, blankets, sheets, and a wig-block', whereas Samuel Plomer, of the same college, left at the value of a future third of £12 4s. a comparatively luxurious collection of items including 'half a dozen chairs with seats of Spanish leather, a steel grate, a press and a chimney-glass, a mahogany stand, a tea-board and a music desk, two other chairs, a sugar-box and a teapot'.[26] Mr Plomer appears to have taken seriously the ironic advice of the author of *General Directions* for young men at Oxford:

> In the choice of your rooms, contrive, if you can procure such an agreeable situation, that they shall look onto the Street. ... Be sure to order a large, soft Sofa, for this obvious reason, you cannot remain alone in your room on a hot or rainy day without falling asleep and this piece of furniture is infinitely more convenient for the purpose than an arm-chair. Procure a flute whether you can play or not, and let it be always in sight, then who-ever sees it will give you credit for an elegant accomplishment. ... Get the most expensive prints you possibly can, they will ornament your sitting room prodigiously, and in the end not cost you more than six-pence to the Porter who carries them back to the print-shop from whence you had them. On the same principle, and at little expense, you may enjoy the luxuries of a handsome Carpet, a set of china ware, chairs, tables, window curtains &c.[27]

Whether the room was a garret or an elegant set, luxuriously or sparsely furnished, the possession of it was exciting and somehow a symbol of the new freedom from parents and the tyranny of schoolmasters and school dis-cipline. Only servants and chosen friends would invade the freshman's rule over this room of one's own. The man's scout would wake him in time for chapel, light the fire, fetch breakfast from the buttery, brush his coat and clean his shoes. In the evening he would be back to serve at any supper parties on his staircase, 'shifting a plate here, drawing a cork there, running to and fro, from one set of chambers to another'.[28] With the scout was the other regular intruder on the undergraduate's privacy, the bedmaker. The freshman who described his tatty room in a verse-letter to his sister, recounts his first encounter with one of this formidable tribe:

> I here sat me down, with my mind quite in gloom,
> When a hideous appearance stalk'd into the room,
> In her left hand a pail, in her right hand a broom; ...
> And she told me at last with a horrible mien,
> 'Sir, I makes your bed up, and keeps your room clean'
> And, sister, this office is wisely contriv'd
> To fall on sage dames who their charms have surviv'd ...
> Such a group I defy Pandemonium to show
> As a bevy of bed-makers all in a row.[29]

Many more agreeable and welcome guests would visit these rooms in the terms to come, friends to talk, to drink and to eat, friends to make music of an evening, to play battledore and shuttlecock, to play cards, to swing on the rope, visiting relatives to be entertained, when the room had been tidied, on 'a slice of cold tongue and ... a Glass of Hock'.[30]

But in these first days it was the simple excitement of ownership and independence which enlivened the freshman and found expression in his first letters home. Remembering his first days at St John's some forty years before, Thomas Frognall Dibden could recall those feelings:

> But who shall describe the inward glow of delight, with which that same scholar first sees the furniture of his rooms as his own – and his rooms a sort of castle, impervious, if he pleases, to the intruding foot! Everything about him begets a spirit of independence. He reads – he writes – he reposes – he carouses, as that spirit induces. All that he puts his hand upon, is his own. The fragrant bohea, the sparkling port; the friends, few or many, which encircle him; while the occupations of the past, and the schemes of the coming day, furnish themes which alternately soothe and animate the enthusiastic coterie.[31]

A more romantic freshman at Queen's wrote home to his father, himself a Queen's man:

To my great joy I am this day in possession of a very comfortable set of chambers, in a staircase adjoining that of Shepherds [his best friend] and pretty quiet. It is a most studious, contemplative place. Right before my window stands St. Peter's Church, and I may meditate upon the tombs below (for mine is a second floor) with vast satisfaction by moonlight ... my furniture is pretty good, and the thirds will run low, I believe. ... I have provided tea equipage, and hope to be tolerably myself presently.

Beneath his manly independence, however, still lurked boyish doubts about housekeeping; 'to what uses,' he asked, 'I must apply the napkins, and to what the towels; how long a pair of sheets must be used before they are washed'.[32] There were no such little doubts in the triumphant entry of Francis Jeffrey into his rooms at Queen's in 1791, even though he was a little homesick, as he wrote to his sister Mary:

It is a noble thing to be independent – to have totally the management and direction of one's person and conduct. ... I am dependent on nobody to boil my kettle or mend my fire. Not I. I am alone in my rooms – for you must know I have no less than three – and need not permit a single soul to come into them except when I please. But you will wish to know how long I have enjoyed this monarchy. . . . The rooms I had chosen could not be ready for me before night.[33]

But they were made ready in time for his brief and not entirely happy, but proudly independent occupation.

The important central place of one's room in Oxford life, for the undergraduate, was emphasized by the lack of any other place in college for easy and accepted social intercourse. No junior common rooms existed, and occasional celebrations in the dining hall bringing the undergraduates together in a social body, were infrequent in the academic year. In New College the scholars were treated to a special meal on Christmas Day when 'The Bursars gave us Scholars 8 bottles of Port Wine to drink at dinner time. They likewise gave us a qutr. of a Cheshire Cheese. We have 2 large Grace Cups between courses. We have rabbits for supper, 1 Rabbit between three at the expense of the Domus.'[34] Less purely carnal were the corporate celebrations in Brasenose College on Shrove Tuesday, when the whole college gathered in the hall, the butler presented a spiced bowl of ale and spoke verses, had money given to him by the house, and no doubt received rousing applause from the undergraduates in credit.[35] In Balliol Hall 'every Freshman on the 1st. of Nov., when they begin to keep Fires, each of them to tell in his turn a story, the seniors being Auditors, and the Dean of the College is present to see things regular. It is done in the Hall at the eagle and there is afterwards a Collation, every junior contributing something. No Gown is excepted.'[36]

For all the pleasure of such occasions and festivities, the undergraduate's own room was his real home in this society, his retreat and the centre of his circle of friends. As it was his first great excitement when as a freshman he took possession, so it was the centre of nostalgic memories when he thought of or revisited the scenes of his youth. 'The bottom of number six,' mused Radcliffe of Queen's years after he had lived there, 'formerly the scene of mirth and joy, is in a manner all forsaken; all unity, friendship and society have been banished it long ago.'[37]

CHAPTER THREE

Eating:
Undergraduates in Hall and Out

The first day dawns for some nervous freshmen in their new rooms, familiar days dawn for the old hands, and the call of the chapel bell as well as the pangs of hunger call them all from their beds. Times of chapel varied, but seven to seven thirty seems to have been the general rule. Only Dr Newton in his *Scheme of Discipline* proposed a time between five and six o'clock as the mornings of spring and summer lightened earlier – one possible cause of the violent opposition to his scheme by his peers.[1] Late awaking and last-minute panic for chapel occur frequently as two of the first hazards of the day in undergraduate memoirs, although hardened spirits brazenly defied the summons of the bell. The ironic advice given in *The Loiterer* was that 'the loiterer should regularly make his appearance at Nine o'clock, in order to be served up with bread and butter, crusts and muffins'[2] and the 'Diary of an Oxford Man' in the same periodical opens with 'Waked at eight o'clock by the scout to tell me the bell was going for prayers ... wonder these scoundrels are suffered to make such a noise ... ten, got up and breakfasted.'[3] Once defiance or tardy compliance was over, came the pleasures of breakfast in one's own room, an occasion often affectionately described, as when on a frosty morning in 1792 John Skinner of Trinity wrote a verse letter to his friend William:

> But to proceed: your friend returns
> To rooms to see if fire burns
>   Or whether water boils. . . .
> Rolls smoking hot at half past eight
> And George and butter on a plate
>   The scarecrow Thomas brings
> Laying a napkin passing white
> Tea equipage he puts in sight
>   While loud the Kettle sings.

It is a meal he shares, as

> Friend Warren takes accustomed seat
> Pours tea on sugar very sweet
>   And cream not over rich;
> And rolls he cleverly does spread
> Or from brown George toasts slice of bread.[4]

Sharing breakfast appears to have been a general habit, and a Queen's undergraduate who had attended chapel at seven o'clock, took a walk until nine, 'at which hour a George (that is to say a round penny roll) is served up, with a bit of butter on a pewter plate, into each of our chambers where we provide our own tea and sugar. We do not often breakfast alone, but generally order our George up to some friend's apartment and breakfast socially.'[5] Another cosy winter breakfast was described by a Christ Church undergraduate who matriculated in 1780, only slightly spoiled by the ice-cold and overstarched table linen. His overzealous scout had similarly treated his bed linen and given him a sleepless and frozen night.

> Having wash'd and scrubb'd myself in the bed chamber, till I was nearly flay'd with the friction, I proceeded to my sitting room, where I found a blazing fire, and a breakfast very neatly laid out; but again I encounter'd the same rigour! ... I dreaded to sit down to hot rolls and butter, lest I should cut my shins against the edge of the table-cloth.[6]

A slightly sadder breakfast story is recorded by James Radcliffe who entered Queen's College in 1745, who missed his northern home, and whose mother wrote anxiously to him: 'You seem to breakfast upon milk, shall we send you some oatmeal, or is there anything we can get you?' It only took a month before the young man gave in and wrote to his worried mother, 'I am disgusted with the water and milk of Oxford', and requested a barrel of oatmeal. Not for him, it seems, the hot rolls and butter of his southern acquaintance, but the wholesome porridge of his home.[7] Breakfast over, this frugal young man no doubt joined his contemporaries at Trinity –

> At half past nine, tea-drinking o'er
> And cups returned thro' pantry door
>   Our books we take instead.[8]

rather than the wicked wastrel who wrote a penitent letter to *The Loiterer*: 'the morning was dissipated in doing nothing, and the evening in doing what was worse: the first part wasted in idleness, the latter drowned in intemperance.'[9]

In whatever way the morning was spent, the next great event in the eating day was dinner. Dinner in this century was a very moveable feast. As the years went by it came ever later in the day. Thomas Hearne, with sour disapproval, records the first moves in this direction in the early 1720s.

'Whereas the University Disputations on Ashwednesday should begin exactly at one Clock, they did not begin this year 'till two, or after, which is owing to several Colleges having altered their hour of dining from eleven to twelve, occasion'd from People lying in bed longer than they us'd to do.'[10] This regrettable move affected his own society, St Edmund Hall, the following year. 'Dr. Felton,' he writes, 'having altered the Hours of Prayers in Edm.Hall, proceeds to make other Alterations, and, among other Things, he hath altered the Hour of Dinner from eleven to twelve a Clock.'[11] Four days later the altered hour of dinner was accompanied by a more grievous omission which Hearne regarded as a serious flouting of tradition:

> It hath been an old Custom in Oxford for the Scholars of all Houses on Shrovetuesday to go to dinner at 10 Clock (at wch time the little Bell call'd Pan-cake Bell rings, or, at least should ring at St.Marie's), and to Supper at four in the Afternoon, and it was always follow'd in Edmund Hall as long as I had been in Oxford 'till yesterday, when we went to dinner at 12 and Supper at six, nor were there any Fritters at Dinner as there us'd always to be. When laudable old Customs alter, 'tis a Sign Learning dwindles.[12]

Nevertheless, despite these rearguard complaints, the hour of dinner continued to advance. At Brasenose the dinner hour had moved from eleven to twelve in 1730, to one o'clock in 1753 and by the end of the century was as late as four in the afternoon.[13] Three o'clock seems to have been the most favoured hour. In 1760 New College dined at two o'clock but by 1768 at three and half an hour later on Sundays.[14] Joseph Pickford, Fellow of Oriel, remembered dressing for dinner at three in the afternoon.[15] At Trinity, too, dinner was served, by 1775, at three. Dr Newton set the Hertford dinner hour at one o'clock in 1747 but the move to a later hour was irresistible. By 1791, after a first move to three o'clock, Hertford men were, as were Merton men by 1795, dining at four.[16]

But before entering upon that meal, the whole college was occupied with the near-frenzied ritual of dressing for dinner. The donning of the required white waistcoat, white stockings and low shoes took comparatively little time, but this was particularly the hour of the college barber. The fashion until the end of the century was to crop the hair and to wear a wig or to dress, curl and powder the hair into a wig-like coiffure. To appear otherwise was to be considered strangely eccentric. 'When I was an Oxonian,' recorded a Christ Church man, 'the hand of Time was forestall'd by the fingers of the Barber, and an English stripling, with his hair flowing over his shoulders, was, in the course of half an hour, metamorphosed into a man, by means of powder, pomartum, the comb, the curling irons, and a bit of black ribbon to make a pigtail.'[17] Robert Southey of Balliol recalls how his father, earlier in the century, to the scandal of the barber, refused to conform:

It was usual for all the members to have their hair regularly dressed and powdered according to the prevailing fashion, and the College barber waited upon the 'freshmen' as a matter of course. My father, however, peremptorily refused to put himself under his hands: and I well remember his speaking of the astonishment depicted in the man's face, and of his earnest remonstrances, on the impropriety he was going to commit in entering the dining hall with his long hair, which curled beautifully, in its primitive state.[18]

Jeremy Bentham, as a twelve-year-old commoner at Queen's in 1760, was another who hated this formal dressing of the hair, although unlike Southey he capitulated to the fashion and emerged with his hair 'turned up in the shape of a kidney'. He had an additional burden to bear in that he 'had a fellow student whose passion it was to dress hair, and he used to employ a part of his mornings in shaping my kidney properly'.[19] For those without such a room-mate, the hand of the barber was required to tidy and refresh the dressed hair of the young and the grizzle wigs of the elderly, and to do it for a sizeable company going in to dinner was a hectic undertaking:

> A quarter wanting now of three
> On entering gates of Trinity
>   For dressing will suffice;
> As Highland Barber, far-famed Duff,
> Within that time will plenty puff
>   Of lime in both my eyes.
> At least he thirty has to dress,
> Who all at the same instant press
>   As clamorous as duns.[20]

These college barbers were men of various talents and callings both within and outside the colleges, and their Worshipful Company highly respected and annually honoured with a dinner or supper by the Vice-Chancellor and Proctors. Hearne records an occasion when the barbers of Oxford attended a feast in the refectory of St Edmund Hall: 'The Master of the Company ... gave a Treat (both dinner for the Men, & Supper for the Women) ... having leave from the Principal of that Place.'[21] They often held other posts within the college, as at Magdalen and Exeter:

> To M-GD-L-N HALL, illustrious Domus,
> K-NE serves as *Tonsor* and as *Promus*;
> Great H-RN-R too with equal Fame
> At EX-T-R performs the same.
> That very Hand which mows their Heads,
> Deals out their Butter and their Bread.[22]

They often offered other services over and above the tonsorial, both academic and entrepreneurial. 'These gentlemen of the comb,' writes an anonymous commentator on Oxford life, 'are in Oxford of the greatest use and consequence: exclusive of their professional abilities, they will procure a theme (or, in case of an urgent necessity, they would not scruple making one themselves) for half a crown, and a good declamation for five shillings. They will get all impositions done, and know where the best horse and the prettiest girl are in all Oxford.'[23] Their ability to relieve the delinquent undergraduate of the tedium of writing impositions for disorderly behaviour is reinforced in verse by the bard of Trinity:

> Which to get done, if he's a ninny
> He gives his barber half a guinea.
> This useful go-between will share it
> With servitor in college garret,
> Who counts these labours sweet as honey
> Which brings to purse some pocket money.[24]

But for the moment, the barber's exclusively professional services completed, the college, properly dressed and gowned, proceeds to dinner.

In the Hall that hierarchy of status and degree, of which we have spoken, finds another outward sign to accompany the strict variations in academic gowns. The young verse epistoler of Trinity depicts this entry into Hall when, the Fellows and gentlemen commoners in their silk gowns safely settled at high table,

> The Batchelors upon the right
> And Scholars' Table standing by't
>   Are lower in the Hall,
> Because some space it does require
> For the large grate and flaming fire
>   Which blazes 'gainst the wall.
>
> Extending from the high raised floor
> In length: we count two tables more
>   For me and my compeers,
> That is, for Youths with leading strings
> And sleeveless gowns, poor awkward things
>   Entitled Commoners.[25]

The methods adopted in various halls to feed these hungry bachelors and commoners seem to have varied. Charles Kirkpatrick Sharpe, who matriculated at Christ Church in 1798, gives this account to his mother of the state of eating at the end of the century:

I resume my pen to give you some small notion of our dinner in hall, which is an immense room with Gothic windows on each side, and a very large one at

8   Christ Church Hall

the end, filled with painted glass. Below it hangs a picture of Henry the Eighth ... and round the room hangs many a sour-looking, ill-painted ancient, frowning as if they grudged one his dinner, and were scandalised at the smooth chins and effeminate grimaces of their degenerated progeny. Indeed the dinner is hardly worth the grudging, being served up on pewter or silver, the Lord knoweth which, at the first course: and a joint of meat is set down at the head of each table, which descends gradually to the bottom, the students cutting huge slices from it all the way down. Then come potatoes; and your beer is put down to you in a stone mug, Then if you choose pudden or a tart you must vociferate for it with the voice of a fishwoman, and often not get it neither. When done, you rise when convenient, waiting for nobody.[26]

It is interesting to place alongside this description by a Christ Church alumnus the impression gained of that same dining hall by a foreign visitor in the early years of the century:

We saw the Hall or dining room, which is fearfully large and high but otherwise poor and ugly in appearance; it also reeks so strongly of bread and meat that one cannot remain in it, and I should find it impossible to dine and live there. The disgust was increased (for the table was already set), when we looked at the coarse and dirty and loathsome table cloths, square wooden plates and the wooden bowls into which the bones are thrown; this odious custom obtains in all the colleges. The *socii collegiorum* as well as the students or scholars must dine here, but the most important have their meals brought to their rooms at an incredibly high cost.[27]

This fastidious visitor was more at ease at St John's: 'The dining Hall is small but fairly clean, and does not stink as the others usually do.'[28]

Other contemporary accounts of dinner in Hall are not so squeamish, sometimes quite happy, but often indicative of a far from dignified and well-mannered occasion. At the very end of the century, a Corpus man, dining now as late as a quarter to five, wrote to tell his father:

The three first tables have joints [presumably high table, batchelors and scholars] but we have what is called Commons; that is, allowances cut in slices. We have generally the choice of two plain dishes, roast and boiled beef, mutton, veal, and pork. When I go into Hall, I enquire what there is for dinner, and desire them to send in half a commons of what I choose, with potatoes or pickles, then I have the other half commons hot afterwards. Then I have pastry occasionally, and cheese and celery, as I seem inclined, and a pint of beer, all excellent of their sorts.[29]

He seems quite happy with what we might call this à la carte ordering of dinner, a sentiment echoed by an undergraduate of Queen's, summoned to dinner when the 'trumpets martial voice proclaims the hour of dinner, to which we all repair in the Common Hall, after having ordered, in our way through the kitchen, whatever part of the bill of fare we may choose'. He adds, to quieten the anxieties of his sister, and incidentally to exonerate his college from the censures of the oversensitive visitor to Christ Church, 'Allow me to satisfy your curiosity by informing you that we have a clean table-cloth every day.'[30] Another Queen's man might be allowed to record not only the quality of the food in Hall – 'I ate the best dinner I remember upon the first Sunday, and starve every day on roast beef and plum pudding' – but also, as a canny northerner, to be glad of the possibility of controlling his expenses in the choice of his commons: 'My eating never almost exceeds one shilling a day, except upon very particular occasions.'[31]

Although Dr Newton's proposed statutes for Hertford were never enacted, his scheme for the serving of dinner no doubt reflects the practice in that college, with a lessening choice of dishes as we move to the lower tables:

Upon the Ringing of the Bell for Dinner and Supper [the Steward] shall go into the *Kitchen* ... shall send up the *Commons* to Every *Table* distinctly: To the *Tutors' Table* consisting of *Masters of Arts* only, in *Messes* or in *Joints* or in

Single Commons, as they shall agree to have them: To the *Other tables* in *Messes* only, *Four Men* being assigned to each *Mess*; the Senior choosing his *Mess* and by that Choice determining his *Three immediate Juniors* to the Same, the Junior of the Mess dividing.[32]

The final impression is a confused one, a mixture of medieval squalor and modern decorum, of solemn discipline and the crude behaviour of such a creature as this 'Raph'[33] or low worthless fellow, so named by the gownsmen of Oxford to such inhabitants of the place: 'At dinner he should scramble to be helped first, and knock down the first who opposes him: or, if he is compelled to wait, he may employ the interval in picking his teeth or nails with a fork, making pills of bread between his thumb and finger, and throwing them in the plates of others who are eating.'[34]

It might have been such behaviour, such less than elegant service, such monotonous and unimaginative food, which encouraged those who could afford the money and the risk of disciplinary action to shun the common hall and dine privately in their own rooms. The century is filled with repeated admonitions against this desertion of the *societas* of the college, in statutes, decrees and orders. In 1723 the Vice-Chancellor and Heads of Houses warned 'all Victuallers or Cooks that if they entertain Scholars in their Houses, for whom there are Commons provided in their Respective Colleges or Halls, that they should be proceeded against with all the rigour and severity which the Laws of the Land and Statutes of the University allow.'[35] They found it necessary to repeat the same order in 1763 and 1766. At a meeting of Heads of Houses on 23 February 1747, notice was taken of disturbances and riotous behaviour and the Proctors, Pro-Proctors and masters were exhorted to be more vigilant:

> We likewise, in aid of our Statutes, in an especial manner recommend a steady Observation of those good Customs and Rules of Discipline which have for many Ages obtained as well within our Colleges and Halls as in the University; and therefore we think it highly necessary to discourage all private Entertainments at improper Times, and to oblige all Persons to attend in the common Hall at the usual Hours of Dinner and Supper.[36]

A year later it is quite clear that this order had been of little effect. The Vice-Chancellor and Heads of Houses repeated themselves in the face of continued disorder:

> And whereas many of the Disorders complained of, have been chiefly and immediately owing to Scholars having Private Entertainments and Company at their Chambers, which are generally attended with great Intemperance and Excess, and always with Expences that are both Needless and Hurtful. We therefore earnestly recommend it to all Bursars, Deans, Censors and Tutors, to prevent as much as in their Power this Unstatuteable and Mischievous

Practice, and to oblige All Persons to attend in the Common Hall at the usual hours of Dinner and Supper.[37]

Some eighteen years later the same Heads of Houses tried again to force the undergraduates to eat in Hall, this time by cutting off one of the main sources of supply for these private feasts. They ordered 'That all Cooks, Coffee-House and inn Keepers be convened before the Vice-Chancellor, Heads of Houses and Proctors, and enjoined, under the Penalties prescribed by the University Statutes, not to send Dinners or Suppers into Colleges or Halls, or dress Dinners or Suppers for the use of Gownsmen.'[38] The college authorities tried to enforce the rules within their own walls with as little success. At Corpus Christi College an attempt was made to check 'the great and enormous extravagence of the Gentlemen Commoners in the article of Battels' and forbade them to continue having private dinners in their rooms without special leave. Clearly this had as little effect as all the other orders and directives, and six years later a complete ban on private dinners was enacted.[39] Dr Newton in his draft statutes for Hertford College proposed a more moderate discipline:

> If a member of the Society wishes to entertain guests not members of the society, he may do so in Hall or, with special permission, in his Chambers ... he may, *at his own Immediate Expence*, in a frugal sort, provide anything else he likes better, and have it dress'd at Seasonable Times, at the Common Fire by the *Cook* ... neither shall he entertain them with *Costly Dishes*, nor with *Wine*, nor any other Liquors than what the *Common Cellar* produces.[40]

But these statutes were never accepted. The private dinner remained a notable part of the social scene, while the powers above thundered and threatened in vain.

The providers of the victuals continued to trade busily and openly. James Sadler, a cook of Lemon Hall near Carfax, advertised a wide range of cooked meats, sausages, tongues, eels, broths and soups and pickles, and that at his establishment could be ordered 'Dinners &c. dressed and sent off in the neatest manner'.[41] Even a college cook, Henry Richards of Trinity, working in his private capacity, announced that he would be dressing 'a very fine lively Chicken Turtle' and that the nobility and gentry could be supplied from the Mitre at 6 shillings a quart or 10s 6d. a tureen, a delicacy which no doubt started many a private dinner in many a college room.[42] One William Puddle of Blackwell Alley off the High was poetically celebrated as the bringer of other good things for these feasts:

> Masters I've sold you many a dainty Dish,
> Tho' small the Lot, most excellent the Fish:
> When piercing Storms do blow thro' College Cloisters
> Immerg'd in Snow, I bring you best of Oysters;

> Lobsters, Prawns and Shrimps, as good as in the Nation,
> 'Tis I procure for your Accommodation.[43]

The nobility and gentlemen commoners who considered themselves exempt from these regulations were especially given to private entertainments on quite a large scale, as when Erasmus Philips, a gentleman commoner at Pembroke, dined with the Marquis of Carnarvon in his apartments at Balliol along with fifteen other guests, where 'The entertainment ... was extreamly Elegant, in every Respect.'[44] At Christ Church, in 1780, the evenings were alive with private dinner parties all over the college to the great exercise of the scouts who had 'upon an average, half-a-dozen parties to attend in the same night, and at the same hour ... running to and fro from one set of chambers to another'.[45] It would certainly appear that the ironic *Advice to the Universities of Oxford and Cambridge* was very near the truth, and that many successfully opposed the decrees of Golgotha throughout the century: 'The Hall he should very seldom see the inside of: if he is not engaged to dine out, or has no company at home, (which should very seldom be the case) let him dine alone, in his own room; for he ought to take every opportunity of appearing to disregard the order of the college.'[46]

Even more popular as a private entertainment, and under no forbidding decree, was dessert in one's rooms, an occasion of varying degrees of sobriety. This took place after three o'clock dinner was over and could take up the rest of the afternoon and evening. Two verse accounts give a detailed and lively picture of these parties, the first by a freshman accepting his first invitation to such a party at Christ Church, and obviously impressed with the exciting new experience:

> So I went to his rooms about four, where I found
> A table, with chairs placed in order around,
> And bottles, replete with the juice of the vine,
> Which clumsier poets would style red port wine;
> A sumptuous dessert then enchanted my eyes
> Ripe oranges, perfect in colour and size –
> Grapes, peaches, and apples, as much as you please,
> Cakes, ruskins, prunelloes, and sweet damson cheese –
> Dry biscuit, that chiefly to Bacchus belongs,
> Delicious when toasted till brown in the tongs –
> And huge lumps of ice which exactly did look
> Like the floating ice-hills in the drawings of Cook.[47]

From Trinity comes an account of another evening where expenses were shared, the host providing the room, wine, glasses and cutlery, the guests finding their own dessert:

For now some ten or dozen get
By fore appointment in a set
   To taste inviter's port;
He glasses, plates, and spoons prepares,
Decanters, knives and forks and chairs,
   But each his own dessert.

For with large baskets enters soon
A wily fruiterer styl'd Baloon,
   Who hands around his store, –
Apples and pears, and chestnuts too,
And oranges deck'd out to view,
   With many a bonne bouche more.

Meanwhile the jovial toasts go round,
The bottles guggle, glasses sound
   As each one drinks his fair.
The Chairman watches, bawls and raps
Should any fill upon heel taps,
   Or his good liquor spill.

The festivities continue, ignoring chapel at five o'clock and teatime at six. By nine o'clock every guest is asleep or tipsy, and the scout arrives with a supper previously ordered from the kitchens,

Boiled fowl, salt herrings, sausages,
Cold beef and brawn and bread and cheese
   With tankards full of ale.

But no one can eat, the scout takes the supper as his perks, and helps his young men safely to bed.[48]

For those not safely in bed, or those who had missed Hall dinner or the lesser meal of supper – which undergraduate memoirs seldom mention – there was other fare to be sought, always recourse to the tempting dishes of the town. Many an evening must have started and ended in the many cookhouses of the streets of Oxford. One such establishment, kept by Mrs Yeoman, brewed its own ale, provided superfine mince pies at Christmas, and advertised an extensive menu:

My *sober Evenings* spend, beguil'd
O'er *wholesome Draughts* of YEOMAN's mild:
While smoaking Steaks, or lucious Pye,
Can each keen Appetite supply ...
Fine large fat Oysters to Command,
Or fresh, or pickled to your Hand;
Beef, Veal, or Mutton, boil'd or fry'd
With thousand other Things beside.

As an extra attraction to student debtors she promised that no duns would be admitted.[49]

The two most favoured items for out-of-college consumption were undoubtedly mutton pies and sausages. Advertisements for these delicacies abound throughout the century, for

> *Oxford* now from all shall bear the Prize,
> Fam'd, as for *Sausages*, for MUTTON PIES.[50]

The best known of the pie-makers was one Benjamin Tyrrell, and either he or his agent had a turn for verse as they announced to the readers of *Jackson's Oxford Journal*:

> All ye that love what's *nice* and *rarish*,
> At *Oxford* in St. *Mary's* Parish
> BEN TYRRELL, Cook of high Renown,
> To please the Palates of the *Gown*,
> At Three-Pence each, makes MUTTON PIES,
> Which thus he begs to advertise.
> He welcomes all his Friends at *Seven*
> Each *Saturday* and *Wedn'sday* Even . . .
> If *liquor* in a MUTTON PIE
> Has any Charms, come taste and try!
> O bear me Witness, *Isis'* Sons!
> Pierce but the Crust, the *Gravy* runs!
> The taster licks his lips and cries,
> O RARE BEN TYRRELL'S MUTTON PIES.[51]

He broke into verse two years later, recommending his pies to the lawyers, jurymen and their ladies gathered for the Oxford assizes:

> For LAWYER'S CLERKS, in wigs so smart,
> A tight warm room is set apart.[52]

Tyrrell appears to have been without many rivals in the mutton pie business, though a lady competitor, Mrs Yeoman, proprietress of the cookhouse already mentioned, sometimes advertised particularly her superb mutton pies[53] and later in the century, in the 1780s the trade continued in the hands of George Pridie, from his shop in the Turl, where at 8 p.m. on Mondays, Wednesdays and Saturdays in the winter season hot mutton pies were on offer.

But the juicy delights of these pies were almost certainly exceeded in popularity by the firmer attraction of the famed Oxford sausage, a solidly meaty creation, unadulterated with crumbs or rusk. Mr Ayres, first cook of

New College, in his recipe book, sets down how 'To make Oxford Sausages':

> ... take of pork and veal an Equall Quantity and let it be free from Sinues & Skin and Chopp it very small, then add to it half as much of good beef suet as meat and Chop it together till the suet is fine then season it with pepper, salt, nutmeg, some sage and thyme minced small, then work it up with 2 or 3 Eggs as you see good.[54]

The making and selling of these sought-after delicacies appears to have been confined to a small and select body of cooks, with a near-hereditary right to a limited monopoly of what was very much a seasonal trade. When the month contained the permissive 'r' which signalled the safety of eating pork, there appeared without fail the advertisements for the opening of the winter season for sausage consumption.

There were two most prestigious sausage purveyors. Charles Dodd, who was a cook at New College, ran his business from the Wheatsheaf in the High Street, opening his season regularly in late September or early October through the latter part of the century. At the Wheatsheaf one could buy sausages for home consumption, or sit down on the premises where 'they will be fried at a moment's notice if desired'.[55] When he died in 1797 the business was continued by Martha Dodd at her house in New College Lane.[56] Dodd's main rival was Mrs Sarah Herbert with her shop near the Angel, and whose advertisements appeared without fail with or slightly after Mr Dodd's. By 1792 Mrs Herbert's daughter, S. Pearson, took over the business and after Mrs Herbert's death one Ann Lockey became the proprietress.[57] Other names appear now and again, evidence of a continuing and steady trade. In 1782 one T. Sadler advertised his sausages as part of his offerings at his shop in St Clement's, where he specialized in potted beef, and was one of those cookhouse proprietors who, defying repeated decrees to the contrary, provided 'Dinners dressed at any Distance from Oxford, on reasonable terms',[58] examples of which doubtless found their way into many a college room. In 1787 T. Davis, claiming the same high quality which he had maintained for thirty years, was selling and frying sausages at his house, and his products could be bought also at Mr Norgrove's in the Corn or at Mr Clements' in Pennyfarthing Lane.[59] Yet another was added to the fraternity in 1793 when a cook at the Angel, James Hilliar, started to advertise.[60] Woodforde, even after the large dinners at New College, was fond of this Oxford speciality, and noted how he had 'Supp'd with Tom Robinson at the King's Head upon Sausages'.[61] He was one of many. All in all, though dinner in Hall had been meagre or missed or seemed a long while ago, there was no need, fortified by a gravy-rich mutton pie or meaty sausages, to go hungry to bed at the end of the eating day.

CHAPTER FOUR

Eating: the Dons on the Dais

For the ageing and the idle, meal times become the high moments of the day and as age and idleness increase, become of increasing importance. Small wonder that they marked the hours of the eighteenth-century don's social day, that the delights of the table occupied his thoughts and management, and that the sin of gluttony should most often have headed his confession of the deadly seven. Eating was his delight and all too often his death.

The eating day started early, for the conscientious Fellow would be up for morning chapel, answering the bell (or the hammering of a mallet at the foot of his staircase)[1] which sounded to call him to his devotions. The drowsy dons were widely understood to be far from regular in answering the call. For them attendance was voluntary, unlike that of their juniors, a fact occasioning this sour comment from a 'Gentleman of Wadham College' in 1730:

> We have a Company of old surly Fellows who take pleasure in making one act contrary to ones Conscience – and tho' for their own part they never see the Inside of a Chappel throughout the Year, yet if one of us miss but two Mornings a Week, they'll set one a plaguey *Greek* Imposition to do – that ne'er a one of them can read when 'tis done.[2]

Thirty years later some verses discover, though in a gentler tone, the same state of affairs:

> Each in his narrow Bed till Morning laid
> The peaceful Fellows of the College sleep. . . .
> The tinkling Bell proclaiming Pray'rs,
> The noisy Servants rattling o'er their Head,
> The calls of Business, and domestic Cares,
> Ne'er rouze these Sleepers from their downy Bed.[3]

But once aroused or returned from chapel, breakfast called them. As we have seen, this was a simple meal, taken in one's own rooms and, though it was affectionately chronicled by many undergraduates it is hardly ever mentioned by the dons. Thomas Warton of Trinity mentions breakfast, but sees the meal predominantly as an occasion for a first good draught of Oxford ale:

> To friendly Buttery, there a smoking Crust
> And foaming ALE to banquet unrestrained,
> Material breakfast.[4]

Woodforde who so carefully recorded other meals, makes only one mention of breakfast after he was elected a Fellow. As an undergraduate he had entertained friends to 'Chocolate for four with bread and Butter' which he had ordered in from Kinnersly's Coffee House, and shortly before his election made a more substantial breakfast of lamb, bread and cheese. In the early years of his fellowship he formed a 'Breakfast Clubb' with his friends Geree and Dyer, taking it by weeks to breakfast in each other's rooms, but solitary breakfasts must have been more congenial, and the club only lasted some three months.[5]

One can only assume that the bread and hot rolls available at the buttery for the servants to carry to rooms, reached both seniors and juniors alike. One satirical comment on the morning scene at Magdalen obliquely confirms this. Scandal pictures 'Little Brats every morning at the Buttery Hatch, calling for hot loaves and Butter in their Papa's Name'.[6] But the minor importance of breakfast in the don's day accounts for this lack of information. It was merely a snack to keep one going through the hours until dinner time, though it no doubt became more substantial as the hour of dinner retreated, and with this growing gap between breakfast and dinner one can sense the approaching invention of luncheon. The lack of that bridging meal may perhaps account for the prodigious consumption at high table, when the dinner bell had rung at last.

Before knife and fork could be wielded, the same preparation for the feast as we have seen for those below high table was *de rigueur*. Wigs had to be dressed and powdered, with priority given of course to the seniors of the college, dark coats and breeches donned, gowns assumed and the procession to high table formed:

> Fellows then march in garments sable
> To upper seat y'clept High Table
>   And range them on each side,
> Where Commoners of first degree
> In silk gowns clad, seem equally
>   With them in state allied.[7]

All settled and Grace said, the long looked-forward-to meal began. Although it was said of the Fellows of All Souls in particular that 'they lived so luxuriantly and indolently, that they did nothing but clean their teeth all the morning and pick them all the evening',[8] the same could be said of the gluttonous Fellows of many a college, and it appears that the Head of the House often set the example. The Warden of All Souls in 1724, Dr Gardiner, 'Being a perfect Epicurean, minding nothing but eating and drinking, and heaping up Money, and doing Mischief, hath got a new way of stuffing a leg of Mutton roasted. He had lately one stuffed by his own order with White Herrings out of the Pickle.'[9] Some forty years earlier Dr Lampshire, Principal of Hart Hall, fell mad and a tutor of Christ Church recorded that 'for my part I attribute it to his gluttony, he being ye greatest eater that ever I knew'.[10]

Frugality and small appetite were more often the subject of satire than praise. The Rector of Exeter, in the same year as the Warden of All Souls was stuffing his leg of mutton, was mocked because

> With half a fowl, and *half a penny small*
> He makes a sober dinner in the Hall,
> (Such slender meals suffice his famish'd nerves,)
> And the minced fragment for his supper serves.[11]

The frugal fare of St Edmund Hall was sneeringly dismissed by Bishop Tanner when he spoke condescendingly to Hearne on Christmas Day 1733: 'I suppose you have no Gaude at Edmund Hall this good day.'[12] Hearne might well have thought again of the absence of pancakes on Shrove Tuesday, and he would have had to admit that the arrival of a simple present of venison from the Duchess of Marlborough made the day remarkable at St Edmund Hall when Dr Mill 'treated his Hall this day with a Haunch of it', rather spoiling the treat in 'that he did not give a glass of Wine or Ale to drink her health'.[13] Certainly Hearne seems always to have accepted invitations to dine out when he could, where the fare at the other high tables was more plenteous and luxurious.

Fortunately for the chronicler, some notable gourmands of the time found a secondary pleasure in recording the menus of the meals they had eaten their way through, and the diary of the foremost of these, the Revd James Woodforde, Fellow of New College, provides us with the fullest picture of the groaning table, not only at New College, but at the many other colleges where he frequently dined out. To heap together these menus is perhaps the best way to experience imaginatively the grossness and extravagance of these gargantuan feasts.

What better start than Christmas dinner at New College, 1773:

> We had for dinner, two fine Codds boiled with fryed Souls round them and oyster sauce, a fine sirloin of Beef roasted, some peas soup and an orange Pudding for the first course, for the second, we had a lease of Wild Ducks rosted, a fore Qu. of lamb and sallad and mince Pies. ... After the second

9   The Dons at dinner

course there was a fine plumb cake brought to the senr. Table as is usual on this day.[14]

When the Warden himself gave dinners for a smaller company, the menu was hardly diminished. On this slightly more modest scale he offered his guests on 6 April 1774 'fish, chine of mutton, a plumb pudding, a couple of wigeon, sweetbreads with force balls, oysters and mushrooms, and some tarts'. For a small company of seven at an elegant little dinner on 22 June in the same year, he provided 'green pea soup, brace of very fine trout, a boiled rump of beef, a roast goose, veal steaks, with tarts etc.'.[15] These were but Lenten meals compared with his 5 December dinner: '1st Course. Cod with oysters, Ham and Fowls, boiled beef, Rabbits smothered with Onions, Haricot of Mutton, Pork griskins, Veal Collops, New College puddings, Mince pies, roots etc.' '2nd. Course, a roast Turkey, haunch of Venison, a brace of woodcocks, some snipes, Veal olive, Trifle, Blancmange, stewed pippins, preserved quinces etc. ...'[16] When Woodforde entertained his friends at a private dinner in the Chequer Room on 27 July 1774, he spread a rich table, and noted afterwards:

We were very merry and pushed the Bottle on very briskly. I gave my company for dinner, some green Pea soup, a chine of Mutton, some New College Puddings, a goose, some Peas, and a Codlin Tart with Cream. Madeira and Port Wine to drink after and at dinner some strong Beer, Cyder, Ale and small Beer ... I had a handsome dish of Fruit after dinner.[17]

10   Dinner being prepared in Christ Church kitchen

There were six to dinner! Now and again the usual bill of fare was supplemented by special treats, as at the annual Venison Feast when 'a neck of Venison and a Breast made into a Pasty' were added to the usual meal of 'a Ham and Fowls and two Pies' or – a more unusual extra – 'a brace of birds called Graus, that came from Williams Junr. out of Wales'. And lest it be thought that the Fellows of New College neglected to observe the penitential season, on 28 February 1775, 'It being Shrove Tuesday we had Lambs Wool to drink, a composition of Ale sugar etc., Lobsters, Pancakes etc ... and the Butler there gives a Plumb Cake with a copy of Verses of his own making upon it.'[18] The ghost of Hearne, deprived of his fritters, might well have hovered sadly over this sumptuous fast.

It was not, of course, only at New College that high table provided these Lucullian feasts. Fortunately Woodforde dined out frequently and left a culinary record neglected by the Fellows of those colleges whose guest he was. Proctors' dinners when they entertained at their installation into or retirement from that high office, were exceptionally splendid. When Mr Barclay the new Proctor from Christ Church entertained, the evening was expansive and heavy.

The first course was part of a large Cod, a chine of Mutton, some soup, a Chicken Pye, Puddings and Roots etc. Second Course, Pidgeons and Asparagus, a Fillet of Veal with Mushrooms and a high Sauce with it, rosted Sweetbreads, hot Lobster, Apricot Tart and in the middle a Pyramid of Syllabubs and Jellies. We had a Desert of Fruit after Dinner, and Madeira, white Port and red to drink as Wine.

He concludes, unsurprisingly, 'We were all very cheerful and merry.'[19] On 9 April 1774 the retiring Proctor from St John's entertained his guests to

1st. Course. Salmon, roast lamb, Sauce a la Mode, Ox cheek a la mode, soup, Orange pudding, garden stuff. 2nd. Course. Pigeons and asparagus, Hot Lobster and sauce, eggs cut in half swimming in some Sauce, hot cream and sweetmeats, some blancmange, and a Pyramid in the middle of Syllabubs and jellies.

After this there was 'cheese to follow'.[20] Two days later his fellow retiring Proctor from Queen's returned this hospitality rather more economically with '1st. Course. a fine turbot, a chine of mutton, an orange pudding, and garden stuff. 2nd. Course. pidgeons and asparagus, a fore quarter of lamb, some roasted sweetbreads, tarts, crawfish and a pyramid of syllabubs and jellies in the middle. A desert of Fruit and Wines.'[21] One week after the dinner at Queen's, New College mounted a fine dinner for their new Proctor Mr Webber in the Proctor's rooms, with some of the obviously favourite dishes of the season. '1st. Course: salmon, a leg of mutton, 3 boiled fowls, a pudding and roots. 2nd. Course: $\frac{1}{2}$ doz. stewed pidgeons and asparagus, roasted sweetbreads, 2 roasted ducks, some veal olive, a fricasse, syllabubs and jellies.'[22] Pro-Proctor Woodforde ate all four dinners!

Finally, to widen the field of colleges where the kitchens laboured to load the board, let us eat at Brasenose through the century. These records, coming more from the kitchens than the high table consumers, give us a better idea of the astonishing amount as well as the variety of food. On Christmas Day 1703 the kitchen used 'A piece of beef, Cabbage and roots, a Racke of veal, a chine of bacon, 1 Turkey, 1 capon, 2 oxtails, 2 cocks, 12 larks, Butter, Anchovies, Wine, Lemons, Grasses, spices, flower, butter and cheese, 2 mince pies.' A year later, at the Tower Dinner, they needed '1 jack, 2 perch, 3 eels, 2 carps, 3 calfs heads, 6 marrow bones, dressed meat, bacon, a 51 lb. surloin of beef, a chine of veal, a marrow pudding, 3 mince pies, 2 wild duck, 2 wood cocks, 12 larks, 2 oxtails, LI cramed chicken, a tansey, oranges, a trotter pie, lemons, oysters'. At a gaudy in the same year, at what might have been a modest cold buffet, among much else '30 great Tarts' were consumed along with 4 custards, as a follow up to 400 sticks of asparagus, a 14 lb. ham and 7 tongues, a gaudy which was overshadowed in 1762 by a huge meal which stretched the resources and patience of the cooks: '23 lb. fresh fish, 36 lb. salmon, 107 lbs of ham, 50 lbs. of lobsters, peas, 32 chickens, 18 ducks, 12 geese, 74 lb mutton, 78 lbs sirloin of beef, 2 tonges and udders, crawfish, roots, currin jelly, 6 dozen tarts, 6 dozen cheese-cakes, 4 doz. custards. Sallad and cucumbers.' A note against ham, lobster and beef records that too much was provided and, against the last item, 'Cucumbers unnecessary'![23] It would be surprising if Woodforde had missed dining out at such a food-loving college, and on 26 January 1775, he noted that Brasenose food was keeping up its reputation, despite an error in the kitchen:

> First course Cod and oyster sauce, Rost Beef, Tongue and boiled Chicken, Peas, Soups and roots. The second course a boiled Turkey by mistake of the Manciple, which should have been rosted, a brace of Partridges rosted, 4 Snipes and some Larkes rosted, also an orange pudding, syllabubs and jellies, Madeira and Port Wines to drink and a dish of Fruit.[24]

It was not only the quantity but the richness and complexity of this high table cuisine which was excessive. Some of the recipes from New College kitchens are preserved in a manuscript recipe book of Mr Ayres who was First Cook of the college from 1721 and probably there for the next thirty years. Let him instruct us how 'To hash a Calves head':

> First boyle the head tendar and pull out all the bones then Cut the meat in thin slices and put it to a stewpan or a fryingpan with half a pint of good beef grauey, a Quarter of a pint of Clarret, a little Cattchup, some nuttmeg, some salt, half a cup of Capors, 2 anchoveys, half a lemmon Cutt in bitts, a little vinegar, and some oysters and musheroomes if you have them, then set it over a fire and when the anchoveys are Dissolved put in half a pound of butter and when it is melted thicken the sauce with the yolkks of 2 Eggs beat with a little vinegar, So your Dish being redy with sippets of white bread barberyes and lemon pour it of, and add some fryd bacon forcemeat balls and if you please sausages put in the middle a roasted foull or 4 veal olives the brains being parboyld Cut them in slices and Dip them in the yolke of an Egge and fry them brown to lay round the Dish.[25]

This savoury richness was certainly equalled by the sweet delights which concluded the second course, such as this famous house delicacy of Woodforde's college:

> To make a Dish of newcollidg puddings. Take the Crumb of 4 penney loaves grated, and add to it one pound of good beef suet shread small put to it as many Currans, some nuttmeg, a little salt, 4 ounces of fine sugar, 5 eggs beat with a little sack or brandey, you may put in a little roasewater if you please, and what Cream will temper it in a pretty stiff paist, so make it in little puddings in the shape of an Egge but longer and this quantity will make a Dozen and a half, and fry ym in half a pound of butter and dish them out with a Quaking puding in the middle then pour over then some butter and strew over some fine suger.[26]

The 'Quaking puding' at the centre when the dish was presented at table was a wobbly concoction, just holding together, of bread, egg, sugar, brandy and nutmeg, boiled in a bag. And if this were too rich and round-flavoured, Mr Ayres had a sharper and tangy delicacy to offer; he records how

> To make a lemon puding or fluoruntine, boyle the rind of 2 lemmons very tender in 2 or 3 waters, then beat it fine in a morter with the meat of the lemmons picked clean from the skin and kernels then add to it 3 Quarters of a pound of loafe suger sifted, 4 grated biskets ye yolks of 10 Eggs beat with a little sack or brandey, then put in half a pound of Clarreyfied butter and keep it stirring all one way till it is Cold then you may put in one ounce of Citteorn and as much Lemmon if you please so your Dish being garnished with puff paist put in your pudding and Cut out a flurantine pattern for the Lidd.[27]

This lemon pie was then baked and served up deliciously tart and piping hot. Further recipes for plum cake, cake icing, apple jellies, potted eels, pigshead, collared beef, custards, pancakes, potted partridges and so on recreate the richness and variety of the meals at high table.

Such recipes also help us to estimate their expense, although this is something which appears to have disturbed only a few stricter commentators. Money was in fact available and was spent with possibly unaccounted ease. Treats, as they were called, in honour of particular honourable college occasions, over and above the daily expenses of common table, were always acceptable. Gaudy reunions and patronal saint's days unquestionably entitled college members to extra-festal eating. Hearne notes an especial gaudy at Queen's: 'This being the Day for celebrating the memory of the Founder of Queen's College, there was a much bigger and more splendid Gaudy than usual, occasion'd by it's being the first of dining in their new Hall on this occasion.'[28] And four years later he writes that the All Soul's dinner at Queen's College 'was very great and very extravagant'.[29] Dr Thomas Wilson, Student of Christ Church, dining at a Corpus Christi gaudy in 1732, enters in his diary that this was 'a very elegant entertainment' which cost at least £60.[30] Hearne is more exact in his costings when he notes that 'The Charges for the eatables at the late Feast at the Vice-Chancellors for the new Chancellor (the earl of Arran) were fifty two pounds, two shillings, & two pence.'[31] But all these feasts seem meagre beside Atterbury's entertainment on becoming Dean of Christ Church. Hearne's note on its splendour has an uncharacteristic tone of approval, which he seldom shows towards such occasions, but this, of course, is a note by one admiring Jacobite on another: ''tis said this treat could not cost less than between two or three Hundred Pounds. ... they never saw any Entertainment manag'd with more consummate Wisdom, exact Decorum, and true Magnificence. Everything was sumptuous, and yet not the least Intemperance or Irregularity.'[32] One last treat at Queen's must find a mention. This was an example of a domestic treat given to the fellowship by three doctors and several masters who were leaving at the end of the Trinity Term, but Hearne notes that Decorum was absent and Irregularity apparent. It was discovered that 'Some Dishes had been put down for the Provost's wife and other in the Lodgings. But the Account being shew'd to one of the Doctors, all was ordered to be struck off, and nothing allow'd for the Lodgings, the Provost himself dining in the Hall.'[33] So Mrs Provost went without her selections from the feast, while the Provost and his Fellows moved, well satisfied, from Hall to the pleasures of the senior common room. Of those varied pleasures we shall speak at length in a later chapter, but meanwhile, there is one more meal to mention, before the high table succumbs sooner or later to the call of bed.

Supper was this last meal of the day which, with dinner, moved steadily later. For those below high table, supper was a set meal at a set time. In 1720 Principal Newton sought to fix this supper-time at six o'clock, but Hearne, ever the praiser of days gone by, asserts that the proper time for supper was four o'clock after a dinner served at ten in the morning. But six o'clock was, it appears, now the accepted norm, although it was inevitable for the senior table, after long gustation and possibly longer imbibing in common room, that supper was a later meal, varied and informal, certainly not a ceremonial high table affair, although it could on occasions assume a more formal mode. In New College, in 1773, at the Christmas feast, after a huge dinner at high table, and the circulation of a grace cup among the bachelors and scholars, supper was served in the Chequer Room, with traditional fare: 'we had Rabbits for supper rosted as is usual on this day. . . . The Sub-Warden has one to himself; the Bursars each one apiece, the Senr. Fellows $\frac{1}{2}$ a one each. The Junr. Fellows a rabbit between three.'[34] More often supper was a private meal eaten in the Fellow's own room or sometimes in the senior common room. Warton shows his 'Fellow of a College' returning home from two hours at the coffee house after dinner, calling in at his room to stir his fire and then 'to Common-room and supped on snipes with Dr. Dry'.[35] Woodforde notes a supper he provided for four friends in his rooms, a moderate cold collation: '2 cold fowls, a plate of brawn, a plate of cold roast beef, a plate of anchovies, a cold apple pie', and elsewhere he supped on more modest snacks, a fine boiled lobster with butter, cold mutton, a venison pasty, a roasted hare with veal collops, and a woodcock.[36] And if hunger remained there were always, outside the college walls, those hot mutton pies and sausages.

So ended the long day's eating, a pattern repeated day in day out, term after term, and the Fellows, whom the morning chapel bell had roused, returned to their 'downy beds' each, we might have supposed

> cram'd from ev'ry dish,
> A Tomb of boil'd, and roast, and flesh, and fish,
> Where Bile, and wind, and phlegm and acid jar,
> And all the Man is one intestine war.[37]

though others, inured by terms of indulgence, settled down as peacefully as Warton's Fellow – 'Returned to my room. Made a tiff of warm punch, and to bed before nine' – even if sleep was delayed for an hour, not by indigestion but by 'a young fellow-commoner being very noisy over my head'.[38]

CHAPTER FIVE

The Society of the Senior Common Room

T he life of eighteenth-century dons could have been solitary and confined were it not for the two places of social gathering around which the day centred: high table, as we have seen, with its food and drink, and common room with its conversation, games and drink. Their own personal chambers varied in size and luxury from college to college, with at least a study, a bedroom and closets for books and wine. The servants brought water in the morning for washing and shaving, and a chamber pot or a commode on the landing, or an open-air walk to the bog-house catered for more fundamental needs. In his rooms, with an armchair, a fire and his books a Fellow could make himself tolerably comfortable to study or to snooze or to drink alone but, in some colleges more than others, he would find the need to escape. When a visitor from abroad, Charles Moritz, met Mr Maud of Corpus Christi, 'he took me to his own room in his own College,' he records, 'which was on the ground floor, very low, and dark, and resembled a cell, at least as much as a place of study.'[1] In such fitting quarters Gibbon's 'Fellows or monks' of his time might have spent their days, but only a rare and small group of scholars did. The majority escaped to the larger confines and conviviality of common room.

The eighteenth century is the period of common room establishment, expansion and embellishment, although the end of the seventeenth century found two already in use. Merton claims the distinction of being the first college to add this amenity, and to change the focus of the social life of the college, in 1661, 'to the end that the Fellows might meet together (chiefly in the evenings after refection), partly about business, but mostly for Society sake, which was before at each chamber by turns'.[2] Four years later Trinity followed suit and the first half of the century finds most colleges emulating these leaders. Wadham common room is first mentioned in 1724. In 1748 Mr Salmon admired Queen's common room, 'a large square Room, wainscotted with Oak, and adorned with a Chimney-piece of excellent vein'd Marble'.[3] By 1759 we read of Lincoln's common room under the library, of

49

Pembroke's in a pleasant garden west of the chapel, with a terrace walk on the city wall, and the guide advises us that at St John's, 'The Common Room on the north side of the Hall, should not be neglected. It's cieling is a good piece of stucco, by Mr. Roberts; and the whole room is handsomely adorned in general.'[4] At Oriel the first common room was in the north-east corner of the old buildings and has since been divided up and altered. It seems to have been quite a Spartan apartment, uncarpeted, and furnished with Windsor chairs, unlike the new common room to which the Fellows moved in 1794, with its mahogany sideboard, new mahogany chairs and a stove and fender. Not until 1800 did the Fellows of Oriel permit themselves the luxury of a carpet. By 1787 a tea-chest had been purchased and so began the notorious habit of tea-drinking in Oriel common room.[5]

Oriel's tea-drinking ranked as notorious because, as we shall see,[6] almost any other potation than tea was the staple in most common rooms. Even Joseph Pickford, an ancient Fellow of tea-drinking Oriel, remembered 'pipes and ale' after the three o'clock dinner, and after eight at night he returned to common room 'to play at cards, and drink brandy and water to a very late hour'.[7] In the earlier years of the century individual fellows made their own selection and purchase of wine for their own reserves. Woodforde at New College, for instance, bought his wine by the hogshead and bottled it, drinking it in his own rooms, or having it brought into dinner or common room or the garden as he wished, but by 1762 a common room cellar was in existence and a new system of clubbing for wine before dinner was agreed, to avoid the unfairness of the unequal contributions of Fellows to wine at table and after.[8] Most colleges by this time had their own valued and guarded wine cellars, their own butlers to care for them, and pride in their reputation. Even *Terrae Filius* recognized 'that the Common Room [of All Souls] was remarkable for the best Port in Oxford', though he offers ironic proof of this claim in that 'Some of the fellows . . . have tost off four Bottles of it a Day, for several Years together, without doing them any Manner of Harm.'[9] The amplitude of these common room cellars and the serious regard in which they were held is demonstrated when the cellar of Brasenose common room was violated by its own common room man, who stole 48 dozen and 4 bottles of red port, and was committed to the castle. The judge, possibly an Oxford man, recognizing the depth of this outrage, sentenced James Bruckner to death. In the following year his sentence was commuted to transportation; he left Oxford and its castle and its common rooms, and was shipped off to Botany Bay.[10]

Drinking, however, was not the only activity of the senior common room, and it would be unfair to omit the variety of social pleasures to be found there. Conversation took up many hours, talk of university politics, local gossip and national affairs, although contemporary accounts make little mention of scholarly or intellectual discussion. In his satirical picture of common room life, Amhurst suggests a mixture of pedantic chat, learned quippery and current affairs, blending finally in the supposed brilliance of alcoholic self-assurance:

> In the same jovial common room I see
> The prim canonic bob and smart *tupee*;
> Grave criticks here on modern authors prey,
> And deep logicians puzzle sense away;
> Pert crambo-wags with subtil school-men joke,
> And punsters and divines in consort smoke . . .
> Of naughty statesmen echoes dismal tales,
> And against WALPOLE, o'er his bottle, rails. . . .
> Say how his soul in conversation shines,
> O'er the third bottle how his wit refines.[11]

At Trinity there were periodic poetic interludes when one of the Fellows was elected Poet Laureate for the year 'whose duty it was to celebrate in a copy of English verses a Lady, likewise annually elected, and distinguished by the title of Lady Patroness'.[12] Thomas Warton was elected in 1747 and 1748 and, crowned with a laurel wreath, read his verses to the assembled company. The common room was the well-loved centre of his life and his gently satirical portrait of an idle don in his *Journal of a Fellow of a College* surely reflects something of his own days as he read his newspaper at six o'clock one evening, and on another sat from two to four in the afternoon with 'Conversation chiefly on the expeditions. Company broke up at four. Dr. Dry and myself played at backgammon for a brace of snipes. Won.' With the same companion he spent many hours of talk. 'Dr. Dry told several stories. Were very merry. Our new Fellow that studies physic very talkative towards twelve.' On another night he 'Got into spirits. Never was more chatter. We sat late at whist.'[13] In that same common room, some thirty years later, he died as he might have wished after a cheerful evening with two other fellows there, suddenly seized with a paralytic stroke.[14] Not only whist diverted the Fellows. Woodforde catalogues the games of New College Fellows – billiards, quadrille, throwing coins into a salt cellar, bragg, cribbage, beat the knave out of doors, Putt, Loo, Lanquinet and backgammon.[15] In the splendid common room of Christ Church with its wealth of silver beakers and candlesticks and the gifts of former noble members of the college, Thomas Wilson records that 2 February 1731 was 'A great day for dancing and singing', though he adds, 'I did neither. Cost us 7s. a piece for the Musick and Entertainment.'[16] The Fellows of Oriel, as their senior common room accounts book shows, added various amenities to their Windsor chairs: maps of Toulon and the Mediterranean in 1744 to help them follow events more closely, cards, dice, oysters and pipes. Only in 1761 did they purchase newspapers, though after that date the number of newspapers and periodicals increased. In 1789, in the midst of revolutionary turmoil, a chess board and men were purchased.[17]

This much-loved club life of the senior common room, and equally of the younger jovial groups in undergraduate rooms, lies behind, and finds its extra-college expression in, the number of clubs and societies which appeared and disappeared through these years, some admitting only senior members, others more particularly gatherings of the young. Thomas Warton the elder was at the centre and presided over the Poetical Club which, in the earlier decades of the century met at the Three Tuns and in its constitution laid down 'That Mr. Bradford would keep good wine, and a pretty wench at the bar', that any member must be distinguished in 'tale, catch, epigram, sonnet, tragedy, or epic', and that only Warton be allowed to smoke, 'the fumigation thereof being supposed to cloud the poetical faculties'.[18] Erasmus Philips visited the club in July 1721 when Dr Evans of St John's was the reader, when he 'Drank Gallicia wine, and was entertained with two Fables of the Doctor's Composition'.[19] The club most favoured by Thomas Warton the younger was the oddly named Jelly Bag Society, whose name was explained and one of its secrets revealed when he dined at the Angel, in June 1762, with his pupil Francis Newberry and his father, and was cheerful and fully at his ease. 'In the course of an evening,' Newberry relates,

> Mr. Warton took out of his pocket a linen cap, striped, which terminated in a point, and pulling off his wig, popped it on his head ... he informed them that a party of wags had established a club called The Jelly Bag Society, of which this was worn as the token of their meetings, and that it had originated from the following epigram written by his friend there, Mr Newberry:-

> One day in Chelsea Meadows walking,
> Of poetry and such things talking,
>   Says Ralph – a merry wag –
> 'An epigram, if smart and good,
> In all its circumstances shou'd
>   Be like a Jelly Bag!'

> 'Your simile I own is new;
> But how wilt make it out?' says Hugh.
>   Quoth Ralph: 'I'll tell thee, friend;
> Make it a top both large and fit
> To hold a budget-full of wit,
>   And point it at the end!'[20]

The Jelly Bag Society remained a popular club and regularly advertised its meetings – though not its secret place of meeting – in *Jackson's Oxford Journal*, often with a neat woodcut of a jelly-bag, at least until 1783. More ephemeral were such clubs as the Free Cynics convened in 1737, 'a kind of Philosophic Club' which had 'a set of symbolical words and grimaces, unintelligible to any but those of their own society', and the Nonsense

Club founded in 1750.[21] The characteristics of all these societies were jovial fellowship, good wine, wit and light-hearted literary exchanges, among a wider and more varied company than one common room provided.

These traditional diversions aside, betting was a popular way of introducing uncertainty into the predictable routine of common room life, providing entertainment and laughter, and, if the bets had been laid in a decent number of bottles, wine for more partakers than the winner. Betting books recorded the details of bets, the stakes and the winners, and the books of Corpus Christi and Lincoln furnish us with a wide variety of topics on which port, claret and Burgundy were staked. Some were of a sporting character: whether Firetail and Pompkin would complete the mile heat in the horse-races; whether Pig or Dutch Sam, Humphries or Mendoza would win their conflicts at fisticuffs. Some were more family affairs between the Fellows: whether Mr Beaver would not get from Corpus common room into Merton with coat, breeches and boots on; whether Mr Model or Mr Weller could hold out the heavier weight at arms length; whether Mr Beaver weighed no more than 17 stone; whether Dr Williams was correct in wagering two bottles of port that he weighed not less than 18 stone 6 pounds. A more energetic bet was accepted by Mr Skelton, no doubt a slimmer Fellow, that he could with the same leg on which he was to hop, touch a mark 6 feet from the ground. Sometimes bets on more significant matters reflected the political and military concerns of England and Europe: whether Mr Pitt would continue to have an armament in a month before 15 October 1792; whether the combined armies would be in possession of Paris before 1 September 1793. That the slave trade would be abolished in the 1790 Parliament; whether there will be a war with America in the course of 1794, or a peace with France before 1795.[22] So the great events of Europe filtered into the common room via the daily papers now purchased through common room subscriptions, to provide food for conversation and subjects for wagers, but nothing to disturb or interrupt the even tenor of its daily life.

That life was the frequent subject of eulogistic poems, nostalgic memoirs, and unashamed enjoyment of its many benefits. Vicesimus Knox, looking back on his Oxford days at St John's, remembered that

> I had been used for thirty years to scarcely any interruption save the tinkling of the chapel and the dinner bell, and could not help being disgusted at the noise of servants and the bustle of a family. Amid the din which was seldom interrupted, how often did I wish myself transported to the blissful region of the common room fire-side! Delightful retreat, where never female shewed her head since the days of the founder![23]

Similar contentment fills a happy college Fellow of twenty years' standing who has not deserted his retreat and writes to *The Loiterer*:

11   Fellows of Merton processing to chapel distracted by ladies

I remember how yesterday passed, I know today will pass in the same manner, and look forward to the morrow with the pleasing expectation that a similar scene will succeed, life elapses in an uninterrupted tranquility, and my time is marked only by the celebration of a gaudy, or the return of a college election.

Though the picture is the same, it is gently touched with irony, for the correspondent signs himself 'Jeremiah Dozeaway'.[24] This is the life which inspires the muse of a contributor to *The Oxford Sausage*, in the measures of Thomas Gray, that melancholy Fellow of combination rooms in another place:

> No chatt'ring Females crowd their social Fire,
> No dread have they of Discord and of Strife;
> Unknown the Names of Husband and of Sire,
> Unfelt the Plagues of matrimonial Life.
>
> Far from the giddy Town's tumultuous Strife,
> Their Wishes yet have never learned to stray;
> Content and happy in a single Life
> They keep the noiseless Tenor of their Way.

There in the Arms of that lethargic Chair,
Which rears it's moth-devoured Back so high,
At noon he quaff'd three Glasses to the Fair,
And por'd upon the News with curious Eye.

Now by the Fire, engaged in serious Talk
Or mirthful Converse, would he loit'ring stand;
Then in the Garden chose a sunny Walk,
Or launch'd the polish'd Bowl with steady Hand.[25]

It is this freedom from cares, domestic, public or financial, which the poets celebrated. How happy was Vice-Chancellor Mather in honour and power, writes Amhurst, though hints of another view lie beneath the praise:

Content to wither in obscure retreat,
And unobserv'd, in plenty drink and eat,
O'er awkward college pedants to preside,
With private grandeur and monastick pride,
In indolence and ease to live unknown,
And nod, like eastern tyrants on their throne. . . .
Nor dost thou only chuse this mongrel life,
Blest with collegiate honours and – no wife.
Sundry besides, thy brethren of the gown,
Like thee, despising fame and wide renown,
Preferring stated meals and frequent prayers
To worldly bustles and domestick cares.[26]

Even the banished Terrae Filius of 1763 had not intended to disturb this comfortable world. 'Let the rosy Doctors and my good *Masters* in every Common-room sleep in Peace,' he would have proclaimed, 'till their next neighbour informs them that the Bottle is at their Elbow! Let them smoke their Pipes in Security . . . I will not, like an unmannerly Dean or Censor of a College, break in upon them to interrupt the Evening's Amusement of Cards or Dice, the brisk Circulation of Toasts, or the *merry merry Round* of Catches in their Rooms.'[27] True, if the comforts of common room and a college life became overshadowed by the tedium and sexual solitariness, the solution was always available. Richard Radcliffe, Fellow of Queen's, put the case quite clearly in a letter of 1773:

The prospect of a Fellowship supported my spirits in poverty, and the possession, thank God, has given me plenty. . . . Besides, you know very well, that we are not bound to this same Foundation by any monkish vows or irreversible decrees. . . . If the prospect at College seems tedious, and we want to settle in the world, the world lies open before us; and we may, if we please, and as is commonly the case, consign ourselves to a school, a wife, and a curacy.[28]

And it is in the character of such a curate that Hurdis, Professor of Poetry, blends criticism and envy of the Oxford life he has left:

> Nor does he envy your ignoble ease,
> Ye pamper'd Priests, that only eat and sleep,
> And sleep and eat, and quaff the tawny juice
> Of vet'ran port; sleep on, and take your rest,
> Nor quit the downy couch preferment strews
> To aid your master. While Alcanor lives,
> Tho' Providence no greater meed design
> To crown his labour, than the scanty sum
> One cure affords, yet will he not regret
> That he renounc'd a life so profitless
> To God and to his country. For he too
> Might still have slumber'd in an easy chair,
> Or idly loll'd upon a sofa, held
> A willing captive in the magic chain
> Of Alma-mater, but in happy time
> Serious occasion cut the golden link,
> And set him free, to taste the nobler sweets
> Of life domestic.[29]

Thomas Warton tries the same tack as he traces 'The Progress of Discontent', but while his rejection of the life of the common room is cleverly assumed, his celebration of that life is the voice of true feeling. At first he speaks like Hurdis's curate:

> These fellowships are pretty things,
> We live indeed like petty kings:
> But who can bear to waste his whole age
> Amid the dulness of a college,
> Debarr'd the common joys of life,
> And that prime bliss – a loving wife!
> O! what's a table richly spread,
> Without a woman at its head!

So he obtains his benefice, moves into his rural life of ease, tythes and gardening, but soon excessive expense and debt overtake him. Then comes the true voice of Warton who loved his common room, spent a long last evening there with congenial friends, and died in his favourite chair:

> Why did I sell my college life
> (He cries) for benefice and wife?
> Return, ye days, when endless pleasure
> I found in reading, or in leisure!

> When calm around the common room
> I puff'd my daily pipe's perfume!
> Rode for a stomach, and inspected
> At annual bottlings, corks selected:
> And din'd untax'd, untroubled, under
> The portrait of our pious Founder!
> When impositions were supply'd
> To light my pipe – or sooth my pride – [30]

But the life of common room and its denizens was not always praised or held in such sentimental esteem. They become a symbol of all that was wrong with the university and its regents. Satirists, serious scholars and disillusioned youth all recorded their disapproval even their disgust at those who

> ... with a clumsy College Pride o'ergrown,
> Sleep life out here a *statutable* Drone.[31]

The inevitable degeneration of these statutable drones is a frequent theme for the satirists, and Terrae Filius, in 1711, hardly surprisingly, makes full use of it.

> When a Person is chosen Fellow of a College, he immediately becomes a *Free-holder*, and is settled for life in Ease and Plenty . . . he wastes the rest of his Days in Luxury and Idleness; he enjoys himself, and is dead to the World; for a *senior Fellow* of a College lives and moulders away in a supine and regular Course of eating, drinking, sleeping, and cheating the Juniors.[32]

Some thirty years later nothing has changed in the way of life or the direction of attack. The college Fellow, according to a correspondence from Cambridge,

> is taught to entertain a sovereign contempt for undergraduates, and, forsooth, scorns to demean himself by conversing with his inferiors. Hence the whole scene of his life is confin'd to those of his own standing: and the college hall, the common-room, the coffee-house, and now and then a ride on Gog-magog hills, is all the variety he has a taste for enjoying ... thus does he gradually degenerate into a mere – what I don't care to name; till at last he has liv'd so long at college, that he is not fit to live anywhere else.[33]

At Wadham, the satirist alleges that

> ... Pride and Dulness to thy Fellows cling,
> And o'er thy whole Foundation spread the Wing.

while at Queen's

> Pride and Ill-nature chiefly o'er them reign,
> Learnedly dull, or ignorantly vain;
> Without Wealth haughty, without Merit proud,

12   Fellows of Magdalen and female attractions

> In Virtue silent, but in Faction loud;
> Upholders of old superstitious Rules,
> Dull in the Pulpit, Triflers in the Schools.[34]

The Fellows of Magdalen found a more famous critic, but his attack presents the same picture. To the fifteen-year-old Gibbon

> The fellows or monks of my time were decent easy men, who supinely enjoyed the gifts of the founder; their days were filled by a series of uniform employments; the chapel and the hall, the coffee-house and the common room, till they retired, weary and self-satisfied, to a long slumber. From the toil of reading, or thinking, or writing, they had absolved their conscience; and the first shoots of learning and ingenuity withered on the ground, without yielding any fruits to the owners or the public. ... Their conversation stagnated in a round of college business, Tory politics, personal anecdotes, and private scandal: their dull and deep potations excused the brisk intemperance of youth.[35]

The audience at the Theatre Royal in 1730 heard much the same thing, but with the more vulgar directness of a character in a Wadham gentleman's comedy: 'O Lord, Madam – why he is a fellow of a College; that's to say, A Rude, Hoggish, Proud, Pedantick, Gormandizing Drone – a dreaming, dull,

Sot, that lives and rots like a Frog in a Ditch.'[36] Such men and such a way of life certainly appear to have shocked and puzzled the more thoughtful youngsters who watched and wondered. John James of Queen's, writing to his friend, described

> The Fellows of a college, that spend half their lives in poring over newspapers and smoking tobacco, seem to live to no end, to be cut off from all the dearer interests of society, to possess, or at least to exert, no benevolence. What in the name of wonder can these men think of themselves when they look back upon a life that has been spent without either receiving or communicating pleasure?[37]

One last example traces, in depressing steps, this degeneration, academic and intellectual, social, emotional and psychological, in the process of donnish decay whereby

> a comfortable subsistence enables the possessors of their liberality to repose from youth to age, in torpid tranquility and unanimated repose. ... One of the first incitements to industry, the apprehension of want is removed; and unless their minds have a strong natural propensity to literature, they soon neglect studies, in the pursuit of which they are not prompted by emulation, or animated by hopes of reward ... those who are far removed from social enjoyments soon forget social habits ... quickly relax into the coarseness of vulgar, or stiffen into the uncouthness of formal manners ... having nothing to demand their attention they sink into drowsy stupidity ... they see every object with a jaundiced eye, they judge of manners from those they observe within the precincts of a common room, and form their estimation of the world, from the appearance of a college ... restrained from the blandishments of female society, and cut off, from every species of domestic enjoyment, with nothing to captivate the affections, with nothing to enlarge the soul, apathy succeeds to feeling; the glow of imagination, the flame of ardour subside, the sweets of friendship, and the smiles of love are unknown, the heart defended from all warm emotions becomes frozen, and the man who has devoted his youth to inactive solitude, too frequently finds spleen, and misanthropy the companions of his age.[38]

This account of the youth and age of a life in college, depressing as it is, and balanced as it must be against the more positive and brighter side of the coin, has nevertheless much truth in it. To the misanthropy and spleen which the writer sees as the companions of age, must be added frequent despair and severe depression. As the happy toping of port and brandy also led to wretched and early deaths, so this life of common room all too often created this lowness of spirits which led to a high frequency of suicides. Hearne records that 'a bedmaker, going to make the Bed of Mr. Thomas Ward A.M. one of the Senior Fellows of Oriel College, found him dead upon the Floor, and his Head shot through. He was cold, so that 'tis supposed he had shot himself the evening before.'[39] Two days later he adds, 'I can now reckon six Clergymen in Oxford that have done so since I have been there (and perhaps there were more, wch I cannot recollect) viz. Dr. Hellyer of Corpus Xti ... who cut his Throat, Mr. Creech of All Souls, who hang'd himself, Mr Will. Hardyng of Trinity Coll., who shot himself, Mr. White ... who cut his throat in Xt. Church., Mr Eyans of Wadham Coll,. who shot himself.'[40] Five years later he reports that 'Last Sunday Morning, between 8 and 9 Clock, when they were at Prayers, at Merton Coll., one Mr. Gardiner, M.A. & Fellow of that College, cut his own Throat in his Chamber, and died of the Wound last Night.'[41] Perhaps without common room and its social life, however cabined and confined it might have been, with only their solitary chambers to brood in and high table to eat at, such deaths might have been even more frequent. Hearne – who lived at a hall without a common room, which survived for over another two centuries before its Fellows obtained one after considerable struggle – filled his life with work in the Bodleian, extensive scholarly work, energetic walking and excursions, a wide circle of learned and youthful friends and a great range of interests. He managed to keep cheerful in his own sour and belligerent way. But Hearne was Hearne, and a rather special person.

CHAPTER SIX

Drinking and Riot

Looking back on his Oxford days in the last decade of the century, Robert Southey wrote that 'Temperance is much wanted; the waters of Helicon are far too much polluted by the wine of Bacchus ever to produce any effect. With respect to its superiors, Oxford only exhibits waste of wigs and want of wisdom; with respect to undergraduates, every species of abandoned excess.'[1] Only one or two voices can be heard claiming otherwise, and they are difficult to believe. Where, one wonders, could James Harris have sheltered himself to assert in 1763 that 'luckily drinking was not the fashion',[2] or where Lewis Holberg, who spent two years in Oxford in the 1730s and recorded in his memoirs 'the benefit which the students derive from this salutary discipline is as striking as is the mischief which results from an opposite system in some other seats of learning, which are at the same time schools for drinking, feasting, gaming, and every species of debauchery'.[3] The evidence to the contrary is too extensive and coherent, whether it be found in specific scandalous comment as Terrae Filius's 'Next for the *Jacobite Toperes* of St. *John's*. How many Bottles of humming double *Coll* did you drink out the last Tenth of *June?* I warrant you swig'd till you were each as drunk as *David's* Sow, from the P[resident] to the *Servitors*',[4] or in the notes of an alleged visitor to Oxford in 1704 that 'Wad. C. is no less famed for liquor than learning; here 'tis at your option to be a Sot or Scholar, Pot and Book are both Exercised.'[5] More generally the truth is unforgettably stated in Pope's famous couplet,

> Till Isis' Elders reel, their pupils' sport
> And Alma Mater lie dissolv'd in Port.[6]

except that pupils as well as elders reeled as well as sported, drank often heavily and sometimes violently.

The only business of a college Fellow, alleged a pamphlet of 1783, 'is, to eat, drink, and sleep; his only care, the means of filling up his idle hours'.[7] And it was surely the idleness of the many hours between dinner and bed, without teaching or serious study, which turned the dons to the pleasures of the bottle to add life to the more muted pleasures of college business, newspapers and gossip. After plentiful imbibing at high table when the Fellows retired to common room, and in the evening after chapel, a stroll or a nap, when common room was the retreat for the hours before bed, it was here that the serious drinking of the seniors was centred. Woodforde's diary tells of many an evening of heavy drinking and drunken quarrelling between Junior Fellows in the bachelors' common room at New College. Shortly before he was elected Fellow he was involved in a fracas with friends from Merton who 'spent their evening in the B.C.R. Croucher was devilish drunk indeed, and made great noise there, but was carried away to Peckham's Bed in triumph. Baker laid with me.'[8] This Peckham was a wild one in his drink as Woodforde found to his discomfort two years later when

> at three in the morning, had my outward doors broken open, my glass door broke, and pulled out of bed, and brought into the B.C.R. where I was obliged to drink and smoak, but not without a good many words. Peckham broke my doors, being very drunk, although they were open, which I do not relish of Peckham much.[9]

Woodforde, as we know, bought his wine in bulk and bottled it for his own use at private dinners in his room or had it brought to common room when he wished to contribute to the jollity. He notes such a party when he

> Had three bottles of Wine out of my room in the B.C.R. Waring was very drunk and Bedford little better. N.B. I was very sober, as I had made a resolution never to get drunk again, when at Geree's rooms in April last, when I fell down dead, and cut my Occiput very bad indeed.[10]

If he kept that resolution, he must have had a very strong head and a large capacity, for he never ceased to keep late and convivial hours as long as he was at New College and among his friends: 'Coker, Townshend, Dan Williams, Blisse Dr. Wall and Webber and myself made a very late night of it being very jolly indeed. We sat up till near 4 in the morning. I fetched 3 bottles of wine out of my Room at 12 o'clock.'[11] When at last he had been elected to the living of Weston he treated his colleagues in style. Wine flowed in the afternoon, wine and Arrack punch in the evening; he treated and drank with the chaplains and clerks, went down to drink with the junior common room from eleven in the morning til twelve, where 'we were exceeding merry in the J.C.R. and had many good songs sung', then back to the senior common room till nearly four o'clock in the morning.[12]

With such large potations a regular part of common room life, it is not surprising that it was frequently violent, quarrelsome and inelegant. Drinking wagers entertained the younger Fellows, as when 'Dyer laid Williams 2s. 6d. that he drank 3 pints of wine in 3 Hours, and that he wrote 5 verses out of the Bible right, but he lost. He did it in the B.C.R., he drank all the Wine, but could not write right for his Life. He was immensley drunk about 5 minutes afterwards.'[13] Woodforde himself was guilty of 'throwing some Wine in Bedford's face in the B.C.R. I was sconced a Bottle of Wine.'[14] On another occasion he quarrelled with a colleague in common room and retired to fight him in the garden 'where he (being full as strong again) beat me unmercifully'.[15] And when he needed to make use of the chamber pot provided in the common room to render a journey to the bog-house unnecessary, he was 'Sconced for breaking Wind while I was making Water in the Looking Glass'.[16]

New College was certainly not alone in its service to Bacchus, but simply more fully documented, thanks to its resident diarist. In the common rooms of most colleges the Fellows drank heavily, often emerged through the college gates much the worse for wear, or staggered home to find refuge behind them. At the very end of the century things had not changed, as the amount of liquor consumed, for example at Queen's, would indicate. In one year 1,470 bottles of port, 171 bottles of sherry, 48 bottles of Madeira, and unaccounted quantities of gin, rum and punch were consumed in common room, not including the wine drunk at high table.[17] No wonder a young undergraduate of Brasenose remembered how he 'often saw my tutor carried off perfectly intoxicated'.[18] Early in the century Hearne, always alert for scandal, noted with disgust that

> Yesterday Morning, at two Clock, the Duke of Beaufort (who is of Univ. Coll.) rid out of Town with that vicious, loose Fellow, Mr. Ward (commonly call'd Jolly Ward) of Univ. Col. ... It is said they had sate up 'till that time drinking. Ward was so drunk that he vomited four times between Queen's Coll. Lane & East Gate.[19]

In lighter satirical mood, a poem of 1713 depicts a reverend doctor seeking but missing his home-college, Magdalen, and finishing up in Magdalen Grove:

> But others elevated to Degrees,
> Above Heav'n's Laws or University's,
> Ne'er flinch till jaded Nature dares reproach,
> Surfeit their only Check upon Debauch. ...
> When Holy Club disperse'd, the Members reel
> To College, full of Liquor as of Zeal.
> The Doctor missing his, did onwards move,
> To meditate himself into the Grove.[20]

There, the poem tells, he met the Devil.

At Corpus Christi Mr Modd the chaplain was notorious for misbehaviour, drunkenness, extravagance and other irregularities. He was admonished twice and finally forbidden to eat, drink, or sleep in college, although it was thought the chapel was safe in his hands and he continued to perform his duties there on full pay. Ames, a Fellow of that same indulgent college, set fire to the furniture of the Fellows' common room, books and pamphlets and college plate. He was allowed to resign quietly, his actions being considered rather 'a sudden impulse of madness than the result of determined villainy'.[21] Even a Pro-Proctor was not exempt from the vice. Harris of Wadham had been abused in the street and struck by one Fletcher of University College. The assailant was carried to the Castle and rapidly expelled. But Hearne adds, 'tho there are not wanting credible Witnesses who say that Harris was more in drink than Fletcher'.[22] Years later and nearer to home he recorded with anger how 'Pearce, Vice-Princ. of Edm. Hall ... staid out with the officers & other Rascall drinking 'till past two Clock this Morning, when he knock'd in at [the] Gate. The writer of these matters was then up. . . . He was quite drunk, and I am well inform'd that this Dog had been before in New Parks.'[23]

Learned doctors, drunken and astray in the streets strove, like the divine of Magdalen, to find their home. Dr Charlett, drunk from an evening at New College, sacked his mischievous servant-boy, equally drunk, for 'lighting him home with a Silver Tankard instead of a dark Lantern'.[24] But perhaps the most endearing of these learned wanderers was a Doctor of Divinity, striving to make his way to Brasenose through Radcliffe Square, who 'had reached the library, a rotunda then without railings, and, unable to support himself except by keeping one hand upon the building, he continued walking round and round' until rescued by a friend and led safely home.[25] No such guiding hand was ever needed by another learned doctor of Pembroke who, when at Oxford, succumbed to many of its ways and pleasures. 'I have drunk three bottles of port without being the worse for it,' boasted Dr Johnson, 'University College has witnessed this.'[26]

The undergraduates, lacking a common room, the scene of so much of their elders' drinking, indulged themselves in college in the rooms they had so proudly taken over on the first exciting day of their arrival. An exception, created late in the century, would be the Phoenix Common Room at Brasenose, but this was much more an exclusive dining club than a general J.C.R. A small meeting of four undergraduates in 1781 expanded to a membership of twelve in 1768, with officers and rules. Later BAs were admitted as honorary members. The members dined together every evening, each member providing the room in turn, where their own common room man waited on them, and where their own decanters, glasses and cutlery were laid out. It also had those other two essentials of a common room – its own newspapers and wine cellar, the latter to furnish the table and the members' needs in their own rooms. The common room rules indicate the not abstemious habits of the members, no single member being allowed to take from the cellar more than two dozen port and six sherry – per week.[27]

Serious voices regretted and explained these youngsters' early resort to the bottle. 'But there is one fault incident to youth,' wrote one solemn but tolerant giver of advice,

> and which in the University, where so many young men are together, often happens: viz. Excess of drinking. – The ease and vivacity of conversation, the openness of thought, and cheerfulness of spirit, which generally circulate with the bottle, are apt to lead us unwarily beyond the bounds limited for the enjoyment of it.... Youth, therefore, to whom the exact limits are not chalked out, as to those of more experience and knowledge, may naturally be expected to fall sometimes into this excess; considering it in this light, it is by most now and then forgiven or passed over.[28]

Other attempts to explain undergraduate drunkenness blame the low spirits brought on by the tedium of college life. A Queen's man, looking back on his time there, recalled how his contemporaries 'Taken from milk, air and exercise, to tea, beef and a sedentary life in College ... become nervous and low-spirited. Assistance is sometimes sought from the bottle, and the bottle, like the Dane, enslaves every Briton who courts its aid and alliance.'[29] Vicesimus Knox believed that 'every one, on putting on the academical dress commences a man in his own opinion, and will often endeavour to support the character by the practice of manly vices'.[30] He is nearer the truth, that these young men felt an exhilaration as they escaped from the discipline and oversight of their schools and parents, from what they saw as the tyranny which oppressed their early years, and now burst out masters of their own rooms, and time and pleasures. True, there were serious and sober youth who hated 'The riot and intemperate mirth, which I am subjected to on one side or other ... at all times disagreeable to me',[31] and who would have agreed with Knox's vision of 'immorality, habitual drunkenness, idleness, ignorance, and vanity, openly and boastingly obtruding themselves on public view. I saw them triumphing without controul over the timidity of modest merit.'[32] But the liveliness and jollity of the accounts of some of these evening undergraduate parties contrast favourably with the dogged excesses of the senior common room, and communicate the joyous kicking over of the traces, and a welcome to social pleasure.

The initiation of the freshman into the world of parties came early, almost on the day he was welcomed by friends and former schoolmates. Nicholas Amhurst in an early number of *Terrae Filius* gives not entirely serious advice and warning to these freshmen:

> You set out in the *Stage*-Coach to OXFORD, with recommendatory Letters in your Pockets to some body or other in the College, where you are to be admitted, who introduce you, as soon as you get there, amongst a Parcel of *honest, merry Fellows*, who think themselves obliged in point of Honour and common Civility to make you *damnable drunk*, and carry you, as they call it, a

CORPSE to Bed; the next Night you are treated as civilly again, and perhaps for three or four Nights afterwards.[33]

One such Freshman in the company of such merry fellows is moved to blank verse as he recalls that first party, its joys and its pains:

> ... The hearty shake,
> The friendly welcome, go alternate round:
> And that blest day, till eve's remotest hour,
> Is sacred to our joys – Its choicest stores
> The genial larder opes; exhausted deep,
> Even to its inmost hoards, the buttery groans.
> But now the bottle rolls its ample round,
> Kindling to rapture each congenial soul:
> The burst of merriment, the joyous catch
> Ring round the roofs incessant – much is talk'd
> Of past exploits, and grievous tasks imposed
> By former Tyrants; tyrants now no more.
> Transported with the thought, in frantic joy
> I raise my arm, and mid surrounding shouts,
> Quaff the full bumper; ah, full dearly rued! ...
>   a deadly hue
> Sudden invests my cheeks, my fainting soul
> Is fill'd with horrid loathings and strange pangs,
> Unfelt before; convulsing all my frame. ...[34]

Once those early days were over and the first experiments made, the freshman found his social group, though strong drink seemed a necessary and almost universal accompaniment to their gatherings. William Shenstone, arriving as a commoner at Pembroke in 1732, found one exception, 'a very sober little party, who amused themselves in the evening with reading Greek, and drinking water', but soon deserted 'this mortified symposium' for the company of 'a set of jolly, sprightly young fellows, most of them west-country lads; who drank ale, smoked tobacco, punned, and sung bacchanalian catches the whole evening; our "pious orgies" generally began with,

> Let's be jovial, fill our glasses,
>   Madness 'tis for us to think,
> How the world is rul'd by asses,
>   And the wisest sway'd by chink.'

He next tried the group of

Some gentlemen-commoners ... who considered the above mentioned as very *low* company (chiefly on account of the liquor they drank) [who] good-naturedly invited me to their party: they treated me with port-wine and arrack punch; and now and then, when they had drunk so much as hardly to distinguish wine from water, they would conclude with a bottle or two of claret. They kept late hours, drank their favourite toasts on their knees; and, in short, were what we called 'bucks of the first head'.[35]

But, as might be expected of a future poet, he chose as his regular evening company a literary circle who, in each other's chambers, 'read plays and poetry, Tatlers and Spectators, and other works of easy digestion; and sipped Florence wine'.[36] An evening at Trinity, with song and music had a similarly moderate alcoholic accompaniment to the consort of harpsichord, viol and flute, when

> The cloth remov'd, some Negus sip
> And some regale on hot egg flip
>   And some sing Catch and Glee.
> For each in turn must something do,
> Attempt old songs or bawl out new
>   By way of harmony.[37]

This evening closed decorously, but the slightest excuse could turn such a moderate evening of pleasure into excess requiring discipline. One young scholar, receiving an affectionate letter from his sweetheart, found himself in 'such spirits, that I invited the chosen Few to my Room; where, being a little too busy with Bumpers, we happened to disturb the Society, for which next Morning Mr. *Trueman* and myself were confined to the Library for a Month, with a swinging Imposition of old *Tully's* to divert us'.[38] It remains for Brasenose, after these few comparatively respectable gatherings, to demonstrate the worst, the noisiest and most violent possibilities of these undergraduate parties. Edmund Botton, an undergraduate from Bolton, attended a punch party in the rooms of Wyndham Napier one December evening in 1725. 'Everyone,' he remembered, 'at first design'd to get drunk soberly, and took their Glasses together very friendly: each drinking his right-hand man's good health over the right thumb.' All went well until another member of the group, one Trogee, considering the pace of things by the glass too slow, decided to swig from the punch bowl. The mood of the party changed. 'Now glasses clash'd with glasses, and pipes with pipes in terrible Confusion, and the punch ran in rapid streams down their throats.' Soon fighting broke out. Trogee who had started it all was 'kick'd from the top of the stairs, and would inevitably have broken his skull'. Luckily a more sober member 'catch'd him at the bottom ... some hurt and some unhurt in the scuffle they went to bed themselves, and so very prettily concluded the Sunday night. ... Trogee is gone down into the Country and has carried with him a terrible black Eye and Bruis'd face.'[39]

New College, too, earned a reputation for noisy and destructive drunkenness. While still an undergraduate, Woodforde had been a troublesome member of his set. 'Hearst, Bell and myself, being in Beer, went under

Whitmore's window, and abused him very much, as being Dean, he came down, and sent us to our Proper Rooms, and then we Huzza'd him again and again. We are to wait upon him tomorrow.'[40] Another time he was the victim when a gang 'about 4 o'clock in the Morning ... broke open my outward Door, and then broke my Bedchamber Door, all to shatters for Funn. N.B. They were all as drunk as Pipers.'[41] Years later, poacher turned gamekeeper, he records continuing drunken disorder. 'In the night there was a great riot in College by the Junior People who broke down Daubenny's doors and broke Jeffries windows.' The Warden summoned the Deans, punishments were meted out and stern threats made, but by the autumn of the same year, with the Warden still thundering threats of rigour, 'We have of many nights past had very great Hallowing etc. in the Courts, what is facetiously called the upright – the He-Up. ... I have been disturbed two or three nights lately by their great disturbance in the Court. The Junior Com. Room Chimney Piece was pulled down Saturday night by the above Rioters.'[42] So it was, within the college walls, in common rooms, under-graduate rooms and quadrangles, but outside lay another world of drink and drunkards, the streets and the drinking haunts of the city, none of them without the patronage and sometimes the riot of the men of the gown.

At the most respectable end of this extensive range of establishments providing liquor, were the numerous coffee houses, customary and well-loved resorts at a certain time in the social day, between the end of dinner and the evening. Routh of Magdalen remembered the time 'when every academic of fashion resorted to the coffee-house during the afternoon,'[43] and every coffee house had its own particular clientele. Tom's coffee house in the High was exclusive and expensive. Its small back room, always known as 'The House of Lords', furnished with Chippendale chairs, was a sanctum for the dons. At Horseman's opposite Brasenose in the High, men from Merton, All Souls, Corpus Christi and Oriel gathered. Harper's at the corner of Queen's Lane catered for Queen's and Magdalen, while Bagg's at the corner of Holywell opposite the King's Arms entertained those from New College, Hertford and Wadham. Malbon's was a tiny house, a little below street level, at the north-east corner of the Turl, and Trinity men crossed the road to drink there.[44] The chief beverages served there were chocolate and coffee at 4*d.* a pot until in 1759 ten proprietors announced a price increase of a penny (only Mr Blowfield of the George coffee house not joining in the rise), but strong liquors were always available and were freely partaken of, not so much in the afternoon session, but by those gathering later in the evening. In 1775 an Irish visitor, Dr Thomas Campbell, a friend of Dr Johnson and the Thrales, noted in his account of his Oxford visit:

> N.B. We went to the Coffee house in the evening, where almost all the Gownsmen we saw were tipsy, and the streets re-echoed with Bacchanalian crys, as we returned from supper with Mr. Barnard. The next night also, we

went to another Coffee house, and there the scene was only shifted, all muzzy. This happily abated my enthusiasm conceived for an Oxford education.[45]

If the reverend doctor had visited the taverns and pot-houses of the city, his enthusiasm would have been totally extinguished. Here, in the less reputable and less elegant houses, the real drinking and the scenes of drunkenness and riot originated. 'We keep up, or at least connive at more than 300 Ale-houses of the very worst Fame and Reputation, without any even the least Offer of discommuning them', complained the proprietors of wine cellars (of whom more anon) in 1734.[46] To chronicle but a few of the three hundred, we find such a picturesque selection as these: the Greyhound, Angel, Mitre, Roebuck, Star, New Inn, Boar, Goats, King's Arms, Cross, Jockey, Chequers, Blue-Cur, Pheasant, Barley-Mow, Ark, Lion, Green Dragon, Seven Deadly Sins, Bells, Nag, Coach, Shoulder of Mutton, Ox, Holly Bush, Swan.[47] Add to these another class of house common in Oxford, 'inns or *tippling houses* . . . not only in the body but in the skirts of the town' such as '*Fox-hall, Lemon Hall, Feather-hall, Stump-hall, Cabbage-Hall, Caterpillar hall* &c.' One deserving particular notice, situated to the north east, a little way out of town, was known by the name of '*Kidney*' Hall, 'which has long been a very noted seminary'.[48] Thomas Hearne, a great walker, would have added Blind Pinnocks at Cumnor, and Louse Hall kept by Mother Louse at the bottom of Headington Hill on the slopes of which both Cabbage Hall and Caterpillar Hall were situated. Nearer town he favoured Antiquity Hall, as might have been expected from one who 'studied and preserved antiquities'. These and others too numerous to mention filled the streets and alleys and environs of Oxford.

Their customers included the whole of the university from don to undergraduate, and it is a don, Fellow of Trinity who, Poet Laureate of his own common room, celebrates in verse the pleasures of the pot-house. Warton had a fondness for the company of working men and the lower orders of society, as well as the relaxing freedom of the ale-bench after the scholarly labours of the day. He celebrates his own twofold life in the imagined person of an undergraduate, in his *Panegyric on Oxford Ale*:

> Meantime, not mindless of the daily task
> Of Tutor sage, upon the learned leaves
> Of deep SMIGLECIUS much I meditate;
> While ALE inspires, and lends its kindred aid,
> The thought-perplexing labour to pursue,
> Sweet Helicon of logic! But if friends
> Congenial call me from the toilsome page,
> To Pot-house I repair, the sacred haunt,
> Where, ALE, thy votaries in full resort
> Hold rites nocturnal. In capacious chair
> Of monumental oak and antique mould. . . .

> Studious of ease, and provident, I place
> My gladsome limbs; while in repeated round
> Returns replenish'd the successive cup,
> And the brisk fire conspires to genial joy.[49]

But this jovial and attractive scene is not what many Oxonians and visitors to Oxford saw or described. Humphrey Prideaux writing to his friend, exposes the other side of Warton's attractive medal: 'There is over against Baliol College a dingy, horrid, scandalous alehouse, fit for none but draymen and tinkers. . . . Here the Baliol men continually ly, and by perpetual bubbeing ad[d] art to their natural stupidity to make themselfes perfect sots.'[50] Charles Moritz, in his reminiscences of a visit to England, describes his arrival in Oxford, just before midnight. Seeking accommodation, he and his companion knocked on the door of what proved to be an ale-house. 'They readilly let us in,' he records, 'but how great was my astonishment, when, on being shown into a room on the left, I saw a great number of clergymen, all with their gowns and their bands on, sitting round a large table, each with his pot of beer before him.' The strangers were made welcome and the conversation turned on discipline and misrule. ' "Oh we are very unruly here too," said one of the clergymen, as he took a hearty draught out of his pot of beer, and knocked on the table with his hand.' Moritz appears to have struck up a special acquaintance with one of the drinkers, Mr Maud of Corpus Christi College, and after many more pots 'At last, when morning drew near, Mr. Maud suddenly exclaimed, damn me, I must read prayers this morning at All Souls!'[51]

Another foreign visitor blamed such men as Mr Moritz had been drinking with for most of the violations of the statutes strictly forbidding the undergraduates to frequent taverns, inns and pot-houses under threat of proctorial discipline. He tells his readers, strange to the Oxford scene,

> In the evening, censors chosen annually, called Proctors, visit all parts of the city, and if any students are discovered in Taverns, or other improper haunts, they are subject to heavy fines and impositions. It is ridiculous enough, however, that these moral regulations do not extend to those who are distinguished by the higher academical degrees: for the doctors and masters of arts enjoy the right of drinking in taverns till daybreak, and the attainment of the superior degrees confers the twofold privilege of disputing and of carousing in public. . . . Certain it is, however, that most of the carousals and drinking bouts in taverns take place under the auspices of masters of arts. I remember the students were often caught in our tavern; but whenever a superior graduate was present, they boldly told the Proctors that they were in the company of masters of arts; upon which the Proctors immediately retired.[52]

Warton asserts that the pot-houses were safer from proctorial visitation than the coffee houses or taverns:

> Nor Proctor thrice with vocal heel alarms
> Our joys secure, nor deigns the lowly roof
> Of Pot-house snug to visit: wiser he
> The splendid tavern haunts, or coffee-house
> Of JAMES or JUGGINS. . . .
> But the lewd spendthrift, falsely deem'd polite,
> While steams around the fragrant Indian bowl,
> Oft damns the vulgar sons of humble ALE:
> In vain – the Proctor's voice arrests their joys.[53]

But a stronger reason for their popularity was simply that, for the young, ale was the favourite out-of-college tipple. A visitor to the King's Head, disgusted by the quality of the wine there, understood why 'Ale is the Prime Commodity that is here afforded, 'tis in it our Gownsmen liquidate their Coin; 'tis on Account of this divine and inspiring Liquid, that they arrive to that Elevated Pitch of Honour, as to render their names worthy of the Dignified Character of *creta Notanda*.'[54] Colleges continued to complain, the Heads of Houses thundered out decrees and orders, the Proctors diligently, though not always soberly, walked the streets, but the undergraduates still haunted their favourite taverns, their potations no doubt gaining spice from the potential danger of proctorial arrest.

Those officers had, perhaps, a more daunting task than visiting the forbidden houses, when the young left their pots and issued forth on to the streets. The noise and destruction of riot and disturbance in college was the concern of the Dean; the violence and rowdiness of the streets had to be tackled by the Proctors and their deputies, and most of it was the direct result of excessive drinking and youthful exuberance. Admittedly there were other causes, the ever-rumbling town-and-gown antagonism, political demonstrations, wild scenes at executions or at the assizes, but, *pace* Lewis Holberg's noting in his memoirs that 'if you go out after ten o'clock at Oxford, it is difficult to imagine that you are in the midst of a populous city, so complete is the solitude, so profound the silence which reigns around you',[55] the larger body of evidence shows that it was with Bacchanalian cries that the streets re-echoed nightly.

The Proctors and their deputies doubtless did their best to repress undergraduate lawlessness and arrest offenders. Their authority frightened and controlled the timid. The law-abiding made for home, out of harm's way, as

> When the Sun darting gentle Western Light,
> Informs fair *Oxford* of approaching Night;
> Releas'd from poring Labours of the Day,
> Her weary'd Youth for Recreation stray;

13   A rag at Carfax as the Proctors arrive

> Just as his ruling Genius each constrains
> To wet his Whistle, or to purge the Reins;
> Till fatally alarm'd by mighty *Tom*,
> Or scar'd by *Velvet Sleeves* they scamper home.[56]

Others, equally timid, were caught, and trembled. Woodforde in his role as Pro-Proctor, called out of a happy night in New College Chequer,

> went to the Swan in George Lane, and unfortunately met with a Gownsman above stairs carousing with some low-life people. We conducted him to his College. He belongs to University College, is a scholar there, and his name is Hawkins, he was terribly frightened and cried almost all the way to his Coll, and was upon his knees very often in the street and bare headed all the way.[57]

The more defiant youth found that pursuit by the Proctors added excitement to their riot, the fun of disobedience and getting away with it, as one who enjoyed 'a famous evening till the Proctors came and told us to go home to our Colleges – went directly the contrary way, eleven to one, went down into St. Thomas's and fought a raff-one, dragged home by somebody, the Lord knows whom, and put to bed.'[58] St Thomas's parish was a favourite if unsavoury retreat from the pursuing powers, but not always a successful one. One young gownsman wandering the streets after many a glass and bottle,

> ... oft by these inspir'd
> From street to street, beneath the moon's pale beam,
> Heedless I stray, if happily *Proctor's* voice
> Check not my progress – *Siste* – dreadful sound,
> *What shou'd I do, or whither turn – amaz'd,*
> *Confounded* down some narrow lane I scower
> Of fam'd *St. Thomas,* virtue's chaste retreat:
> But vain my flight, for ruffians' cruel palms
> Arrest my steps, and to the offended power
> Force me reluctant. ... [59]

His escapade ended in his being gated and given a heavy imposition. At least he surrendered peacefully.

Sometimes the Proctors faced more serious and dangerous opponents. Witness this notice issued by Thomas Leigh, the Vice-Chancellor, on 20 March 1750:

> Whereas on *Friday* Evening ... between the Hours of Eight and Nine o'clock, a most notorious Insult was offer'd to one of the Senior proctors in the Execution of his Office, by a Person throwing at Him a large Stone, whereby he received a violent Blow on the Head; this is therefore to give Notice that if any one will discover the said Person, he shall upon his conviction be entitled to a Reward of Ten Guineas.[60]

Subsequent investigations discovered certain undergraduate delinquents who were punished, though not as severely as they might have been 'on account of some favourable Representations on Their behalf' – of wealth, connections, nobility, who knows?

Neither the streets nor the night time were the only settings for drunken riot. One of the most picturesque took place at the heart of the university, in the Sheldonian Theatre, at the height of solemn university ceremonial, and presented a very difficult problem for the Proctors:

> Mr. Woodhouse a gent: com. of University College was very drunk at the Theatre and cascaded [i.e. vomited] in the midst of the Theatre. Mr. Highway one of the nominal Proctors for this week desired him to withdraw very civilly but was desired by one Mr. Pedley a gent: comm. of St. Mary Hall not to mind him, my seeing Highway in that distress I went to them myself and insisted upon Woodhouse going away immediately from the Theatre, and then Peddley behaved very impertinently to me, at which I insisted upon his coming to me tomorrow morning. Mr. Woodhouse after some little time retired, but Peddley remained and behaved very impertinently.[61]

His name was intended for the Black Book of university infamy. Such gentlemen commoners as this Mr Peddley, not subject to the stricter rules and disciplines, are often blamed for inciting and leading such drunken wildness – 'a pert and pampered race', as we have seen them described, 'too froward for controul, too headstrong for persuasion, too independent for chastisement; privileged prodigals'.[62]

Juvenile debauchery and donnish sottishness may have their elements of grotesque comedy or gloomy pathos, but excessive drinking in eighteenth-century Oxford had often only an unrelieved black and squalid face. Death from drink was commonplace, in the young and the old, sometimes caused by drunken violence, sometimes finding its victim in solitary drunkenness. Hearne notes a few of them in a cool offhand way reserved for recording the ordinary:

> On Sunday Night last Mr. Thomas a Welch man Commoner of Queen's Coll. being drinking with three or four more of the same College, and continuing at it till 2 or 3 Clock in the Morning, at last a Quarrell arose, & Thomas receiv'd a Wound near one of his Eyes, wch threw him into a violent Feaver of wch he died on Tuesday following afternoon.

> This afternoon was buried in St. Peter's in the East Dr. Lawrence Hyde (S.T.P.) of Madg. Coll. (of wch he was a fellow), he dying a Day or two since of a Consumption, occasion'd in great measure by Hard Drinking.

> This Morning between 12 and 1 Clock died suddenly in High-Street, as he was coming with his Companions from a drinking Bout at the Blew Bore, one Mr. Cletheroe, a Commoner of Queen's College.

> This morning died Mr. John Isham (Son of Sr. Justinian Isham) A.M. and Fellow of All-Souls, a Young Gent. who killed himself purely by hard drinking, as not long since did his great Comrade, one Mr. Williams, A.B. and fellow of the same College.[63]

Humphrey Prideaux wrote to his friend of one David Whitford, student of Christ Church who 'was found fallen back upon his bed halfe dressed, with a brandy bottle in one hand, and the cork in the other; He findeing himself ill, as it seemeth, was going to take a dram for refreshment, but death came between the cup and his lips'.[64] And death came for many between the bottle and the lips, in drunken accident, quarrel, apoplexy and stroke and decayed liver. This was the other side to the joviality and comradeship of wine party and tavern and common room, the unpleasant reality behind the melancholy irony of Thomas Gray's sketch of common room life, albeit in another place: 'We shall smoke, we shall tipple, we shall doze together, we shall have our little Jokes, like other People, and our Long Stories; Brandy will finish what Port begun.'[65]

CHAPTER SEVEN

Women and Love

The truth was that this society was almost exclusively male: the myth was
that, with a few permitted exceptions, it was celibate. Between the truth and
the myth are the many slips from grace, concealments and subterfuges, open
and notorious scandals, which make as fascinating reading today as they
provided endless gossip for their own time.

A lady of pleasure in George Colman's *The Oxonian in Town* exclaims, 'I
wish to die, if I don't wonder how they do live there. A pack of men together
without any women among them.'[1] She would soon have discovered that
many hands, young and old, reached out for the forbidden fruit of female
company and love. The freshman, released from the male confines of school
and fired with new desires, looked round eagerly and often awkwardly to
fulfil them:

> In vain the sober Tutors swear and curse
> And spend in unregarded Chat their Hours;
> In vain they syllogistically prove,
> That 'tis a childish thing for Boys to love;
> Their Art will ne'er the giddy Youth reclaim,
> They'll still hunt after Girls, be still the same.[2]

One of these giddy boys, awakening to the call, inspired a poet of Wadham
to describe

> ... the dull *Freshman* just arrived from School,
> (A Coxcomb rip'ning from a rustic fool)
> Whilst in his sabbath-suit he treads the mall,
> Staring, and star'd at too alike by all,
> If a bewitching *Syren* catch his eyes,
> In his wrapt breast *poetic* transports rise;
> Straight, the pert *sonnet* frames her all divine,
> Bids her a *Muse*, a *Grace*, a *Venus* shine.[3]

75

14   Gentlemen-commoners going a-wooing

Others of less poetic turn roam the streets 'staring with all eyes a young man has, at everything in the shape of a woman that happens to walk the street or to look out of an inn'[4] or indulge themselves inside the inn where among congenial company they can boast of amorous conquests real or imaginary:

> But with his Friends, when Nightly-Mists arise,
> To *Juniper's Magpye*, or *Town-Hall* repairs:
> Where, mindful of the Nymph, whose wanton Eye
> Transfix'd his Soul, and kindled amorous Flames,
> CHLOE, or PHILLIS; he each circling Glass
> Wisheth her Health, and Joy, and equal Love.[5]

There was no lack of ladies upon the watch for these eager and unpractised youths, '*Kidnapping Females*', as one satirist warned, 'upon the watch, and *seeking whom they may devour*' bringing about 'the almost universal Corruption of our Youth, which is to be imputed to nothing so much as to that Multitude of Female *Residentuaries*, who have of late infected our Learned retirements, and draw off Numbers of unwary young Persons from their studies.'[6] And not only the raw youth. The higher ranks of the academic community were not immune to the amorous flame or the machinations of these kidnapping females. Noblemen with their gold tassels and gentlemen commoners in their silk gowns had their attractions, and greater freedom to respond:

> Fresh from the Schools, behold an Oxford Smart!
> No dupe of Science, no dull slave of Art.
> As to our dress, faith ladies, to say Truth.
> It is a little awkward and uncouth.
> No Sword, Cockade, to lure you to our Arms –
> But then this airy Tassel has its Charms.
> What mortal Oxford laundress can withstand
> This, and the Graces of a well-starch'd Band?[7]

Respond it seems they did, as a lady in the same play confesses to her friend. 'It was a gentleman-commoner of *Marlin's College* (a sweet, pretty, dear, good-natured man as ever lived) that first *ruined* me; and has been a particular good friend to me ever since.'[8] As we shall see in greater detail later, college Fellows, young and aged, were not behindhand in the race. Indeed the ladies, according to one fictional witness, preferred the good times the more opulent fellows could offer them: 'Believe me, Sir, we scorn to look or speak to an Under-graduate, when engag'd in a Pleasure-Boat with the Fellows of *Baliol*; there's glorious living, good Ham and Chickens, sparkling Wines, ravishing Musick, then we can sip and tip and smack our Lips all round with some Satisfaction.'[9] Another fictional sister, however, writing 'from experience', suggests that though the picnics might have been scrumptious, the love-making was pretty shy and reserved: 'I avow that the seniors are IN THEIR WAY, as gallant and as amorous as the younger collegians ... [but they] seem asham'd of our good graces; and instead of open congees in a walk or assembly, content themselves with a tacit adoration of their mistress during tea or a Sunday's dinner at her fathers.'[10] An opinion expressed more crudely and directly by Alicia D'Anvers some fifty years before:

> Not one of their Young Senior Fellows,
> But's of his Chastity so jealous,
> Should you a Naked Woman shew 'em
> You'd fright 'em so, 'Twould quite undo 'em.[11]

The years pass by. The shy young Fellow ages into the decrepit but lofty Rector of Exeter College, and the youthful amorous ineptitude declines into pathetic pursuit of rougher trade:

> Yet thus disabled, for the longing dame
> He feels the pangs of love, though not the flame;
> Fair RAGGABEL, that near his college-gate
> Fine china sells, and tea, and chocolate,
> Or mends old tatter'd gowns with matchless art,
> Shines in his eye, and triumphs in his heart;
> Oft to her shop the feeble lecher strays,
> Toys with her hand, or with her bubbies plays.[12]

Allowing for the exaggerations of satire and gossip, it is quite clear that the pursuit of women in this male society was an absorbing pastime, involving young and old, exploring various sources of supply, near at hand or safely distant from the officers of discipline, moderately respectable, but often definitely sordid.

A pamphlet published in 1779, a copy of which was sent to the Vice-Chancellor and Proctors and every common room, faced the problems of, and suggested a daring way of dealing with, the most disreputable of these, the brothels and prostitutes of Oxford. 'The passions of young men in such a seminary *will* be gratified', it asserted. 'It is to be Questioned whether connivance at the crime, under certain limitations and conditions were not preferable to compelling young men either to the ruinous expences of *London* and other expeditions, or to injure their constitutions by means of the Dregs of Prostitution that remain in the University.'[13] Such a suggestion for the legalizing and the supervision of permitted brothels could have aroused nothing short of outraged disbelief among the rulers of the place, and the squalid resorts remained as before and after, well known to all, whether visitors or officers of the university or civic law. They find frequent mention in the literature of the town:

> The stench of Brothels, and the filth of Stews.
> Call loud for Censure, and demand the Muse;
> Within our Walls a num'rous, shameless Race
> (To useful Arts and Learning a Disgrace)
> Secure to Folly the unpractis'd Youth
> And turn his Footsteps from the Paths of Truth.[14]

Notorious within the city was Bullocks Lane which even the author of these lines found too horrid to describe:

> I pass in Silence all the Rubbish-Train,
> Nurs'd in the filthy Stews of *Bullock's-Lane*.[15]

Filthy indeed they must have been, as Amhurst's *Terrae Filius* reports three years later: '*Bullock's Lane*. The contagious Distemper which raged so violently at this Place, last Summer, is pretty well abated, and the *Toasts* begin to appear in publick again.'[16] Those same Toasts figure, coupled with the denizens of another well-known haunt, in a poem of these same years:

> But, above all, record the female race,
> The reigning Toasts and beauties of the place,
> Whether in *Bullock's lane* they choose to rove
> Or Kidney-hall, the soft retreat of Love.[17]

The margin glosses Bullock's Lane as 'Oxford's Drury Lane' and Kidney-hall as 'a publick house near Oxford, dedicated to love'. Another such place, a little out of Oxford, was at the top of the favourite walk up Headington Hill, where lived 'honest Joan of *Headingtons*' who

> . . . boasts she has been a *Beginner*
> With many an after-harden'd *Sinner*[18]

As well as these notorious houses there were others where services beyond coffee and spirits were available at a more amateur level. Hearne records

> a Coffee house newly set up in St. Clements, kept by one Bygge, who hath a very beautiful, comely Wife (of a loose life) & a beautiful sister (unmarried) living with them, wch sister is also very loose, and 'tis for this reason that young gentlemen frequent the House, a thing which has been much complained of.[19]

On high days and holidays, especially at Encaenia, when local provision might prove inadequate, it was not only nobility, parents and relations who flocked to Oxford for the ceremonies, concerts and balls. 'Why faith,' exclaims a gentleman commoner in an early comedy, 'this publick Act has drawn hither half the nation', among whom he lists 'Vacation Whores, which the Proctors are very busy in discovering, first to – examine 'em, and then cart 'em out o' Town'.[20] Another comedy, later in the century, features such a vacation whore rather nervous about making such a trip. 'Charlotte and I,' she says, 'were going to take a post-chaise, and go down to Oxford to pay you a visit; only the what d'ye-call-em's, the *doctors*, would take us up they said.'[21] Another regular date for such visitors was the annual Oxford Races on Port Meadow. Hearne had seen this occasion developing in length and in the diversity of entertainments there which he thought were 'nothing else but incentives to Idleness and Vice, and doing a great deal of harm to the Youth of the University and others'.[22] His outrage increased when 'that which is scandalous is, that Booths (particularly one) were erected in the Meadow six or seven weeks before the Races began'.[23] The following year the extent of that scandal came to light when it was revealed that in that particular booth three commoners of Exeter College 'and many besides, to the number of about 30, lay with a young woman all together one night (The Woman's Maiden Name Cradock, she being married, a most impudent slut) in the said Meadow, whilst all the people in the Meadow stood around to see them.'[24] The Exeter men were expelled along with two from Queen's College. One Queen's man hanged himself: one of the Exeter men, doubtless to Hearne's outrage, was entered a commoner at St Edmund Hall!

The university and the officers of the city had authority to seek out and punish both those who managed and those who worked at these houses of ill fame. The Proctors had power to expel the delinquents or commit them to Bridewell for discipline. Jeremiah Milles of Balliol, during his Proctorship records that he 'was in pursuit of an ill woman to put her in Bridewell, but failed'. A few months later, after walking his proctorial rounds until one in the morning, he managed to put two whores in Bridewell.[25] Bridewell was indeed a place to be dreaded. In 1726 one of the Proctors found a girl and another lewd companion in the rooms of a gentleman of Jesus. Hearne tells of their fate:

> The said Wigans was whipp'd, having fourty lashes in Bridewell and dismissed, though she would confess nothing. Next day she was seen again in Town, finely dress'd (in lac'd stockings) and patch'd. Her Companion was whipp'd at the same time, & after about 5 lashes, she began to confess, and after 5 more, she told all, viz. that Wigans had lay with 5 or six Gentlemen of the College, and had been from Sunday till the Thursday in the College.[26]

Keepers of houses of ill fame suffered less painfully. Two such men before the magistrates in 1781 were fined 20 shillings each and sent down for six months. William Blake who kept a brothel in St Giles's parish provoked a resolution 'to prosecute all Offenders of this kind in the future with the utmost rigour'. He was imprisoned for six months after standing in the pillory. But the sympathetic onlookers showed little rigour. He was not molested and, as it was raining, he was allowed to wear his hat.[27]

There was no need, of course, to visit such houses of resort, sordid or deceptively respectable, for the freelance girls of pleasure roamed the streets and their favourite walks and resorts. They could be found 'Ambling at every *College* Gate,'[28] round the tennis courts, at concerts and even in church, where

> O! how demure the list'ning Harlots leer,
> And drink the Musick in at either Ear;
> How the Sluts languish with deceitful Pride,
> And ogling drop the pretty head aside:
> In Church they practice each new Female Air.
> And to a *Playhouse* turn the *House of Prayer*.[29]

They had their favourite walks where they could catch new customers or make assignations with old ones. Christ Church Meadow, Trinity Wilderness, or Merton Grove were favourite haunts.

> Where there were Youths so bright, and Nymphs so fair,
> T'was fitting she shou'd fix Loves Empire There....
> Of *Ida's* Hill no more let Poets sing,
> And from the Skies contending Beauties bring;
> In *Merton* Groves a nobler Strife is seen,
> A claim more doubtful, and a brighter Scene.
> O! *Merton* cou'd I sing in equal lays,
> Not *These* alone shou'd boast *Eternal* Praise,
> Thy soft Recesses, and thy cool Retreats,
> Of *Albion's* brighter Nymphs the blissful Seats.[30]

The Fellows of Merton finally found this invasion of college ground too much to bear, and shut the Garden Gate, an act inspiring a stricter Oxford bard to reply to the author of *Merton Walks*:

> Well, O! ye Sons of Merton, you exclude,
> From your Recesses this licentious Brood:
> No more by Day they haunt your crowded Groves.
> Nor stain by Night with their unhallow'd Loves;
> Henceforth some other publick Walk they seek.
> To meet their blust'ring Coxcomb once a week.[31]

Some years later Hearne added his prosaic account to these poetic effusions:

> Some Years agoe came out at Oxford a poem, call'd *Merton Walks*, the Walks in the Garden of that Place being every Sunday Night, in the pleasant time of the Year, throng'd with young Gentlemen and young Gentlewomen, wch growing scandalous, the Garden Gate was at last shut up quite, and thereupon the young Gentlemen & others betook themselves to Magdalen College Walk, wch is now every Sunday Night strangely fill'd, just like a Fair.[32]

For those who found brothel-visiting or love in the open air unattractive, there was the exciting challenge of smuggling the desired female into college under the eyes of porters, Deans and Proctors, and many are the anecdotes of the discovery of these violations of discipline. Disguise sometimes aided these illegal entries. Charles Wake of Corpus Christi College dressed his lewd woman in a scholar's gown and managed to keep her in college for two nights before being discovered.[33] Even more ingeniously contrived was the scandal at Hart Hall which Hearne, who had a relish for such stories, tells in detail:

> A gentleman entered himself Commoner, and with him at the same time, another person Gentleman-Commoner of that Hall. These two were

15 Smuggling in the
ladies, the Proctors lurking

Chamber-Fellows, or (as the common Phrase is) Chums. But it seems, the
Gentleman-Commoner was not really of the Male, but Female, Sex; and
therefore she was properly to be called a Gentlewoman-Commoner. She
dressed herself in Man's Apparel, and so passed without any suspicion, till
some time for a Man ... She had continued long undiscovered had she not
been found with Child, by means of her Copulation with the aforesaid
Commoner.[34]

But it seems that such long successful concealment was the exception rather
than the rule. Information from a variety of sources led to searches and
searches often to discovery. One William Eldridge, for instance, had given
what proved to be false information that the under-porter of Brasenose had
been bringing girls into college. He had later to make a public apology for
this falsehood 'in consequence of which several Gentlemen's Rooms were
entered and searched'.[35] Other searches were more successful. The Vice-
Chancellor himself 'catch'd Mrs. Gratiana Crook's black Wench in a
Gentleman-Commoner's Chamber in Queen's Coll. & broke open the Door

upon them'. Hearne, the Jacobite High Churchman could not resist adding 'Memorandum that the said Gratiana Crook is the daughter of a Presbyterian.'[36] At one swoop Hearne denounces three dons for the same offences:

> George Ward ... A.M. of University College, & a Tutor of the House, and in priests orders, was found with a common strumpet in his Chamber of the College, in the time of Evening Service in the Afternoon. ... She was with this Ward two or three Hours, & was convey'd to him by an elderly woman that he imployed. The same Strumpet hath been often with one Fiddes, A.M. & Fellow of All Souls, and also with our debauched & irreligious (for so he is) professor of Astronomy, Dr. John Keil.[37]

A splendid public row followed such a discovery in Hearne's own Hall where, he says, there was a 'Strange Neglect of Discipline ... which makes those few young gentlemen that are there loose'. Apparently 'one Rice (a Batch. of Arts) a Welchman of ill Character ... kept in his room in the Hall all night on Wednesd. Night last a comely [lass] (from Begbroke), called Huntingdon Peg, & yesterday had her to dinner at his Chamber.' Here a gentleman commoner of the Hall, Walter, joined the company. Whereupon Sam the under-butler discovered the scandal to the Principal and his wife, and Walter, outraged at this betrayal, attacked Sam in the quad. The Principal's wife and then the Principal descended from the Lodgings to attempt in vain to end the fray. When the Vice-Principal, Mr Creed, joined them, Walter threw kitchen plates at his head, telling him to get back to Queen's where he had been only a poor pitiful servitor. In the midst of the tumult Huntingdon Peg escaped before a Proctor could be found to lead her away to punishment.[38] Hearne would not be thought a mere scandal-monger in his chronicling of these escapades. 'I put these things down,' he writes, 'not that I think the University ought to be reflected on upon this Account, but only some particular Men who encourage Idleness & Debauchery & the greatest wickedness.'[39] But the evidence is that the sinners were far from few, and the university and its life could not escape being reflected on.

Another class of less disreputable available female company was comprised under the title 'Oxford Toasts', a title which too often covered these women of the brothels and the streets, but also included the daughters of the tradesmen and the lower bourgeois of the city, outwardly respectable but covertly intriguing to trap a promising young member of the gown and conclude a marriage above her station. These were 'the Tea-giving Belles of the Town who have Danglers in square caps and hanging Sleeves' and 'put the Pit-a-patation of their dear little Bosoms into a Flutter'.[40] These are 'those gaudy *Things* which flutter about *Oxford* in prodigious Numbers, in Summer-Time' haunting not the back streets of low reputation but the more fashionably favoured walks of the university, to try their seductive powers. 'Let her,' advises an observer of 1750, 'frequently vary the place of her walking ... and if she is still follow'd by the same idle tribe of gaping lowngers, I may venture to pronounce her a *celebrated* Oxford BEAUTY.'[41] The birth and breeding of these predatory girls are described at length and in detail in Nicholas Amhurst's character of a typical specimen:

> *She* is born ... of *mean Estate* being the daughter of some insolent *Mechanick*, who fancies himself a *Gentleman*, and resolves to keep up his *Family* by marrying his Girl to a *Parson* or a *Schoolmaster*: to which end, *he* and his *Wife* call her *pretty Miss*, as soon as she knows what it means, and send her to the *Dancing-school* to learn to hold up her Head, and turn out her Toes; she is taught, from a Child, not to play with, nor talk to any of the dirty Boys and Girls in the Neighbourhood; but to mind her *Dancing*, and have a great respect for the *Gown*. This Foundation being laid, she goes on fast enough of herself, without any further Assistance, except an *Hoop*, a *gay Suit of Cloaths*, and *two* or *three* new *Holland Shifts*. Thus equipt, she frequents all the *Balls* and *publick Walks* in *Oxford* where it is a great Chance if she does not, in *Time*, meet with some raw Coxcomb or other, who is her *humble servant*, waits upon her Home calls her again the next Day, dangles after her from Place to Place, and is at last, with some Art and Management, drawn in to *marry* her.[42]

There is sufficient evidence to show that, despite the efforts of the Heads of Houses and their statute 'prohibiting all Scholars, as well *Graduates* as *Undergraduates*, of whatever Faculty, to frequent the Houses and Shops of any Townsman by Day or especially by night' many a raw coxcomb and many not so raw were ensnared by a successful 'Toast'.

There was yet another race of women who, though they lacked the appeal of the 'Toasts', needed no disguise nor smuggling, but had full freedom to enter college premises without let or hindrance, to enter rooms and the most intimate chambers – the race of Bedmakers. We have already met one of this tribe, terrifying a freshman by her sudden appearance in his room, armed with pail and broom, whose 'terrible mien' led him to persuade his sister that she offered not the slightest amorous temptation,

> And, sister, this office is wisely contriv'd
> To fall on sage dames who their charms have surviv'd;
> For were it bestow'd on each careless young jade,
> 'Tis certain our beds would be seldom well made.[43]

But it was only too true that when this naive freshman matured into an Oxford scholar who 'in the Mouths of most Women of sense, is only another Word for a wild, raking, ill-bred, awkward Animal', then 'whatever Conquests they might formerly boast of, the chief FAVOURS they receive now are from their *Laundresses* and *Bedmakers*, or from their *Daughters* who are the TOASTS of the University, and the only Objects of their Gallantry.'[44] This same satirist constantly voices these innuendoes alluding to what he

16 A don with his bedmaker – and knowing undergraduates

considers a widespread wickedness among juniors and seniors alike, of 'a venerable Head of a College ... coaxing his Bedmaker's Girl out of her Maidenhead', or how 'a certain Doctor got his Bedmaker with Child, and plaid several other unlucky Pranks'.[45] Hearne frequently records such liaisons and their results as facts well known throughout the university. He writes,

> When it was debated amongst the Fellows of Magd. College, that the Women Bed-makers (who had been scandalously lewd and vitious) should be discarded and for ever kept out of the College, Dr Fayrer ... shew'd himself the great Patron of these loose Women, which was severely reflected upon by some of the fellows, who knew he labour'd under the flagrant suspicion with regard to some of them.[46]

A Fellow of the same college, George Cox, finally made an honest woman of his bedmaker's pretty daughter, the mother of his children, and married her.[47] Yet another Magdalen man, this time a Bachelor of Arts, Mr Stephen Richardson, had married a bedmaker of Exeter College, just before she was brought to bed. It was, adds Hearne, 'a great vexation to his Father, that he should marry a Bedmaker, that is worth nothing'.[48]

Some bedmakers exerted power behind the scenes over those to whom they granted favours, and Hearne suspected that Dr Mill, Principal of St Edmund Hall, was guided by the directions and instigation of a Bedmaker there. Others, the majority, had a sadder time and often a wretched end. Witness Hearne's account of love betrayed:

> Docea Jordan ... a young Girl of about twenty six years of age, and made beds at Queen's-College. ... Her mother was a very comely body, & so was this Girl wch was the reason that she (this Girl) was much caress'd by some of the Gentlemen of Queen's-College, particularly one Morland, a Batchelor of Arts, who went from Oxford three or four years ago, & used afterwards to send the Girl (with whom he had been too familiar) money, sometimes a Guinea, sometimes half a Guinea, at a time, & promised to send for her to London, but at last he failed her, and sent her word that he was going beyond Sea, where 'tis said he is now. This broke the Girl's heart, as she declared when she was dying.[49]

The inevitable result of these relationships, the production of numbers of illegitimate children, was a well-known fact and accepted as a not unusual or outrageous part of academic life. These unfortunate accidents were managed in a variety of ways. The most honourable was, as we have already seen in other cases, to accept paternity and marry the mother. A further example was Mr Thomas Hunt, a clergyman and tutor of Hart Hall, who fathered a son and married the mother, a Mrs Sarah Adkins, 'a large and comely laundress'. She had until then taken in the washing of this reverend scholar in oriental tongues, who had been 'looked upon (before this Thing) as a virtuous man, tho' I have heard of other sly Intrigues of his with Girls'.[50] Other solutions of the problem were less worthy. If the girl could be fobbed off with a small maintenance payment, all might be well, as with the young mother who appears among the duns crowding at the door of an undergraduate:

> ... a kind Girl beside, who had
> Made him a *Twelve--month* since a *Dad*;
> Good reason why she came to seek him,
> For something towards the *Infants* keeping.[51]

Sometimes a surrogate father could be found as arranged by a Mr Hannes, a BA of Magdalen who 'had a Bastard ... by a Bedmaker, wch Girl he got marryed to a Taylor of St. Peters in the East, Oxford'.[52] When a young gentleman of Queen's College, Mr Potter, sinned similarly with his bedmaker's servant, Sarah Smith, and after she had been locked in the college kitchen until she confessed, in tears, the identity of the father, the matter was settled by a Fellow of the college, Mr Hill, who contrived a marriage for her with an ale-house keeper of Stanton St Johns. She was but a young lass of fifteen or sixteen, and her husband, who was about sixty, had been given twenty guineas to have her, and lead her to the altar in St Clement's Church.[53]

Such were a few cases in this part of the social scene, a part seized upon and no doubt exaggerated by the satirists of the town, who could suggest that All Souls should be 'translated over the Way and that the *Three tuns* Tavern was All Souls College. ... Within these Walls inhabit your *Smarts*, your *Gallant gentlemen*, who have debauched more Girls than they have read Books', while 'These Gentlemen of Maudlin, are always Maudling, and therefore no wonder they are always prepared for the *Delights* of Venus. ... Here you may see *little brats* every Morning at the Buttery Hatch, calling for hot Loaves and Butter in their *Papa's Name*.'[54] Nick Amhurst's couplets sum up the whole business, sad and rather sordid as it was:

> By no such borrow'd charms, nor spurious arts,
> Our *Oxford* ladies reign o'er youthful hearts;
> In their own native, naked charms they shine,
> Smug chamber maids and sempstresses divine,
> Smart laundresses on *Saturdays* so clean,
> And bed-makers on every day between,
> The beggar's offspring to the parish left,
> And college bastards of their sires bereft.[55]

Some of these anecdotes throw an interesting light on another aspect of the gap between the truth and the myth of the statutes and discipline of the academic single life. By rights a Fellow of a college resigned his fellowship when he married, moved possibly into schoolteaching or, if he were so fortunate, moved with his wife to be instituted in one of the college livings. In fact there appears to have been a widespread ignoring of the statutes, with Fellows' wives of long standing being known to the college without any action being taken. Hearne records many instances at many colleges where the favour of granting a Fellow on his marriage a period of grace of one or two years before resigning his fellowship was usual, but often exceeded quite blatantly:

Mr. William Smith late Fellow of [University College] after he had a year and half's Grace, (tho' publickly known to be married several Years, & had a Child by his wife kept at Windsor) ... ask'd three Years at least more, and had certainly been granted to him, unless Mr. Allen had most vigorously oppos'd the request. ... Mr. Greenwood had a year's Grace after he had a Parsonage of above 200 libs per annum, wch is the more remarkable because a Bastard-Child was laid to him much about the time the living fell to him by Brown the Coffee-man's Daughter, of wch he never very well clear'd himself.[56]

Mr Knot, a Fellow of Wadham, died leaving a widow and two or three children, whom he had kept at Thame. 'His Marriage was conniv'd at, as is usual in Colleges.'[57] At Magdalen Henry Stephens resigned his Fellowship but not before he had 'been married about eight years before to one Mrs. Betty Gardiner, an Oxford wench, of a large, stropping Make, but of little Sense'.[58] At the same college many years later George Cox 'married a pretty Girl, his Bedmaker's daughter, by whom he hath children. Notwithstanding his marriage he kept his Fellowship.'[59] Little wonder that the Terrae Filius of 1733 should choose as one of his victims one who 'having tasted the Delights of Marriage, and the Sweets of a Senior Fellowship for sixteen years together without Mistrust ... resigned his Fellowship in Favour of his Eldest Son'![60] Hearne's rage boiled over when, contrary to 'the Statutes and design of the Founder', the Warden of New College married. 'These are things,' he fumed, 'that are evaded all over the University, with Shame be it spoken, and Colleges and Halls are turn'd into Cunny-boroughs.'[61]

In some darker places of the university were darker sins, and stranger flesh was sought than that favoured in Cunny-boroughs. Hearne believed that 'this Practise of Marriage is much to the Prejudice of Colleges', and that the duty of a don was to do good in his society, a duty which 'marry'd Men are not known to do ... at least not known that they do it so effectually as single men.'[62] But there were also temptations in the way of the single man living in a close society of men, many of them young and attractive, and there is evidence that the temptations were not always resisted. One such scandal broke at Merton in 1732 when

> Mr. John Pointer, Chaplain of Merton College, was examined before the Warden of that College, Dr. John Holland, on the point of sodomy, he having been accused of sodomistical practises. Two persons of the College, Post-masters, I hear, of a good reputation, were ready to make their oath, and there were not wanting other proofs, but the oaths were foreborn, and for quietness Pointer was advised to go off from the College, and forbid reading Prayers as Chaplain any more.

Hearne could not resist making a Jacobite point of this lenient cover-up: 'He has been guilty of this abominable vice many years ... but this and other Vices are become so common in England, being spread from beyond sea and from a most loose Court in London where there is no Religion, that they are not by many looked upon as sins.'[63] News of the affair soon spread throughout Oxford. Thomas Wilson of Christ Church noted in his diary the day after the examination,

> This evening I hear that Mr. Pointer Chaplain of Merton 40 years standing was called before the Warden and Fellows upon a complaint made by one of the Commoners of the House whom he had got into his chamber, and after urging him to drink, would have offered some very indecent things to him. He

has been long suspected of Sodomistical Practices, but could never be fairly convicted of them.[64]

But this event appears trivial, and certainly attracted less interest and excitement than the notorious Wadham sodomy case.

The Reverend Robert Thistlethwaite, Doctor of Divinity, became Warden of Wadham in 1724 but not until 1739 were the scandalous doings in the lodgings discovered in a mounting series of disclosures, beginning when, after evening prayers, the Warden saw Mr French, a handsome second year undergraduate, talking with friends in the quad, and summoned him to his rooms. There, after plying the young man with wine and locking the doors, he made a 'Sodomitical Attempt' upon him. French's distraught behaviour when he escaped puzzled his friends and finally he confessed the cause to a Fellow of the college. An investigation by a group of Fellows brought more affairs to light as other victims of the Warden gave evidence. The college Butler, William Langford, had been frequently importuned and had been reduced to sneaking out of college by the back way to avoid the Warden's seeing him from his study window, and summoning him up. A young Fellow, William Boxley, confessed to passive sodomy with the Warden. Finally, and most grotesquely, a young barber while shaving the Warden, who was in full splendour of his cassock and gown, felt the Warden's hand, beneath the white sheet, groping into his breeches whilst making suggestive enquiries about their contents. When he persisted in his advances, the barber knocked him down and escaped. Despite Thistlethwaite's repeated attempts to persuade French to withdraw his accusations, and to bribe the butler into silence, the scandals were brought to a grand jury who found a bill nem. con., and it was sent to the assizes. Thistlethwaite disappeared and never reappeared for trial. Wadham had more to suffer. There was another chapter to be added to this sordid story.

Alarmed by the scandal of the Warden, an old member of the college wrote to Mr Baker, who had been a leading member of the group of Fellows investigating the Warden's doings, alerting him to the behaviour of the Revd John Swinton, a Fellow and close friend of the former Warden. Swinton had taken a ragged and lousy lad, Robert Trustin, to live in his rooms in college, under the pretext of giving him physic. Under examination by Baker and other Fellows the lad alleged that he had often slept with Swinton, that mutual fondling had taken place and that Swinton had femoral and anal intercourse with him. He was taken before the Vice-Chancellor and repeated his allegations. Whilst the investigation was adjourned, the boy was approached by Swinton's bedmaker, John Kimber, at a secret meeting in Friars Entry, and promised a reward if he denied all his previous evidence. At the next session before the Vice-Chancellor the boy obeyed, declaring that Mr Baker had given him money to make his allegations. The case was dropped, and Swinton insisted that Baker should sign a recantation, denying all his accusations and admitting intentional defamation of Swinton's character. This he had printed in *The Daily Advertizer* and the *London Evening Post*, for the affair had aroused interest beyond the walls of Oxford.[65]

Before the interest faded and the market diminished, there appeared a further, but this time poetical, contribution to the scandal, suggesting that Swinton's inclinations and practice – referred to throughout as 'his ancient art' – had found a wider range of victims than young Bob:

> After his ART with great Success
> He'd taught to twenty more or less,
> Some Rich, some Poor, as he could find
> Their Genius was thereto inclin'd. ...[66]

With obvious enjoyment and fun the poet set out to add his light-hearted supplement to the more serious 'A Faithful Narrative', and possibly captured something closer to the tone of college gossip over the whole squalid affair:

> Attend, I'll paint you out a Case,
> Which happen'd in that Learned Place.
> Not Pembroke's Warden; no, 'tis W–dh–m,
> The Word, I' faith, sounds much like *Sodom*.[67]

And was this the first appearance of the 'Wadham–Sodom' rhyme, so useful to future generations of Oxford limerick-makers?

Looking back over this whole dark picture of lust, sodomy, bastards, subterfuge, prostitution, forced and improbable marriages, relieved only by the occasional female visits by mothers, sisters and lady cousins, one recalls the shocked comment of the lady of pleasure with which this chapter began: 'I wish to die, if I don't wonder how they do to live there. A pack of men together, without any women among them.' The answer must be that they did not do very well. It would take the next century and the family houses of north Oxford to bring to the senior members of the university a life at least one important step nearer to normality. As for the junior members, it would need another century after that.

CHAPTER EIGHT

Walking and Sauntering

This Oxford was still a

> Towery city and branchy between towers;
> Cuckoo-echoing, bell-swarmed, lark-charmed, rook-racked,
>   river-rounded;

Another century would see the building of its 'base and brickish skirt', but for these hundred years country and town met and mingled. Over Magdalen Bridge beyond the few buildings of St Clement's and Mr Spencer's Riding Ground was open land of heath and trees, the remnant of the Royal Forest of Shotover, rising up to

> Where Shotover erects his head
> A shapeless mass o're Oxford towers.[1]

Two roads forked off, the left to London by way of Shotover and Wycombe, the right to Henley, while an ancient footway lined with trees climbed the hill to Headington. Northwards, beyond St Giles Church the country opened out on to Bullingdon Common, a landscape of open fields and scattered villages and their church spires. To the south, across the water meadows rose the hills of Hinksey and Cumnor and Boar's Hill, Cumnor still heavily forested, with the tiny villages of the Hinkseys, Wytham and Binsey below, while to the west, just beyond the encircling branch of the river, a countryside coppice, down and woodland, the area of the ancient Forest of Wychwood, came right up to the city. The Oxford scholar, seeking rural peace and beauty, need only make a short excursion beyond the walls of a city in which it was no unpleasant place to saunter, so long as one sauntered in the more salubrious streets and quarters.

A pamphlet of 1764 describes the mixture of splendour and meanness which went to make up eighteenth-century Oxford: 'It has long been obvious to the Inhabitants, and is now, to our Shame, become the

91

17   Rural Oxford from the south west, 1767

18   Entering Oxford from the north, up St Giles, 1779

Observation and Wonder of Strangers also; That no City whose Streets are so spacious, and whose Public Buildings so magnificent, is so ill swept, and so meanly lighted, as the Town of OXFORD.' The author deplores 'those prodigious Heaps of Dirt, and Rubbish, which are scattered all about the City, to the great Impediment of, not only clean, but also safe Walking', and 'those heaps of Dung from Stables, Mortar from old Houses, and of rotten Vegetables from the Stalls'. He contrasts the flat pavements of Bath and London with the cobbled streets of Oxford where 'the weary Fair-one … justly accuses the sharp Points of our Pebbles, for making so rough a Return to the Pressure of so much Beauty'.[2] Much of Oxford, away from the spacious streets and magnificent public buildings, was a warren of jumbled buildings and alleys:

> The whole area between Jesus College Lane and the High Street was covered with dwelling houses and their ordinary appurtenances, stables, stable-yards, and gardens. The interior of this portion of the town was approached by various passages on the north and south sides and by two openings in the Turl, one of which was called Maidenhead Lane.[3]

This was the area destined to be cleared to build the New Market after 1771, before which the west end of the High had been anything but a salubrious place to saunter, as a foreign visitor to Oxford in 1748 recorded:

> The East End goes by the Name of *High-Street*, the Middle of it is called *Old Butcher Row*, and the West End *Castle-Street*. The East End forms a very spacious Street, clean and well paved, and illuminated with lamps in the Winter. … The Houses which stand East of that elegant Edifice of *Queen's College* would disgrace an ordinary Market-Town … the Butcher-Market, held here every *Wednesday* and *Saturday*, when the Stalls extend half the Length of this fine Street. … Farmers incumber the other principal Streets with their Waggons and Corn; and Fish and Poultry are sold in both.[4]

The Act of Parliament of 1771 initiated many improvements on the main streets of the city and especially on the High. Ten years later the East Bridge had been replaced by the wider and more imposing Magdalen Bridge, and the approach to it had been widened and beautified. The High Street had been newly paved and, most importantly, the New Market had been completed and the stalls and trade of Butcher Row moved there. In 1781 a new Act authorized further work and controls. The High was to be widened 'in the upper part thereof' (i.e., the end towards Carfax) by the demolition of buildings on the north side. The Turl – the narrow end of Lincoln Street opening on to the Broad – was to be widened to enable carriages to go through. All unpaved roads, ways and streets were to be paved. Now the Butter and Eggs Market which had cluttered the streets had to join the butchers in the New Market, together with the merchants of fruit, flesh, fish

19 Town and Gown in Radcliffe Square

20 The Conduit and the Butter Market at Carfax

and garden stuff. The riding or leading of horses on the newly cleared streets 'for the purpose only of exercising such horses' was forbidden, and progressive fines for breaking these regulations were imposed, as were those for punishing the citizens who persisted in throwing rubbish on to the streets. Stricter times for the emptying of bog-houses sweetened the general air for the walkers and saunterers on this widened and beautiful central promenade.[5]

The High resembled a communal quadrangle for the denizens of the separate colleges and, especially for the elderly, was the most convenient place for a short stroll in its proper place in the day's timetable. Joseph Pickford, an ancient Fellow of Oriel, remembered how he and his colleagues 'After dinner ... went to the common room ... and had pipes and ale. Then they walked up and down High Street till five, when they read and wrote in their rooms till seven or eight.'[6] The youth of the place spent longer, it seems, on the street, for the ironically intended advice to young gentlemen rather describes the truth:

> You may venture ... at last into the High Street which is to be so often the scene of action whilst you reside in the University ... watching the arrival of stage coaches ... fasten your face to the window of a print-shop for half an hour ... the delight of parading up and down this beautiful avenue during the whole day.[7]

And if walking increased thirst, the parade was packed with establishments to ease the thirst and rest the feet, coffee houses at frequent intervals – the Angel, Tom's, Horseman's, Harpers among them – and ale-houses between them – the Mitre, the Chequers, the Ark. Here one met colleagues, gathered the news, showed off one's new wig and rustling gown and, as we shall see,[8] frequently encountered bizarre and entertaining spectacles to enliven the day and provide topics for talk in common room.

Further afield, but not too far, were other pleasant resorts and walks. Opposite Magdalen was the Physic Garden, with its splendid arched gateway, with gravelled paths and beds of herbs and flowers. Uffenbach in 1710 walked round the garden, describing its other main features which pleased those not primarily interested in genus and species,

> ... we passed the Physic Garden or *Hortus Medicus* we entered to have a look at it. It is opposite Magdalen College, not very large, and fairly well laid out, but it is ill kept and everything in the flower-beds appeared wild and overgrown. The large yews provide the chief ornament; I have nowhere met with finer or better-trained specimens than here. One finds many different figures made out of them, and two especially; of unheard of size just at the entrance of the gates are exceptionally fine trees cut with shears to represent, one Hercules with the club, the other a man with a spear. Both are about thirty

21 The Physic Garden

feet high. Finally there are two pilasters of the same work each with a vase of flowers artistically cut and very pretty.

He crossed the road to explore the other pleasant walk at the east end of the High. 'As it was still fairly early', he writes,

> we went for a walk at the back of Magdalen College. There is an avenue here skirting a beautiful meadow which is entirely encircled by a little river. It takes over a quarter of an hour to walk round the avenue, and though it is not quite even, it is very pleasant.... To the right of the college is a park belonging to it, a pleasant spot. There are numerous white and other stags and deer amongst which two, white spotted with brown, were as beautiful and tame creatures as I ever saw.[9]

Also popular and close at hand were the walks of Christ Church Meadow, explored and described by another foreign traveller. Broad Walk he admired,

22   Merton College from the meadows, with Dead Man's Walk

'their long Gravel walk, planted on each side with Elms. . . . This is much the
finest Walk about *Oxford*, and yet it is not so much frequented as some others
that are in all respects inferior to it' and that other sheltered walk beneath
the south walls of Merton, 'much resorted to in bright frosty weather . . .
covered from the North Winds by the colleges above-mentioned, and
warm'd at the same time by the Reflexion of the Sun from these Walls.'[10]
Here the aged and infirm took their short stroll, convinced that its warm
shelter could even give life to a dead man.

Away from the High and on the edge of the city stretched the University
Parks to the north of Wadham, not so cultivated and footpathed as they were
to become. A map of 1733 shows some tree-planting, but large areas of what
appears to be ploughland, a fact confirmed in a poem of 1793 by a Trinity
undergraduate who has walked,

> Seeking the Parks:– for so they style
> A certain track of well-ploughed fields
> Which ample grain to Farmer yields.[11]

Obviously the Parks were a step to the wilder open country to the north, but
another public resort to the east of the city provided a more cultivated end to
the walk, the Paradise Gardens. At the bottom of Penny Farthing Lane was a
small promontory of land bordered to the north and east by branches of the

23   The Parks

river. From that same map of 1733 it appears to be divided by walks or hedges into a number of rectangular plots, some with flower beds, some with trees, some empty. These gardens were run partly as a market garden and orchard, partly as a pleasure garden. Contemporary visitors fill out the details of this pleasant spot. The indefatigable Uffenbach had not failed to visit. 'We then went', he records,

> into another garden, called the Paradise Garden. This is almost at one extreme end of the town at an inn, behind which by the waterside are countless little retreats, close to each other, of cropped hedge, where the Fellows drink in the summer. The inn itself is furnished in the same fashion. The garden is otherwise nothing in particular and is chiefly dedicated to cookery, though it has fine fruit trees and yews.[12]

The other observant foreign tourist, Mr Salmon, had also visited this 'pleasant Garden, which goes by the name of *Paradise*, in which are Camomile and Grass Walks, planted with Evergreens, and almost all manner of Fruit-trees and Flowers'.[13] It was still as pleasant a spot in 1762 when Woodforde 'walked all over Paradise Gardens, and ate some Fruit there. ... They are the compleatest Gardens I ever saw in my Life.'[14] Which is a surprisingly enthusiastic compliment from a Fellow of New College, whose own college garden together with those of many other colleges formed a

24   A working farm between New College and Wadham

collection of elegant and highly cultivated pleasure resorts for the sauntering, not only of the university, but the more respectable citizens, and the not
so respectable ladies of the city.

The college gardens of the university, like its politics, were conservative.
In a century when the freer more natural gardening of Kent and Brown was
to conquer and transform estates and parks, Oxford resisted the new taste
longer than most noble and rich men. Garden after garden shows a fondness
for formality, geometric patterning, topiary, parterres and gravel paths,
where

> Grove nods at grove, each Alley has a brother,
> And half the platform just reflects the other.
> The suff'ring eye inverted Nature sees,
> Trees cut to statues, statues thick as trees.[15]

The old taste, for the most part, held to the end of the century, as the
historian of Wadham College wrote: 'These gardens had survived until now
the falling out of fashion of formal gardening and topiary. Capability Brown
had risen and ruled and been dead for some thirteen years before the new
gardening conquered.'[16] These gardens have all disappeared and survive only
– though in fascinating detail – in contemporary prints: David Loggans's
Oxonia Illustrata of 1675 and William Williams's *Oxonia Depicta* of 1733.

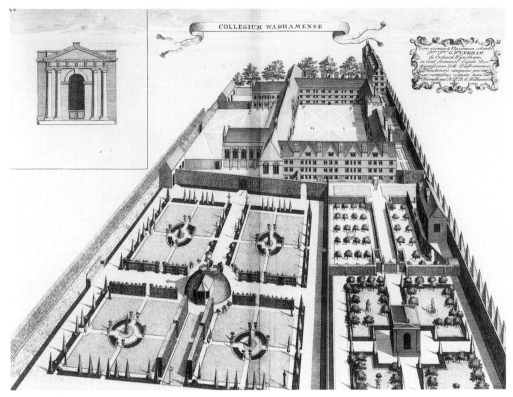

25   A plan of Wadham College garden, 1733

With their help and the comments of contemporary visitors, we can reconstruct something of the development and something of the final eighteenth-century state of these enclosed college enclaves which, despite the mocking lines of Pope, must have been pleasurable resorts for after-dinner saunters and summer evening talk.

Wadham gardens in 1675 still retained something of the less disciplined style. The part of the garden towards what is now Parks Road was a completely informal plantation of quite large deciduous trees, and by 1733 it retained something of its earlier freedom, but now freedom restrained. One half was more informal, looking more like an orchard but with neatly lined trees and amongst them a stone table, doubtless for wine and talk on a warm summer evening. This was separated by large ornamental gates from a garden laid out with largish trees, geometric areas of lawn, two statues and, at the centre, a largish building looking like a small rectangular Greek temple, columned and pedimented. The opposing half of the garden was highly formal and regular. The area was divided into four sections, each section subdivided into four, the parts all separated by gravel paths, and the smaller parts centred on a circular flower bed, itself centred on a clipped pointed spire of a tree. At the centre of the whole area was a domed mount with an entrance at the side with porch and door. The dome was crowned with a hexagonal balustraded terrace around a statue of Atlas with his globe. Uffenbach thought the garden 'well laid out and very pleasant', and added the detail that Atlas's globe was gilded and had on it a sun dial without a pointer.[17] In a great storm in 1753 Atlas was blown down, and the central mound removed. In 1796 evolving taste rather than tempest brought about the first great changes in this formal garden, when 'it was agreed to adopt the plan of alterations in the Fellows's Garden, recommended by Mr. Shipley, the Duke of Marlborough's Gardener; and it was ordered that all the Trees marked by Mr. Shipley should be immediately cut down.'[18]

Trinity garden followed the same Oxford pattern of development from the seventeenth into the eighteenth century. In 1675 it appears as a meadow-like area, completely undesigned, with many large well-grown and untrimmed trees, but in 1706 alterations to this grove-like garden began. By 1733 we are shown a garden of varied complexities. If we had viewed the garden from Parks Road through the great gate, we would have seen on the left, running the whole length of the garden, a maze of complex geometrical regularity formed of clipped hedges with, at its centre, some undecipherable object resembling a pole with pendent parts. A long gravel walk, leading up to the gate, separates the maze from a tall slim clipped hedge, beyond which are four rows of twenty-one pointed trees clipped to shape, with gravel walks on each side of the rows. Another clipped hedge separates this arboretum from a large area of lawns and parterres, with a generous scattering of topiary trees in square columns, pyramids, round columns and globes, while in the middle of the two parterres which form the two centres of this area, are two domed mounts. Uffenbach must have been fatigued and unobservant, or the early years of the century up to 1710 must have seen little development from the earlier natural meadow walk, if his description of the garden is accurate: 'At the side of the second court is a great garden, in which, however, there are neither trees nor shrubs, nothing but grass plots and several small yews, which are not unpleasant.'[19] He possibly saw the early stages of the development of the garden towards that which Williams depicts in 1733, and which a later visitor in 1748 is obviously describing, noting other pleasurable and social additions, especially the much favoured tables:

> The Gardens of this College are large, and well laid out, containing about three Acres of Ground; They are divided into three parts; the first, which we enter from the grand Quadrangle, consists of fine Gravel-walks and Grass plots, adorned with Ever-greens; and the Walls entirely covered with them, as those in other College-Gardens generally are. Adjoining to this, on the South, is another Garden, with shady Walks of *Dutch* Elms; and beyond a wilderness, adorned with Fountains, close Arbours, round stone Tables, and other Embellishments.[20]

26   Detail of a plan of New College garden, 1733

Whatever our gardening philosophy, this variety, these dry gravel paths for Fellows in their ankle-length gowns, these arbours for rest and talk, these rustic tables for a social bottle, create the perfect ambience for those who designed them.

Next door at St John's informality reigned, with a planting of larger mature trees. Looking from Parks Road, the left half of the Fellows' garden was turfed and divided into four rectangles, down the middle of which the central avenue was bordered by an avenue of lime trees, and the four lawns enclosed by pleached and cut lime trees. An avenue of large untrimmed deciduous trees separates this area from another, rich in large trees, elms along the side walks and two groups of beautiful chestnut trees in the middle. There was a rotunda at each end of a terrace walk at the Parks Road end which was bordered by large trees, possibly firs, trained into a flat wall-like screen. Only the small President's garden contrasted with this freer horticulture, with its small parterres and topiary trees.[21]

New College garden was smaller but had its own unique feature around which it was laid out, the Mound. It also contained a most popular item (as did the gardens of Queen's, Pembroke and Magdalen) – its private bowling green. This was a garden which changed very little between the pictures of it in 1675 and 1733, mainly because the central mound dictated its main layout. The area around the mound was divided into four parterres, laid out with no doubt a variety of plants, sands and gravels to present in one the arms of Charles I, in the others the arms of William of Wykeham, a sun dial and, as if local relevance had been exhausted, an abstract convoluted pattern. In the midst of this rose the square-based mound, rising in square terraces, with walks at each level guarded with clipped yew hedges, and at the summit a 'prospect'. The rest of the garden, outside the mound and its parterres, was not extensive but imaginatively planted. A description from 1761 records that

> on the North Side in particular there is a *serpentine Walk* [shades of Kent] planted with *flowering Shrubs*. Behind the Mount likewise is a fine Collection of Shrubs, so contrived as to rise gradually one above the other, and over them, a Row of Horse Chestnut Trees, which spread in such a Manner as to cover the Garden wall, and carry the Eye on to a most beautiful Mantle of tall Elms, which terminate the view.[22]

Uffenbach was not impressed with what was in his opinion 'a very mediocre garden', though he added a few details to our imaginative reconstruction. In the midst of the sun dial, cut out in box trees, was 'a great wooden stake supplying the index finger. Above, as the circle is not quite filled up by the twelve hours appear the words: *Sic vita* also cut out of box.' The mound itself, he tells us, was called Parnassus.[23] One charming addition to the social life of the Fellows was the construction in the hedge wall at each side of the mound, of little summer houses with arched entrances and, around the large bowling green, approached by an opening to the right of the mound, further semi-circular summer houses. In these shady retreats the Fellows of New College would sit to watch the bowls, to cool after a game, and to drink a bottle of wine brought out from their private stocks.[24]

The improvement and care of these pleasant gardens was an important part of college business. Merton built a summer house in 1706 and in the following year the terrace walk along the south wall of the Grove, with its view over the Meadows, and a circular bench in the projecting tower. Extensive alterations at Brasenose quite changed its character. Loggan's print shows the quadrangle filled by two elaborate parterres of serpentine patterns, edged with box and enclosed by a balustrade. In the earlier years of the century trees must have been planted and flourished around the edges if Hearne's outrage at the alterations of 1727 are to be understood. 'Last Week', he writes,

> they cut down the fine pleasant Garden in Brasenose College Quadrangle, wch was not only a great Ornament to it, and was agreeable to the Quadrangle of our old Monasteries, but was a delightful & pleasant Shade in Summer Time, & made the rooms, in hot Seasons, much cooler than otherwise they would have been. This is done by the direction of the Principal, and some others, purely to turn it into a Grass Plot, & to erect some silly Statue there.[25]

The hint of senior common room discord is violently explicit in the garden controversy at University College earlier in the century. Hearne's account of the complex motives in this episode is worth quoting in full:

As soon as Dr. Hudson was made Bursar of University College, he took care to regulate divers disorders relating to his Office ... among these laudable Undertakings is chiefly to be mentioned the College Garden wch having been almost ruinated and quite out of Repair, he order'd to be cover'd with Green Turff, planted with Trees & flowers, and the Walks to be gravell'd, to the great Beauty of the Place & Satisfaction of the rest of the Fellows; and there was no one of the College appear'd at present displeas'd with it but the Master; wch perhaps being known to one Robinson (a Commoner of that House, & Nephew to Mr. Smith lately Senior Fellow and now in London, who it seems was always averse to this Reform) a day or two after it was finish'd with two or three more of the College got into the Garden in the Night time, pull'd up some of the Ews spoil'd others, and did other Mischief to the no small Grief of the Doctor & the rest of the Fellows ... one reason which instigated him I hear is because the Dr. and the rest of the Society had taken care that all the undergraduates & Bachelors should dine and sup in the Hall, or undergo a penalty for it.[26]

Alongside other topics of college business and planning, food, wine and the disposition of college benefices, these gardens, offering escape from chambers and common room and a pleasant scene for gentle exercise, were the object of careful guardianship by the Fellows, not only of University but of all the colleges.

Not that the use of these gardens was exclusive to those Fellows. Some of them were popular haunts of all the members of the University and the citizens of the town, convenient places for the two to meet and mingle. 'The *Beau Monde*', one guide book tells us, 'have different Places for different Times of the Year.'[27] They also had favourite places. Merton Grove, as we have seen,[28] was not only popular but somewhat disreputable, 'the seat of nymphs and love', and in the end the Fellows of Merton closed the gate and kept their lime trees and terrace walk to themselves. Magdalen walks received many of the banished crowd of Oxford 'Toasts' and their distant chatter disturbed the peace of the satirist:

> If thro' the lonely, smiling Meads I stray,
> And by the *Charwel* pace my Thoughtful Way,
> Loud Female Laughters reach my distant Ears,
> Before my Eyes the tawdry Manteau glares.[29]

The wilderness of Trinity College was another well-visited spot,[30] but St John's garden appears to have been the main place of rendezvous. It was to this retreat that a young Oxford scholar of 1756, accompanied by his sweetheart, proceeded 'and found the Gay and Young of both Sexes parading it',[31] while the foreign visitor, Mr Salmon, recorded that

the Outer Garden is become the general Rendezvous of Gentlemen and Ladies every *Sunday* Evening in Summer; Here we have an opportunity of seeing the whole University together almost, as well as the better sort of Townsmen and Ladies, who seldom fail of making their Appearance here at the same time, unless the Weather prevents them.[32]

Inevitably St John's was included in the advice on the most advantageous places to walk given to the aspiring daughter no doubt of one of those 'better sort of Townsmen and Ladies' – 'But lastly, to try her utmost power, let her frequently vary the place of her walking: this evening let her be in *St. John's Grove*, tomorrow in *Christ Church Walk*, the next day let her go *up the Hill*.'[33]

Had her dainty feet completed the walk up the ancient footpath to the top of Headington Hill, she would certainly have encountered many a member of the University, who walked this popular route beyond the sauntering gardens, over Magdalen Bridge, through St Clement's and up the steep path to Josiah Pullen's tree and the open country beyond. She might have overtaken such an undergraduate as James of Queen's who, though convinced of the beneficial effects of exercise, had to confess that 'It was but last Friday that I was overpowered with heat in labouring up Heddington Hill', even though it was February.[34] She might more easily have caught up with 'those slow pac'd Sires who climb the steep of Headington'.[35] It was a favourite walk with many an Oxford tutor, and one small book of advice warns young gentlemen that they will probably be 'indulged by your destin'd Tutor with an entertaining walk to the top of Headington Hill', although the author admits St John's garden as a less strenuous alternative.[36] That ungrateful son of Magdalen, Edward Gibbon, and his tutor Dr Waldegrave were regular climbers of the road up the hill and, amid his sour memories of his time at college, 'the most idle and unprofitable of my whole life', he remembers that he 'preferred his society to that of the younger students, and in our evening walks together to the top of Headington Hill we freely conversed on a variety of subjects'.[37] It was a walk with a worthy destination, in Thomas Warton's words, '*Jo Pullen's Tree* on Heddington-Hill ... all our young *Antiquarians*, who constantly visit it Morning and Afternoon ... that venerable Elm, in consideration of its learned Planter, its Beauty, its eminent Situation, and other respectable Circumstances.'[38] Here one could rest 'Beside Joe Pullen's fav'rite tree',[39] or refresh oneself at one of the available taverns and pot-houses. Before the ascent an inspiring draught could be drunk at Mother Louse's pot-house, Louse Hall at the foot of the hill. On the way up was Cabbage Hall and higher up the hill was Caterpillar Hall, the resting place for those to whom the Headington walk was long enough.

Longer walks seem to have been the exception rather than the general rule, although some stalwarts ventured further afield than the gardens and the Hill. Erasmus Philips of Pembroke recorded in his diary that he 'Walked to Pert's with Mr. Wilder; this is a pleasant Tour from Oxford, whereof from this Hill one has a good Prospect'.[40] In the spring of 1763 Woodforde celebrated the mild weather following a very bitter winter with a series of walks, over

Shotover, out to Hinksey, to Godstow, and to Bays Water and back via
Headington.[41] A more romantic spirit from St John's with his Milton, Shakespeare or Thomson in his pocket, remembered in later years his long youthful
rambles: 'How many "summer suns have rolled unperceived away" while, in
the deepening glooms of Bagley Wood or near the magnificent expanse of
water at Blenheim, I have been seated with some one of the above authors in
my lap!'[42] But the great walker of the first decades of the century was
undoubtedly Thomas Hearne, visiting and noting monuments, inscriptions
and antiquities, but not neglecting the pleasures and adventures of the road.
On the day of the Pretender's birthday in 1715 the inveterate Jacobite, to
avoid threatening trouble, 'walk'd out of Town to Foxcomb with honest Will.
Fullerton, & Mr. Sterling, and Mr. Eccles.' After the pleasures of the walk the
group returned home to find themselves in trouble.

> We were very merry at Foxcombe, & came home between 9 and 10. Honest
> Will. Fullerton & my self (it being very near ten clock) were taken by the
> Proctor ... just this side Christ Church as we were coming to Cairfax. ... No
> sooner had we got from him, but we met Dr. Charlett [the pro-Vice-Chan-
> cellor] with Will Rawlins the Yeoman Beadle before him.[43]

Their MA status, of course, ensured their safe escape.

A long walk from Oxford made its return route through Wytham and
provided another adventure. 'From Wightham,' he recorded, 'I went to
Oxford by Binsey, But the Bridge, before we come to Binsey, being broke
down lately by some young Scholars ... I was forced to be carry'd over upon a
Man's Back.'[44] Whenever he could plan it, some refreshment was an interlude
in or the goal of these excursions. When he had walked out to Horsepath he
turned for home but 'called and dined at Iffley at the Ale-house kept by one
Jackson, by the great Elm Tree, now near an Hundred Years old, as they say.'[45]
A walk to Woodstock had a social pleasure at its end for there 'I met and din'd
with the Reverend Mr. Ralph Bridges, and two young Gentlemen of Xt.
Church. We din'd at the Bear.'[46] The diary does not record how he got back
over the eight odd miles between the Bear and Edmund Hall. Not that this
inveterate walker over great distances spurned the local favourites. He often
climbed Headington Hill along with his peers such as Dyer and Ward of Oriel,
but once at the top 'we dined upon Beans and Bacon'.[47] Could that trio have
been around a table at Caterpillar Hall? Nowhere in his diaries does Hearne
record that he had ever been upon a horse. His reliance on his own two legs for
these longer excursions beyond St Clement's and St Giles and St Aldates
makes him a notable exception to the horsemen of Oxford, young and old,
who needed four legs beneath them to visit more distant scenes, more distant
pleasures and more various ways of defying both parental and university
authority. But they are characters for another chapter.

CHAPTER NINE

Sports and Pastimes

Sport in the university had to wait until the following century before it became organized and regimented, before the spirit of competition and team transformed the world of individual exercise for the sheer pleasure of it into a group activity of dedicated seriousness. And as these young individuals, with the time and money for sport and leisure, brought with them the customs and pleasures of their fathers, the nobility, the landed gentry small and great, the rural parson or the successful bourgeois, so their sport at university was for the most part a replica of that of their riding, hunting, shooting, killing forbears.

At the centre of much of their activity was, inevitably, the horse, and opposed to their dedication to equestrian pleasure was, continually, the stern forbiddings of university authority and the worried advice of some anxious parents of more serious and sedentary lives and occupations. Typical are the doubts expressed by Stephen Penton, whose reign as Principal of St Edmund Hall had given him experience to advise with authority. In his *The Guardian's Instruction*, which must have echoed many an anxious parent's thoughts on his son's future and his own purse, he writes:

> ... now I will tell you the use of an horse in *Oxford*, and then do as you think fit. The horse must be kept at an *ale-house*, or an *inn*, and he must have leave to go once *every day*, to see him eat oats, because the master's eye makes him fat; and it will not be *genteel* to go often to an house and spend nothing; and then there may be some danger of the horse growing *resty* if he be not used often, so that you must give him leave to go to *Abingdon* once every week to look out of the tavern window, and see the maids selling turnips. ...[1]

Penton's serious advice is echoed with irony in a pamphlet sold in Broad Street a century later:

> You are nothing without a Horse and a Servant to attend him, so take care to become Master of both immediately; they will do you credit if they are

27   Setting off for a badger-baiting

expensive, and the Horse will afford you a good diurnal amusement perfectly conformable to the rules of the university, as riding every day from breakfast to dinner implies neither idleness nor extravagance.[2]

If the horse was more highly mettled than a mere hack, the hunt called to faster sport and greater waste of time. 'Fox-hunting is another requisite', writes the ironic but informed adviser, 'this ought to employ three mornings in the week at least; you may fan a hack to Woodstock or chapel for the sake of more commodious hunting next morning; the other three mornings may very reasonably be spent in bed after the fatigue of the previous day.'[3]

To the parental anxiety over time-wasting and expense, the powers of the university in statutes and decrees added their attempt to outlaw and punish the keeping and riding of a horse. A statute of 11 July 1772 forbade all those below the degree of BA, always excepting barons and above, sons of barons and baronets, 'Equum alere, seu proprium, sive alienum, aut conductitium, sub quovis praetextu' and laid down penalties of three months', six months', and a year's rustication for successive violations of the rule. The city, exercising powers granted to it by Act of Parliament, forbade any person to ride or lead a horse in the streets merely for exercise.[4] Four years later in a

28 A smock race

statute of 16 December 1785, the authorities proposed even stricter and more inclusive controls, forbidding any member of the university under the rank of MA 'to keep or cause to be kept for him, a horse without leave and, if granted, insertion in a Register with penalties set forth for violation'. This edict was set to come into effect in January of the following year and all Heads of Houses were enjoined to be vigilant in its enforcement. A 'Member of Congregation', no doubt wiser through knowledge of all the previous decades of the century's ignoring of the edicts of authority, 'opined that such statutes as the above would never hold', that 'The good-natured and liberal *Collegiorum & Aularum Praefecti* ... will permit it softly to sink, like its much-injured Parent, into sweet oblivion.'[5] From what we can see, it did. The whole thing, as they ought to have realized, was a losing battle against deeply entrenched belief and practice. Whatever the Golgotha of the Heads of Houses pronounced, this sport carried on unheeding. Horseriding, as a young man of Queen's told his friend, 'is universally understood and pursued here, that no study is so generally or perseveringly prosecuted, and that for some months in the spring a large meadow adjoining to Oxford is nothing but a riding school'.[6]

The city was riddled with stables and horse-hiring establishments to cater for these, for the most part, unlawful riders, and the country around Oxford afforded the most pleasant, open and tempting riding – the wide level expanse of Port Meadow, the open country across Magdalen Bridge and on Bullingdon Common to the north. The area north of the High, where the New Market was later to be built, was filled with stables and stable yards between the maze of houses and gardens. Christ Church had its own stables down by 'a shallow place of the Ditch' where Hearne was used to 'go over to the Wheat Sheaf and Anker',[7] and New College too maintained its own stabling. There was a large stable for ten to eleven horses opposite Wadham and at the New Inn the proprietor Charles Tilson hired out horses and four-wheeled post-chaises.[8] One Blagrave was 'well known at *Oxford* for letting out Carriages'.[9] It was possible to hire a horse 'once a day at the rate of 5s. per week',[10] though one could pay more if one patronized Mr Dry of the Eastgate who charged £15 for ten days.[11] Woodforde hired his horse from the nearby stables of Jonathan Jackson in Holywell for 2s. a day and pronounced it 'a very good Hack indeed',[12] unlike Erasmus Philips who risked buying a horse from Mr Reeves the painter for £3 8s. which 'died after riding about ten miles'.[13] Stabling one's own horse could be an expensive business, and when Woodforde brought his own grey up to Oxford, Jackson charged 5 shillings a week for livery.[14] Daily then, from these many stables, the hired hacks and the private steeds trotted out of town, exercising their masters and defying the authorities, while the ostlers and stable lads shovelled out the heaps of dung which, for a greater part of the century, filled the back streets and alleys.

Two typical riders out were Woodforde and Erasmus Philips. Woodforde was fond of a solitary ride in the evening to Abingdon on his own grey, and in the fine spring weather took long rides to Dorchester, over Shotover to Stanton St John, over to Foxcombe, through Abingdon and home by way of Dorchester. As the spring warmed into summer he rode regularly and no doubt returned with his appetite honed to face the enormous meals he relished.[15] Erasmus Philips, son and heir of Sir John Philips, was well connected and had access to distinguished Oxford company with whom he often dined elegantly and whom he accompanied on frequent riding expeditions, sometimes only to Port Meadow to watch the races, but often further afield, with some pleasant or entertaining motive for the ride. His diary records many of these days away from Pembroke. 'Rode with Mr. Wilder and Mr. le Merchant to Newnham, where dined upon Fish at the pleasant place [I] mentioned.' 'Rode with Mr. le Merchant and Mr. Clerk to Sr. John D'Oyley's seat about six miles from Oxford.' When his father came to stay, the couple spent many days in the saddle. 'Rid out with my Father, Mr. Jorden, and Bro. John to Shotover Hill, whence a good view of Col. Tyrell's beautiful seat. Din'd at Wheatly'; 'Rode with my Father &c. to Woodstock and Blenheim'; 'Rode with ditto to Fyfield ... passing Hincksey, Sandford &c. .... At Fyfield din'd at Ralph Wilder's. This is a pleasant Jaunt.'

Sometimes these jaunts, when his father had left, ended with more romantic rewards: 'Rode out with Mr. Clayton to Basisley.... Near here met Mr. Clayton's three Sisters (all fine bred Women) ... walk'd with the Ladies about two hours, and then return'd.' He rode out to watch the races at Burford where he 'Lay at a Private House here, and next morning breakfasted with Mr. Wm. Linto at Mrs. Clerk's here, where saw a very pretty Miss, her daughter.'[16]

Mention of the races at Burford introduces another part of this equine scene. Though attendance at horse races, riding in them or placing bets on them were all forbidden to scholars by statute, this was again an interdict openly and universally ignored by the gown, and pastimes extremely popular with the town. Lord Carteret of Christ Church in 1709 reports a great exodus to Burford to see the races: 'There is to be a famous Horse-match this week at Burford for a Hundred Guineas, if the lameness of one of the Horses does not prevent it: all the Hacks are already taken up, and I don't question but the schollars will make a very great appearance in Buck-skin Boots.'[17] Bicester held its race meetings with evening ball, handsome entertainment and plays,[18] and there was an annual meeting at Woodstock which, however, early in the century suffered from the strain in politics and later the uncertain temper of the Duchess of Marlborough. Hearne notes in his diary in 1706 that

> Upon the Turning out from Court of the Earl of Abingdon, the Earl remov'd the Horse-Race wch. us'd to be yearly for a Plate wch he gave, at Woodstock, to Port Meadow by Oxford. Upon which the Dutchess of Marlborough continu'd it, beginning last year, when only a parcel of Whiggish, Mobbish People appear'd.... [This year] was a Race at Oxon in the said Meadow, where was a great appearance of Nobility &c.[19]

The races at Woodstock continued but not without further trouble from the fury of Sarah. Erasmus Philips, a great race-goer, set out thither in September 1722 to discover that 'The Races this year were run upon Campsfield downs, near Woodstock, & not in the Park as usual, the Duchess of Marlborough having taken offence at something that happened at the Races last year.'[20] Interestingly enough, a later duchess, at her own expense, levelled the course and improved the approaches, making it, according to the reporter, 'the best flat course in Europe'.[21] The Oxford races on Port Meadow were, from 1706, to become the main meeting of the year and one of the great events of the social calendar. They were held every September until 1721 when Hearne recorded that 'because that season is generally wet, it was agreed last Year to begin for the future the first Tuesday in August'. The races soon started to run over more and more days, more prizes were established, and more fringe entertainments sprang up, to the fascination of some but to the scandalized disapproval of conservatives like Hearne. In

1710 the visitor Uffenbach made sure not to miss this Oxford spectacle and obviously enjoyed it when

> In the afternoon of the 16 September a race meeting was held about a mile and a half away from the City. ... Many booths had been set up, where beer was sold, each of which had its sign, a hat, a glove and such like. Nearly all the people from the town were there, and also many strangers, some riding, some driving, some in boats. The horses which were to run were six in number, and had to race twice round the whole course – five English miles, which took inside ten minutes.

He did not go out the next day, but would have done if as is customary on the third day, there had been a smock-race; that is when the women in nothing but a shirt and petticoatt without a blouse and the men shirtless and in short breeches run a race for the prize of a shirt; but this time the race did not take place.[22]

Other diversions were introduced as the years went by. In 1755 there was a contest of single-stick with prizes of a gold-laced hat and a pair of buckskin breeches, and in 1767 foot races, wrestling, leaping, sack races, and catching a loose pig by its tail.[23] Such booths and such vulgarities already aroused Hearne's fears and anger. The booths were being erected far too soon and the whole event extended too long. 'Even yesterday,' he said,

> 'twas talked of that there would be another Race of two horses, and some said a Foot-Race for either a smock or a hoop-Petticoat, and some said also that there would be bull-baiting, but the excessive Rains wch fell yestereday ... prevented any farther Sports. And indeed 'twas time to have done these Diversions ... being nothing else but incentives to Idleness and Vice, and doing a great deal of harm to the youth of the University and others.

By 1729 the races lasted eight days 'all wch time there were booths and revellings in the meadow, and one booth was put up 3 weeks before the Race began'. The following year the offending booths were in place six or seven weeks before the races. At the races of 1732 'Booths and vicious living were there for about seven weeks, to the no small scandal of virtuous people' as well as puppet shows and rope-dancing 'to the debauching and corrupting of youth'.[24]

Hearne's sour voice was, however, unheard in the general approval of this festive event which grew almost to equal Encaenia as a social attraction to the university and even more so to the citizens of the town. More and more ladies began to visit, and with them their necessary entourage. The hairdressers, Messrs Mesnard and Stroud and Mr Presto announced their arrival to attend upon the ladies at the races of 1790. For their greater comfort at the actual races of that year a special stand was erected for them with a full view of the whole course. In the evenings the company repaired to dinners and balls. In the early years the Angel was the scene of these assemblies and dances, but in 1753 the ball was held in the new town hall and was a brilliant affair. In 1767 a splendid ball was held in Christ Church hall. In 1768, 165 people joined in country dancing at the town hall, at 5 shillings a head, and to illuminate the Race Balls of 1790 in the town hall there was installed a magnificent gilt chandelier, the gift of the Duke of Marlborough. Throughout these weeks there were public breakfasts at the town hall, public suppers at the Star Inn, venison ordinaries at the King's Head in the Cornmarket, and every sort of entertainment, cock-fights and even an exhibition in 1798 of two creatures 'from a new discovered part of the world'. No name was given, but the close description ensures that they were the animals which fascinated the end of the century, the kangaroo.[25]

The better-off scholars and no doubt constant attenders at the races also enjoyed the more exciting and less gentle pursuit of the fox and the hare. Philips with his noble friends had ample opportunities to join the hunt – 'went a foxhunting with Geo. Henry Lee Earl of Litchfield etc. etc. ... din'd at Woodstock'.[26] With him hunted many an undergraduate brought up to the chase and with means to hire a hunter and perhaps buy a red coat or a velvet hunting cap. Now and again the hunt brought excitement and confusion to those dwellers in city and college who had never followed hounds, when the close propinquity of open country and city created unusual and sometimes dangerous incursions. Hearne records how

> One Hart of Beckley, being driving a Waggon, loaded with corn, out of the Field, a Hare, started by some Grey Hounds that two or three Gentlemen had brought out (Scholars, I think) happen'd in Passing to fright the Horses, & thereby the Waggon overturn'd, fell upon the Man, & crush'd him to death.

Less disastrous was another excitement when

> On Friday last my Lord Abingdon being hunting several Miles from Oxford, the Deer, being pursued by the Dogs, came through the water by Magdalen College, and so went to Merton Coll. Field & so to Corpus Xti Coll. back Gate, & so into the College, where it was killed by the College before ye Dogs came out, against which the Gate was shut.[27]

One hopes that the inhabitants of Corpus were granted the venison.

Less edible but equally exciting quarry appeared when 'A Hare, started by spaniels at the Castle mount, ran up George Street, past Balliol and Trinity, now pursued by all the dogs and curs of the neighbourhood, turned past Wadham and escaped into the Parks, all to the great alarm of the populace.'[28] The spaniels involved in this escapade were, as *The Loiterer* noted later in the century, among '(all the animals, which an Oxford man is

29   Caught bringing his dog into college

ever-possessed of) two or three *Pointers, and Spaniels, a Hunter, and a Pony*'.[29] The same source reports another hunting scene but with different dogs, up by Pullen's Tree on Headington Hill, when 'a large party of very *dashing* Men rode by, mounted on cropt ponies, and followed by no inconsiderable number of Tarriers, of all sorts, colours and sizes; and as they did not ride very fast, and talked very loud, we easily discovered that the object of the grand cavalcade had been a *Badger-baiting* on *Bullingdon-Green*'.[30]

Those spaniels and terriers are part of another power struggle between the authorities with their decrees, and country bred youths of the university with their inherited love of dogs and the need to have one for companionship and sport. How else could the country resound with

> The Shouts of many an academic Buck
> O'er diving Spaniels and the quaking Duck?

Statutes and decrees on the subject were clear and unequivocal, and the dislike and forbidding of dog-keeping went back to the seventeenth century. When the Bishop of Winchester's commission visited New College, it was, we are told, interested to discover whether the scholars of that place kept dogs.[31] The authorities of the following century, along with many others, knew they did, and forbade it. The Vice-Chancellor and the Heads of

Houses, in an order of 14 January 1734, ordained that 'No scholar ... shall ... be allowed to have Dogs, Guns, or Nets, for the destroying of Game, to the Injury of others, and the loss of their own Time.' Nearly forty years later they were still waging an obviously losing battle, and ruling that no undergraduate could be allowed to keep a dog or dogs of any breed under penalty of rustication for three months, six months or a year for successive offences against the statute.[32] When Richard Newton, Principal of Hart Hall, devised his *Scheme of Discipline* earlier in the century he would have embodied such prohibition in his college rules, that a member of Hart Hall 'does not keep any Dogs to defile his Rooms, or multiply his Care, or spend his Time Improperly'.[33] Other colleges were equally severe in their intentions. Gentlemen of Trinity put 1 shilling a time into the pocket of the porter whenever their dogs were seen in college – nothing being said about their owning them. Worcester in 1785 fined any undergraduate owning a dog 2s. 6d. The ruling thirteen Fellows of New College with, as might be expected, gentler manners, made an order to sconce all the dogs seen in college.[34] Before he was elected to his Fellowship, Woodforde had owned a dog he was proud of. 'I had out my dog'. he notes, 'being the first time, and he did pretty well.'[35] Later in his diary he chronicles the difficulties he had in keeping another dog there. His colleague Hirst's bitch, Chloe, gave birth to six pups and he presented one to Woodforde, who named it Pero. At first he boarded it out with a servant Dods at 9d. a week, but relented at this banishment, and Pero returned to college, 'My little dog Pero laid in my bed Chamber. I have taken him away from Dods these two days,' he notes, and that he has bought him his own meat for 1 shilling. But this arrangement proving unsatisfactory, Pero was then chained up behind the stables, and when Woodforde was sconced 2s. 6d. by his colleague Whitmore for his dog being in the quad, it was banished to its kennel behind the stables. Later he acquired another dog Nero whom he fed luxuriously on sheeps' paunches, bones and sheep heads.[36]

It was not, however these few colleges where the flagrant violation of the anti-canine laws took place. Frequent advertisements for lost Oxford dogs, an obviously vagrant and untrustworthy breed, filled the local newspapers, and give some evidence of the widespread blatant failure to take decrees and orders seriously. The wandering beasts came from all over the university, Queen's, University College, Magdalen Hall, St John's, Lincoln, Christ Church, Hertford, All Souls, New College and St Edmund Hall. Spaniels, especially the red and white, were the favourite breed, but pointers, greyhounds, foxhounds, harriers and terriers were also among the lost and strayed, answering to such names as Dash, Hector, Ponto and Dido, Phyllis, Vixen, Pepper, Rover and Grog.[37]

These forbidden dogs often accompanied their masters on forbidden shooting expeditions. Alicia D'Anvers enumerated this pleasure among many others:

116   *University Life in Eighteenth-Century Oxford*

> Now for their *Way* of going a *Shooting*,
> Sometimes a *Horse-back*, sometimes *Footing*.

Her young ruffians finished their day stealing a farmer's bacon and then shooting his ducks and hens.[38] Small wonder the authorities anathematized the possession and use of guns by such members of the university. Statute Tit. xv. Sect. 7 of the university forbade shooting, and the Vice-Chancellor's order of 14 January 1734 had forbidden all scholars to own a gun or to 'appear in the Streets, or any other Place within the Precincts of the University, with any sort of Arms, under pretence of exercise or recreation'. Vice-Chancellor Bernard Gardiner attempted severe measures to stamp out the sport when he ordered

> All Gunsmiths and others … to take notice, that if they lend or set to hire any Guns to Scholars, which they shall be found to use for their Recreation, or to put to any Unstatutable uses, the said Guns are by the Statutes of the University forfeited, and shall be seiz'd accordingly.

Despite these thunderings, gentlemen went a-shooting. Woodforde enjoyed the sport. The sober and unhappy Jeremy Bentham at Queen's did a little fishing and now and again shooting, though he disliked both.[39] We read of a party of gentlemen being taken up river to Port Meadow to shoot swallows.[40]

At a safer distance from the Proctors were frequent pigeon-shoots in the country. Before the days of 'clay-pigeons' and the sling, real pigeons were released from a box as targets. At one such contest at the Oxford Arms at Thame a prize of a silver cup went to the best of three shots, and all contestants had to eat and pay for an obligatory dinner at the pub. The Dog House at Abingdon was another scene for such contests,[41] while rooks also provided a favourite target for wandering shooters. Hearne records the tragic end of one such expedition when 'On Tuesday last … one Mr. Newby, Commoner of Lincoln Coll., being at Cassington, with two or three other gentlemen, on purpose to shoot Rooks, happened to lean upon the mouth of his Gun, wch was cock'd, and it went off, & shot him through the Heart, & he died immediately.'[42] He tells of an even more shocking incident when,

> Mr Dalton, one of the Junior Fellows of All Souls College, going out two or three days to divert himself shooting, met with some High-Constable, who not giving way, there was some Justleing, but at last Dalton being forc'd to break way, he was so concern'd that he turn'd back presently, & shot the Constable, who being a lusty stout Man made up to him (not withstanding his wound) and took his Gun from him.[43]

Such incidents as these doubtless strengthened the determination of the Heads of Houses in their continued but vain struggle against guns and gunmen.

30   The Cockpit in Longwall

Equally vain were their attempts to control the one other sport which came under their banning edicts – cockfighting. In 1739 Vice-Chancellor Leigh issued an order announcing that 'All Persons are hereby strictly Forbidden to keep or to Frequent any Cock-Pit, or to beat any drum, calling to such unlawful Game, within the University or City of Oxford.'[44] The statute of 1772 'de reprimendis sumptibus non academicis' forbade, amongst all its other bannings, those games at which bets were laid and referred especially to horse racing and cockfighting. Penalties ranging from three months' rustication to being sent down were threatened on any gownsmen who were apprehended at cockfights or taking any part in them. All in vain. In Holywell there were two well-established cockpits, the Great and the Lower, which were the main venues for the sport, although later in the century we find fights being staged in the pit at the Cock and Bottle. Mr Eaton, proprietor of the Great Cockpit ran fights for over twenty years, while Mr Johnson ruled the Lower Pit, both of them regularly and openly advertising matches in the local paper, with special three-day events to coincide with the Oxford horse races in August. In 1753, for example, each morning at the Great Pit there fought '21 cocks on each side in the Main . . . and 15 for Byes'. After the fights an ordinary was provided for the hungry audience. The matches were between the cocks of local and visiting teams.

31   A cockpit in action

In 1755 the gents of Oxford challenged the gents of Wiltshire with thirty-one cocks a side, and the Oxford gents, two years later, took on the gents of Bucks.[45] When Lord Carteret, a noble undergraduate of Christ Church, went to a fight in 1709 he enthusiastically recorded the contest:

> The Green has lately been so rough, that I have been forced to retire into the Cockpit, where wee have had a noble engagement between Oxfordshire and our neighbouring county Berkshire, and indeed the Oxford Fowl behaved themselves very bravely, and generally put their Enimys to flight the first or second stroke.[46]

Erasmus Philips in 1722, supporting one of his noble friends, 'Went to the Great Cockmatch in Holywell, fought between other Windsor Hickman, Earl of Plymouth, & the Town Cocks, which beat his Lordship.'[47] Any scholar who was more daunted by the veto of authority could more safely find his sport in the neighbouring countryside, at Wheatley or Stokenchurch, where an ordinary was usually laid on for the travelling enthusiasts.

These grim forbiddings of the Vice-Chancellor and Heads of Houses thankfully left other sports and pleasures free and unconfined. Bowls was a popular game with young and old, the staider fellows of fortunate colleges playing on their own college greens, while the young scholars not allowed to use those privileged lawns resorted to the public bowling green in Holywell Lane, a place remembered by Stephen Penton with somewhat mixed feelings. 'After dinner,' he writes, 'I went to the publick *bowling-green*, it being the only recreation I can affect. Coming in, I saw half a score of the finest youths the sun, I think, ever shined upon. They walked to and fro, with their hands in their pockets, to see a match played by some scholars and gentlemen famed for their skill.' This idyll was soon interrupted by the terrible swearing of a rough yokel, and Penton was constrained to forbid his son ever to attend such a public place.[48]

Tennis attracted most of the athletic young, and was well provided for. Thomas Warton in his humorous 'guide' to the notable sights and pleasures of Oxford, insisted that among them we must reckon 'three spacious and superb Edifices, situated to the southward of the High-Street, 100 feet long, by 30 in breadth, vulgarly called *Tennis Courts*, where *Exercise* is regularly performed both morning and afternoon.'[49] These three courts remained from numerous courts in use in the seventeenth century; one was in Merton Street, one at the corner of Blue Boar Lane and St Aldates on Christ Church land, and one in Oriel Street.[50]

Cricket was another sport emerging as a popular game in the period, not only for the undergraduates but, even more, for the youth of the country surrounding Oxford. Woodforde writes of the earliest formation of a cricket team and organized matches, and was himself an enthusiastic cricketer. On 29 April 1760 he notes in his diary: 'Went and play'd Crikett, being the first time of our Clubb's playing NB. we play'd in Port Meadow.' An entry the following month reveals that the club was a team of Winchester-schooled New College men – 'Plaid at Crickett in Port Meadow, the Winchester against Eaton, and we Winton: beat them.' He was out on the field with the club again in June and July. The two teams later united to take on more serious opposition when 'The Eaton and Winchester People plaid at Crickett against the whole University 11 on each side, and the latter were shamefully beat off the Field.'[51] Two years later he records a widening of the game, bringing together town and gown, when he 'Took a ride ... to Bullington Green to see a match at Crickett, between some Milton Men and some Gownsmen, Eleven a side'.[52] Bullingdon Green, part of the great common east of Magdalen Bridge was the favoured venue for cricket as well as riding, and the Milton men were one team among many in the country around. Thame had an active team whose matches were organized by the Oxford Arms, with prizes of silver cups and laced hats for the winners and a compulsory dinner at the inn. Princes Risborough offered velvet hats with gold tassels for winners and, for 2s. 6d., the customary compulsory dinner. Wycombe Rye and West Wycombe had cricket grounds, the latter the scene of a challenge match between Risborough and Maidenhead for a silver cup:

32   A fencing school, the students in action

Benson challenged any team which might turn up on the day and staged a match between the gentlemen of Berkshire and the gentlemen of Oxfordshire. Gentlemen players were invited to make up teams at Great Milton, while Bicester and Witney and Woodstock organized matches and invited gentlemen players. Nor was spectator interest lacking. We read of some thousands of spectators at Longworth Lodge to see Cumnor parish defeated by Viscount Longworth's servants.[53] Without violating the statutes and with a hack available, Oxford scholars joined these teams and established the game's popularity, marked by the founding of the Bullingdon Club who played 'The Marylebone' in 1795 and 1796, being defeated in both matches, even though at one stage they were allowed sixteen players. Only after the turn of the century was this easy-going and haphazard organization of the game transformed into the Oxford University Cricket Club, and the flannelled gentlemen dedicated to serious pleasure.[54]

Little can be said of football of either code. The Laudian statutes had forbidden the game within or without the precincts of the University, with heavy penalties for violating the statute, and it seems that the game was an informal and often rough struggle among youths of the artisan and labouring classes. It was many years ahead, many miles north of Oxford, that a boy would pick up the ball and inaugurate the long road to Twickenham.

Other pleasures and exercises which tougher sportsmen of our day might have avoided with suspicion were much sought after by their predecessors, activity which could be called the exercise of deportment and genteel agility – fencing, dancing and disciplined horsemanship. Fencing masters established their schools in the city and received pupils for instruction in the art. Richard Lovell Edgeworth, a gentleman commoner of Corpus, attended one of the best known, 'the fencing school of Paniotti, a native of one of the Greek islands, a fine old Grecian, full of sentiments of honor and courage, and of a most independent spirit'. Thirty years later his death was announced in *Jackson's Oxford Journal* with some variation in the spelling of his name and the exact place of birth of 'Paynyoty Ballachev, 84, an eminent fencing master in the University, born in Sparta. a widely travelled mercenary, a master of languages, affable and well mannered.'[55]

Fencing masters were also frequently dancing masters and catered for a large clientele of scholars, judging by the number of academies advertised, and the establishment of new teachers as the years passed by. In 1755 Mr Tate, who had studied under the best masters in Paris, taught at Mrs Lanyon's in St Ebbs, and offered private lessons in the houses of ladies and gentlemen. Woodforde attended Matthew Towle's Dancing School in 1760 with his friend Tom Robinson, staying till ten at night, before adjourning to the King's Head for a supper of sausages.[56] Mr Monro set up his school in New Inn Lane, moved to Holywell Lane and was still teaching in 1774. Some of these teachers, like Mr Hart, were peripatetic. He had a large circuit in the county and came once a week to Oxford. Prospective pupils could enroll at the Star Inn. Later in the century Mr C. Cullen took up residence at Mr Ley's in Catte Street and specialized in teaching the new style of Scottish dancing 'now all the fashion', while Mr Charriere, in his room at Mr Randall's in the High was equally up-to-date in modern dances, reels and Irish steps. When the lessons were learned, the young men had plenty of opportunities to put their accomplishments to the test and to meet the ladies at the balls and assemblies which at the time of Encaenia and the races were held nightly, at smaller card and dancing assemblies like one held at the Bear Inn where the 6 shilling ticket included tea, coffee, negus and a carriage home for the ladies,[57] or even at much smaller parties as when Woodforde 'Went this evening to a Private Hopp at Mr. Orthmens' and met the ladies who were the daughters of well-to-do tradesmen.[58]

The building of a riding school where the finer arts of horsemanship could be taught was a scheme of the 1770s founded on the Clarendon Bequest to the university, which mainly consisted of the profits of the *Life of Clarendon* which the University Press published in 1759. The bequest was administered by three Clarendon trustees, of whom the most famous to take an active and enthusiastic interest was Dr Samuel Johnson. He put forward the name of Mr Carter, a protégé of the Thrales, to be appointed Riding Master. When Lord Mansfield had doubts about the sufficiency of the fund to establish this as a salaried post, Johnson consulted the Heads of Houses who supported Carter's

33   Grown gentlemen taught to dance

petition that he only 'be enabled to profess horsemanship in Oxford, at such prices and under such regulations as shall be fixed by the Magistrates of the University'. He found a prospective builder and submitted to the trustees an estimate of £875 for building the riding house, stables and a house for the Master. His hopes were high in 1776 when he wrote to the treasurer of the trust at Windsor:

> The Vice-Chancellor and Proctors of Oxford have approved a Master of Horsemanship recommended by me, as a proper man to put in practice the design for which Lord Clarendon left a provision. The trustees have been

34   A satirical view of a riding house

consulted and have agreed to issue money for the erection of a Riding house, and the business is at a stand only till the Bishop of Chester can be informed how much money the Book has produced.

The reply told him that the account stood only at £150, and in deep disappointment he told Mrs Thrale 'that the last spark of hope is now extinguished'.[59] Terrae Filius would have joined him in that disappointment, but for different reasons. Early in the discussions he had expressed a wish 'to see the intended Scheme of a Riding-house ... carried into immediate Execution. He forsees great Advantage accruing to the Church Militant, from our Doctors in Divinity being taught to ride the Great Horse. ...'[60]

To turn from land-borne diversions to those of the Isis. That river, in summer and in winter, was the scene of exercise and pleasure for generations of undergraduates as well as the elders of their colleges. Days spent on the water, more than in any other sports, are the most frequent memories in their nostalgic moments. Robert Southey's father 'used to say he learned two things only at Oxford, to row and to swim'.[61] The Village Curate, proud to have resisted the temptation of the idle life of a fellowship, still cherishes days when

> ... on thy bank too, Isis, have I stray'd,
> A tassel'd student. Witness you who shar'd

> My morning walk, my ramble at high noon,
> My evening voyage, an unskilful tar,
> To Godstow bound, or some inferior port,
> For strawberries and cream.

And then the slow silent return home with only the sound of New College bells over the meadow:

> And so too have I paused and held my oar,
> And suffer'd the slow stream to bear me home,
> No speed requir'd while Wykeham's peal was up.[62]

River memories, more than many other, inspired the Oxford muse to recall these pleasures passed away with youth:

> What now can every Wish avail,
> To guide, as erst, the spreading Sail,
> Or ply, amid the jocund Roar,
> On ISIS Flood, the dashing Oar! ...
> In Memory's Eye he views the Day,
> Light as his *Skiff* that danc'd away
> When bent to MEDLEY's lov'd Retreat,
> Or BINSEY's shade-surrounded Seat;
> Or antique GODSTOWE's mould'ring Walls
> Where oft the hoary Fragment falls.[63]

Another nostalgic Oxonian, disappointed in the hoped-for pleasures of married life, lets his memory return to such carefree river days:

> Nor seldom, where the Skiff light-glancing flew
> Or flash'd the Colors of the gay Canoe,
> The summer's swift-descending Hour we gave
> To social pastime on the classic Wave;
> The Paddler's Evolutions pleas'd to mark
> From the broad Benches of our safer Bark,
> Whether beneath the wide-spread Awning glow'd
> Our circling Glass, while trowser'd Rustics row'd;
> Or to hale exercise we strove to pour
> The fluid Silver from each feather'd Oar;
> Or strait becalm'd, where low-incumbent Trees
> Wav'd to the Whisper of the shifting breeze,
> Among the rustling Sedge and Lilies moist
> Mourn'd our rude Efforts that essay'd to hoist
> The slacken'd Sails no more by Zephyrs fill'd,
> And ran aground, in Steerage all unskill'd.[64]

35   Gownsmen boating from Folly Bridge

The boats featuring in these fondly remembered outings were hired from a firm at Folly Bridge run by a well-known Oxford character, Mrs Hooper:

> Right to the River, where a dame
> Hooper yclep'd, at station waits
> For Gownsmen, whom she aptly freights
> In various Vessels moor'd in view,
> Skiff, Gig, and Cutter or Canoe.
> Selection made, each in a trice
> Becomes transform'd, with trousers nice
> Jacket and Catskin Cap supplied
> (Black Gowns and Trenchers chuck'd aside)
> From students lo! see sailors rise.[65]

In the seventeenth century the scholars hired a boat and a boatman to row them, as George Wither sings in his love-song of 1620:

> In summer time to Medley
>   My love and I would go,
> The boatman stood there ready
>   My love and I to row.[66]

But by the eighteenth century the undergraduates had discovered the joy of rowing rather than being rowed, and the easier enjoyment of picnics and bathing without the inhibiting presence of servants. The growth in solitary rowing for the sheer joy of pushing the boat along –

Straining each nerve, I urge the dancing skiff – [67]

made the skiff an increasingly popular craft, light, but not too easy or safe to handle, as Robert Southey, together with many generations of young oarsmen, found when

> On the water I went yesterday, in a little skiff, which the least deviation from the balance would overset. To manage two oars and yet unable to handle one! My first setting off was curious. I did not step exactly in the middle, the boat tilted up, and a large barge from which I embarked alone saved me from a good ducking; my arm, however, got completely wet. I tugged at the oar very much like a bear in a boat.[68]

Southey, as we shall see, was luckier than many a young man in skiff or canoe who did not live to tell of his failure to control these delicate little vessels. In contrast, the largest boats to be hired, though not without their own dangers, were the wherrys which held five passengers, four rowing and one steering, sometimes overloaded with seven or eight, and the most popular vessel for convivial voyages by a group of friends bound for some pleasurable destination.

Those destinations were few and exceedingly popular. Fondly remembered, widely chronicled and often celebrated in song, was Medley, the first port upstream the rowers came to, as Port Meadow widened out before them. Hearne is quietly enthusiastic about the place: 'Medley is a single House nearer the water than Binsey is, and not so far up the River. The House is much frequented in Summer time by Scholars and others, there being good Accommodation there, & it being wonderfully pleasant.'[69] Thomas Warton later fills out the picture in his *Companion to the Guide*:

> about a mile north-west of this City, stands the Seat of Mr. Potter, called MEDLEY-HOUSE, delightfully situated on the Banks of the *Isis*. It is elegantly built of hewn-stone, having two beautiful Wings, with commodious Offices. The front, besides the River, and a Walk shaded with Horse-Chestnuts, commands an *extensive* Prospect over *Port-Meadow*. On the North is a delightful *Grove*. – Mr. Potter, who, in consideration of his distinguished Eminence in that Profession, was the first *Tooth-Drawer* that ever *retired* from business, keeps an hospitable House, and is always glad to wait upon his friends.[70]

The place had a long reputation for good refreshments. A century before Withers had treated his love to cream and cakes and prunes there, and a later voyager

... sails that afternoon to medly,
Near half a mile, or such a matter,
It lyes as you go down by Water;
A place at which they never fail,
Of *Custard*, *Cyder*, *Cakes*, and *Ale*,
Cream, *Tarts*, and *Cheese-Cakes*, good *Neats Tongues*
And pretty *Girls* to wait upon's.[71]

Upstream, not far from Medley, was the inn at Binsey, set a little back from the water. Woodforde, the night before he was elected Fellow, went there up water with a party of comrades. He rowed up in a skiff which he had hired for 6d. It must have been a good celebratory party, for he records that 'I was in the water coming down 20 times.' Further upstream was the inn at Godstowe which Woodforde refers to as 'Old Jerrys', where he refreshed himself on 'bread & Cheese & Strong Beer'[72] and where Hearne often went, though he walked there on dry land, 'to eat a fish' or met a friend there 'and had a Fish dinner and enjoyed one another's Company with great pleasure and satisfaction for about four hours'.[73] Erasmus Philips and his companions played music and took wine to refresh themselves en route, as they made their way to Godstowe.[74]

Dowstream there were also favourite places of refreshment along the river route through Iffley, Kennington, Littlemore and Sandford and on to Nuneham. Erasmus Philips had taken his father along this 'most agreeable passage',[75] but without the restraint of a visiting father, the voyagers stopped sooner and more often. Iffley was a favourite port of call, where there was food and drink and skittles.[76] Further downstream was the next stop on the way to Nuneham:

We visit Sandford next, and there
Beckley provides accustom'd fare
Of eels and perch and brown beef-steak –
Dainties we taste of twice a week,
Whilst Hebe-like, his daughter waits,
Froths our full bumpers, changes plates. . . .
A game of quoits will oft our stay
Awhile at Sandford Inn delay
Or rustic nine-pins; then once more
We hoist the sail or tug the oar,
To Nuneham bound.[77]

Picnics and barbecues became increasingly popular along with these visits to well-known hostelries. Erasmus Philips with a party of friends 'Went up the river a fishing ... as far as Burnt Island, whereon we landed, and dressed a leg of Mutton, which after we dispatched in the wherry. The passage to this diminutive Island is wonderfully sweet and pleasant.'[78] Woodforde went out fishing for barbel and took cold meat with him for a dinner in the boat.[79] And we have already met the party of Oxford 'Toasts' boasting of their pleasure-boat voyages with the Fellows of Balliol, supping on the water on 'good Ham and Chickens, sparkling wines'.[80] Another picnic came to a sadder end when two Oriel men, on a party of pleasure to Nuneham, dined on the banks of the river and bathed. Getting by accident into a deep hole, they both drowned.

This much-loved river claimed many such victims, in boats or bathing, for the undergraduates' ability to swim appears to have been even less than their skill in handling boats. The newspapers record these accidents with an awful regularity throughout the century; two young fellows, sailing a wherry with a sail, drowned between Oxford and Medley; a party of seven or eight on a river party of pleasure stayed late at Iffley and when five had re-embarked in their wherry, just above the mill, it was carried over the sluice; Edward Taylor of Christ Church rowing a skiff was carried over the weir at Iffley and drowned; William Farrer of Lincoln was drowned while bathing near Wolvercote; an undergraduate of Christ Church leapt from his skiff to avoid disaster at the weir and drowned; three Merton men were drowned when a sudden gust overturned their sailing boat at Kennington; an overturned canoe drowned a gentleman commoner of Hertford; and when young James Sparrow Chapman of Balliol was drowned while bathing in the Cherwell, the whole college turned out to attend his funeral in the church of St Mary Magdalen.[81]

The river in winter, together with its flood waters, was the scene of lively pleasures and safer than those attempted in the more dangerous waters of the spring and summer terms. The century suffered many severe winters. In 1739 there were 103 days of frost; in 1763 there were 94 days of frost; in 1784 there were 89 days of frost and the following year the freeze continued until 25 March with few days above freezing and some recording 18 degrees of frost.[82] In the first month of 1789 the temperature fell to 6 degrees Fahrenheit, and the waterworks froze solid.[83] It was when the shallowly flooded Christ Church Meadow froze that the first sport began and town and gown turned out to skate:

> Here graceful gownsmen silent glide
> Or noisy louts on hobnails slide
>   While lads the confines keep
> Exacting pence from every one
> As payment due for labour done
>   As constantly they sweep. ...[84]

John Scott, later Lord Eldon, remembered 'that when Christ Church Meadows was overflowed and sufficiently frozen for skating, people used to ply the ice with kegs of brandy and other cordials'. He managed to fall through the ice with no serious effect.[85] Woodforde, a great skater, was often on the frozen meadow, but preferred longer excursions on the frozen Isis. In the winter of 1762 he skated through the whole month of January and with friends he 'skated down to Abingdon where we dined and for our dinners there etc. each of us pd. 2s. 6d. We were going down about an hour and a half; NB. We walked above 2 miles out of it. It is about ten miles by water.'[86]

In the following year in the long freeze-up Woodforde skated nearly every day of January, often from Folly Bridge to Iffley, with refreshing ale at Iffley or from some booth set up on the ice. Sometimes he skated for a whole day, learning what he calls 'the out stroke' and dining at Iffley on beef and ale or pork and ale, and paying his penny to have the ice swept. Once he skated as far as Sandford. When there were fireworks at Folly Bridge he stayed on the ice until seven o'clock, and to finish the day skated to Iffley and back until nine and the sound of Tom.[87] The town joined the gown in various ice-treats beside fireworks. In January 1763 a whole sheep was roasted on the ice at High Bridge amidst a vast concourse of people, and various games and contests were organized. A sweepstake was held on a race between Iffley and Sandford, a young apprentice cook from Corpus carrying off the prize. In another game the contestants had to pick up stones from the ice at speed, 100 stones set a yard apart, and return to the start with each stone separately. A boy won in 37 minutes.[88]

With field and heath on every side, a fine river flowing through the city, with horses and races, tennis and fencing, bathing and boating, it was a good place to be young and healthy. It was a good place to find other pleasures than the pot-house and tavern, to frolic, cap and gown cast aside, without the frowning presence of Proctors and statutes, and with only the occasional don making his sober way up Headington Hill or along the river bank to the refreshing delights of Medley or Godstowe.

CHAPTER TEN

The Theatre and Music

To chronicle only the pleasures of high table, the somnolent indulgences of common room, the gossip of coffee house and the jollity of the ale-house, the gentle saunterings in parks and gardens, the more strenuous sporting joys of horse and river, is yet to omit much of the exuberance and excitement of the city in which the University took an active part and wielded much power. This gave to its social life a more outgoing dimension, an escape from the cloistered and exclusive life of college rooms and college acquaintance, where town and gown met more often and more easily, without the furtive and sordid aspects of the world of brothels and bedmakers, and a life with an open and often earthy simplicity.

One notable absence in this wider scene of social pleasure and enter-tainment was the theatre. In a university which had nourished and encouraged the play and the production of plays as part of the full education of a scholar and gentleman from the early days of British drama, the shadows of disapproval began to gather at the close of the seventeenth century. There was no purpose-built theatre in Oxford, and any production took place in the courtyard of such an inn as the King's Arms or in the tennis courts and dancing schools temporarily converted. Added to the hardship of the lack of a permanent playhouse, the players were now condemned as the source of riot and immorality. Wrote Humphrey Prideaux of Christ Church in 1674,

> The players parted from us with small gains which I hope will give them noe encouragement to come again. Neither, I suppose, will the University for the future permit them here, if they can be kept out, since they were guilty of such great rudenesses before they left us, going about the town in the night breaking windows, and committing many other unpardonable rudenesses.[1]

Moreover the converted tennis courts where the undergraduates came into the dangerous company of women, were seen as a source of vice and corruption. Alicia D'Anvers celebrates the adjournment of the young from the celebrations in the Sheldonian Theatre to the less permanent but more attractive scene:

> In this Employ the Day well worn,
> They to the *Tennis-Court* adjourn.
> A *Theatre*, tho' far less spiteful
> Than is their old, far more delightful;
> Where the young *Lads* that never ventur'd,
> Never till now, are fairly enter'd;
> What there they do among the Wenches
> Say, O ye Stools, O speak ye Benches.[2]

In the face of such threats to morality, the authorities acted. In 1710 the players were refused permission to come to Oxford, which Hearne records with obvious approval: 'Dr. Lancaster wrote to Dr. Charlett "I have had the players and Pinkerton with me, but I have refused everybody leave to show at [the Act]."' Nelson also remarks 'we are very much pleased in town with the VCr. resolution in not suffering the players to have the opportunity to corrupt the youth of the University'.[3]

Someone must have softened and relented for in 1713, at the Act, the players were allowed back, with the irrepressible Colley Cibber as their leader and historian. 'I cannot,' he writes, 'pass over the good Fortune of the Company that followed us to the Act at *Oxford*.' He records the visit as a triumph, firstly because he could doctor the script at this 'Accademical Jubilee' to suit the gossip of the day, how 'Tony Leigh the Commedian took [a liberty] with the character of the well known *Obadiah Walker*, then Head of *University college* who in that Prince's Reign [James II] had turn'd *Roman Catholic*.' Leigh, explaining why the Obadiah in the comedy *The Committee* should be hung, inserted the line 'Upon my Shoule, he has shange his religion.' Cibber adds that this local reference was 'received with all the Triumph of Applause'. His whole account of this visit to Oxford is worth repeating for its professional hard-headedness and pride:

> It had been a Custom for the Comedians while at *Oxford* to act twice a Day; the first Play ending every morning before the College Hours of dining, and the other never to break into the time of shutting their Gates in the Evening. This extraordinary labour gave all the hired Actors a Title to double Pay, which, at the Act in King *William's* Time I had accordingly receiv'd there. But then present Menegers considering that, by acting only once a day, their Spirits might be fresher for every single Performance, and that by this Means they might be able to fill up the Term of their Residence, without the Repetition of their best and strongest Plays; and as their Theatre was contrived to hold a full third more than the usual form it had done, one House fill'd might answer the Profits of two but moderately taken up.

The new scheme paid off:

The fact was, that on our first Day of acting it [Addison's *Cato*] our House was in a manner invested, and entrance demanded by twelve a Clock at Noon, and before one it was not wide enough for many to come too late for Places. The same Crowds continued for three days together.... To conclude, our reception at *Oxford*, whatever our merit might be, exceeded our Expectation. At our taking Leave we had the Thanks of the Vice-Chancellor for the decency and Order observ'd by our whole Society.... Our Receipts had not only enabled us ... to double the Pay of every Actor, but to afford out of them towards the repair of St. *Mary's* Church the Contribution of fifty Pounds.

He concludes with a valedictory comment on the taste of his Oxford audiences:

A great deal of that false, flashy Wit and forc'd Humour, which had been the Delight of our Metropolitan Multitude, was only rated there at its bare intrinsic Value. Applause was not to be purchased there, but by the true Sterling, the *Sal Atticum* of a Genius.... The elegant Follies of higher Life were not at *Oxford* among their Acquaintance, and consequently might not be so good Company to a Learned Audience as Nature, in her plain Dress and unornamented in Her Pursuits and Inclinations seemed to be.[4]

When the players left Oxford after this last visit, Miss Willis spoke their farewell Epilogue:

> My Orders were, our humble Thanks to pay
> For Lavish Favours done to ev'ry Play.
> Beyond our Hopes we've found a Welcome here,
> And wish (with some of you) it might be ev'ry Year:
> 'Tis hard, methinks, Old Rules we should not follow,
> Since *Semel in anno ridet Apollo*.
> But since your learned Jubilees are scarce,
> We must be humbly patient for some Years;
> Then I, perhaps, may see you less to Love inclin'd;
> And be reveng'd on all the Golden Tufts I leave behind.[5]

Alas, Miss Willis's epilogue and Cibber's report on the warm reception of the players appear to have failed to receive wide approval, though one member of the academic community, tired but happy at the end of the official ceremonies of the Act, wrote to his friend: 'Our Act is over and without the least disorder; nothing more to be done, but seeing plays and eating and drinking for a few days more.'[6] Hearne records that by 1733 the players were still refused permission to come to Oxford, and had moved their activities into the wider countryside. 'The Players being denied coming to Oxford by the Vice-Chancellor and that very rightly, tho' they might as well have been here as Handel and (his lowsy Crew) a great number of foreign fidlers, they went to Abbingdon, and yesterday began to act there, at which were present many Gownsmen from Oxford.'[7]

The establishment of the players at Abingdon and Hearne's reported presence of the gownsmen there, is the key to the way in which the theatre, despite its physical absence in Oxford, still played an important part in the social life of the gown. It flourished in an area around Oxford within easy reach of carriage or horseback, or even tempted young scholars to a night away from college and the Proctors. The theatre at Abingdon continued to be a favourite destination for the theatre-loving – and lady-loving – members of the university. Woodforde noted in 1774 that 'There were two gownsmen at the Play in Boxes with two noted Ladies of Pleasure, a Miss Allen & a Lady who goes by the name of Miss Burford.'[8] Some visitors from Oxford were apparently well known, and not always charitably treated. We hear that

> certain reverend Persons, of very great Weight and Person in the University, being pleas'd to mount their sober Steeds, and trot over to Abingdon, to see a play acted by some *Strollers* [Congreve's *The Double Dealer*]. A special prologue was written for them by a saucy Spark of Merton which infuriated them. After threats to the players and useless complaint to the Mayor, they rode home.[9]

But such temporary breakdowns in the proper treatment of Oxford audiences did little to hinder the stability and growth of the Abingdon theatre as a welcome outlet for Oxford's theatre-loving clientele. The stage was situated in the town hall and this was the venue of the players until December 1786 when a new theatre was opened at the Lamb Inn. This was a custom-built affair with pit, boxes and gallery, and the audiences were promised good fires to warm them. Unfortunately, eight days after the opening performance of 18 December and as the final curtain came down, the gallery gave way and fell into the pit, the audience escaping with many bruises and one fractured leg.[10] By January 1787 the gallery was rebuilt 'on a new construction' and the theatre re-opened with an aptly chosen comedy, *The Chapter of Accidents*.[11]

Abingdon was but one of many theatres within easy reach of Oxford, suggesting a thriving provincial theatre supplied by touring companies and generously attended by junior and senior members of the university. Theatres advertised performances in Banbury, Bicester, Wallingford, Witney, Henley, Woodstock, High Wycombe, Wantage and Chipping Norton. Some of these took place in conversions of the larger rooms in the more spacious inns of the town such as the George at Bicester, the Catherine Wheel at High Wycombe, the George at Wallingford and, in 1778, a second theatre in Woodstock at the Six Bells with a fully fitted stage with pit and gallery. Thus, the general picture is one of prosperity and expansion in the theatre around Oxford. At Woodstock the players moved from the town hall to a new theatre fully equipped with boxes and gallery; at Witney in 1767 they transferred from the Little Theatre to the New Theatre; and in 1769 a newcomer on the scene sounds to have been a forceful entrepreneur manager. Mr Stow's company of comedians took over a large place at Wantage and announced that they were fitting it out as a stage in a genteel manner, promising a repertoire beyond the reach of country companies. Three years later he and his company were at Abingdon, already well supplied with its new theatre, and had taken a place there with proposals to fit it up as a theatre, again 'in a most genteel manner' and boasting that his company 'will look upon the other Pretenders, as mere shadows'.[12]

Mr Stow's company was one of the groups of players, each under their actor-manager, which travelled the Oxford circuit, offering seasons of plays throughout the year. Among the regular companies Mr Linnett's was possibly the longest active, 'universally allowed to be the best that was ever seen in these parts',[13] performing throughout the whole area from 1754 to 1774, after which their advertisements no longer appear in the newspapers. In the 1750s Mr Williams's company was active. Audiences in the 1760s were entertained by the actors of Mr Penhard, Mr Foster and the Portsmouth Company. Mr Wood's troop travelled widely in the 1770s and in the 1780s there were at least three active companies under the management of Mr Richardson, Mr Bower and Mr White. In the last decade of the century the company of the Royal Theatre at Cheltenham, where Mrs Siddons gave her last performance, toured in the area.[14]

Once arrived the companies usually settled in for a season of plays, sometimes for only a fortnight but frequently for two or three weeks with three performances a week, covering the year with spring, summer and winter visits.[15] These hardworking seasoned players had time therefore to provide a wide repertoire for their audiences, the backbone of which was the frequent presentation of a rather limited group of Shakespeare's plays. *Romeo and Juliet* and *Hamlet* were the favourites, closely followed by *Richard III*, *Henry IV* and *The Merchant of Venice*, with *Othello*, *King Lear* and *The Merry Wives* at the lower end of performance figures, and no other plays from the Shakespearian canon being advertised in the regional press. The great plays of the eighteenth century formed the next substantial group of productions, with *She Stoops to Conquer* and *School for Scandal* leading a field containing *The Provok'd Husband*, *The Beaux' Stratagem*, *The Recruiting Officer* and *The Rivals*. A less sophisticated public taste was apparently satisfied with such offerings as *Love in a Village*, *The Maid of the Mill*, *The West Indian* and *The Child of Nature*.

One other development in this provincial theatre, of interest in itself but relevant to our theme because we read that 'There were members of the University in the numerous and polite audience', was the appearance of private theatres with plays mounted by an amateur cast drawn from the families of local gentry, sometimes reinforced by the household servants and local yokels, and by a number of professional actors and actresses. These genteel and elegant establishments, free from the rough and tumble of the town playhouses, were more to the taste of the senior and staid members of the university, and all within convenient carriage distance. In February 1773, in his house at North Aston, Oldfield Bowles furnished out a theatre where he could present private theatricals, opening with a production of *The Upholsterers*, 'to great applause from a polite and numerous company'. After the play the company was treated to a collation and a ball.[16] In January of the following year he put on a performance of *The Merchant of Venice* and in February, as part of another social evening, *The Fair Penitent* was staged.[17] January 1775 saw a production of *Every Man in his Humour* where members of the university were in the audience and no doubt stayed for the elegant collation after the show before driving back to Oxford.[18] By this time it appears that an autumn season was a regular event at North Aston. November 1776 saw a production of *The Siege of Scutari*, a tragedy, with wine and confectionery between the acts to relieve the gloom.[19] For autumn 1777 we have a full programme of three plays, *Hamlet* in October, *The Merchant of Venice* and *Jane Shore* as the closing piece in November, with a gushing report on the beauty of the theatre and the presentation 'as perfect as those which are in use in the established Theatres in Town'.[20] In December 1779 *Jane Shore* was possibly Mr Bowles's last production. He died in August 1780, though we read that the theatre continued after his death with a young Mr and Mrs Bowles acting in *Venice Preserved* before an audience of neighbouring nobility and gentry 'and members of the University'.[21]

In 1786 at his home, Faringdon House, Mr Pye followed this fashion of amateur theatricals with his family and friends mounting a production of *Tancred and Sigismunda*,[22] while a grander affair appeared at Blenheim. The noble lords and ladies of the Marlborough family had previously performed a play before an audience of family and friends in the Bow Window room of the palace but in 1786 a conservatory was converted into a proper theatre, 'fitted up in a style of peculiar elegance, and with appendages correspondent to the munificence and fortune of the owner. The stage is large and is furnished with proper changes of scenery and fixtures: the seats for the audience are easy and commodious, and capable of accommodating two hundred persons, without including the side boxes. The whole has a grand and pleasing effect.' In this new theatre, until 1789, plays were regularly produced and *Jackson's Oxford Journal* at the end of the 1787/8 season enthusiastically reported of the audience how 'every look spoke the exquisite satisfaction which was felt', though other reports criticize the productions for the usual amateur faults of forgotten lines, inaudibility and unrehearsed giggles.[23] At the end of the year the same noble cast opened a week's season with *The Provok'd Husband*, and the same autumn programme was mounted in 1789 with the Marquis of Blandford added to the brilliant cast. The theatre was a favourite and favoured resort of the university. On the last two nights of the 1788 season the gentry and clergy of the county and the university were supplied with tickets on application, and Thomas Warton was present on one of these nights to see 'one of the Blenheim Theatricals'. He proved to be one of the severer critics. 'I must confess,' he wrote to Charlotte Warton, 'that the scenes and decorations were better than the performances. ... The chief actor was Lord William Russel, a young lad of Christ-Church. Lady Charlotte Spenser was feeble and frightened.'[24] At the opening of the 1789 season the second night was devoted to the members of the university. After 1789 there were no more productions. The theatre was dismantled and no trace of it remains, though the conservatory still stands.[25]

A year later another possibility of a more splendid theatrical evening away from Oxford was provided by Lord Barrymore at his house at Wargrave. This young peer, brought up to a life of extravagance and prodigality, and an early friend of the Prince of Wales, started his theatricals about 1786 in one of his barns, with a cast of family and yokels, but a year and a half later began to build his theatre at a cost, some report, of £60,000. It opened in 1789 with a cast of actresses from professional companies reinforcing family and friends. His enthusiasm led him to rebuild his theatre on a grander scale with room for an audience of four hundred 'on the model of the late Opera House'. It was an elaborate and extensive building of stone, with two tiers of boxes, five boxes a side, a large stage and fore-stage with a fore-stage curtain, with facilities for complicated and spectacular scenic effects. In 1791 plays were staged every Tuesday and Saturday for some months 'to the great entertainment of the neighbouring gentry' and on Christmas Eve the Prince of Wales attended 'with a convention of provincial fashionables'. The play was a prelude to further revels, when the bottle went round till seven the next morning.

After this brilliant season the theatre had a sudden and sad end. The Earl's extravagance had led him into deep financial troubles, with bills unpaid and actions threatening. The complete contents of the theatre were put up for auction on 10 July 1792 and, although the sale was postponed, it was announced for the following October when the whole theatre, building materials and fittings, came under the hammer. The sale included 'The superb and elegant Dresses, Decorations, Cut Glass Lustres, beautiful Scenery, excellent Dressing Room, Ball and Green Room Furniture, compleat Printing Apparatus ... Tastefully selected at an immense expense, and recently executed in very superior and masterly stile, by some of the finest artists in the Kingdom.'[26] Something of the rich elegance of these private additions to the theatrical life of the Oxford neighbourhood is suggested by one item in the catalogue of sale – '28 crystal Chandeliers'.[27] In 1793 at the age of twenty-four its builder was killed by the accidental explosion of a gun while he was on duty with the militia. Nothing remains of his theatre on its site, now part of the kitchen garden of Barrymore House.[28]

In 1763 Terrae Filius, alias George Colman, had announced a plan 'once more to convert the Tennis-Court into a Playhouse, and, in defiance of the

Statute *De Ludis prohibitis* to bring down a Company of Comedians (*funambulos et histriones*),[29] but it was not until the closing years of the century that the theatre returned to Oxford, albeit a theatre in disguise, providing the excitement and pleasure of the drama without necessary carriage-drives to Aston, Blenheim or Wargrave, and without, apparently, the disapproval of Vice-Chancellor or Heads of Houses.[30] At the Rackett Court opposite Merton, extensively converted with pit, a gallery and boxes, their Majesty's Servants from the Theatre Royal, Windsor, under their actor-manager Henry Ford Thornton, opened with a series of 'Readings' from *She Stoops to Conquer*, *High Life below Stairs* and *A Cure for the Heart-ache* before a 'large and elegant attendance'. Later in the month, before an audience increased in fashion and brilliancy, the readings continued. These were far more elaborate productions than mere static dramatic readings. For form's sake the fiction of 'a Reading' was maintained but 'plays and farces are exhibited in an entire state, the actors only now and then affecting to look at their parts which they carry in their hands'.[31] A play *Blue Beard* was now preparing for presentation 'in a manner the most splendid and superb'. There were indeed spectacular scenic effects recreating Bluebeard's castle, a Turkish mountain village, luxurious palace chambers and, at the climax, Bluebeard mounted on an elephant (in London a real live one, but on these provincial tours a walking mechanical creation). In the following month, after news of packed houses and many being turned away, we read of a coming performance of Mr Sheridan's *Pizarro*, for which 'splendid scenery, dresses and decorations are preparing', along with other references to new scenery and dresses.[32] The 'readings' continued until 1815, after a move to another tennis court in Blue Boar Lane, but with trouble from rebellious players and also from horses brought in for some productions, the new manager, Russell, gave up the struggle, and from then onwards for many decades Oxford, as a resort for plays and players, was a barren land.

Music, however, flourished in Oxford without the forbidding frown of authority or the stigma of moral danger and studying time misspent, and never more splendidly and extensively than when it accompanied academic ceremony and celebration. In the early years of the century the occasion at which music added pleasure to solemnity was the Act. The academic year would end with several days of exercises in early July, to be undergone before men graduated to become Bachelors of Arts, and when these were over the Act Day was celebrated in the Sheldonian Theatre with musical concerts and a satirical, often scandalous, speech by the Terrae Filius, an under-graduate chosen for the occasion. After the Act of 1713 there was a gap in these celebrations until they were revived in 1733. Oxford was packed with visitors and special arrangements were made in the theatre for the accommodation of ladies, and the occasion was made memorable by the presence of Handel and the playing of his music, his Utrecht *Te Deum*, the oratorios *Esther*, *Deborah*, *Acis and Galatea* and, as one contemporary noted, 'a spick

36   The great Encaenia of 1759

and span new *Oratorio* called *Athalia*.[33] Not everyone was pleased. Thomas
Hearne grumbled that 'One Handel, a forreigner (who, they say, was born at
Hanover) being desired to come to Oxford to perform in Musick this act'
was, in his opinion, out merely to line his own pocket by numerous benefit
concerts at 5 shillings a ticket, and too mean to pay the fee for the honorary
degree he refused. Better to have had the players, Hearne thought, than
these 'foreign fidlers' who were little more than 'a parcel of Pickpockets
[brought hither] to run away with the money'.[34] Nor was Hearne alone in his
disapproval. We read that 'One of the Royal and Ample had been saying,
that truly, 'twas his Opinion, that the Theater was erected for other-guise
Purposes, than to be prostituted to a company of squeaking, bawling out-
landish singsters, let the agreement be what it wou'd.'[35]

After this Act of 1733 the Commemoration of Benefactors or Encaenia
became the climax, both academic and musical, of the university's social
year, with the Doctors partaking of Lord Crewe's Benefaction before
processing, sometimes a little unsteadily, to the Theatre, for the conferring of

honorary degrees, the speech of the Professor of Poetry, the reading of prize poems and exercises and, in large quantities, music, before and after the ceremonial. The concert programmes were indeed substantial, divided into two or three acts with a variety of overtures, oratorios, songs and instrumental music for solo instruments or concertos for cello, violin, flute, harp and orchestra. Particularly memorable was the visit of Haydn in 1791 when the *Oxford* symphony received its first performance and Haydn, unlike his parsimonious predecessor, received his honorary degree with pride. The brilliant audiences of nobility and ladies, as well as citizens and undergraduates, filled the Theatre, for this and every Encaenia. A visit to Oxford for this event and attendance at the concerts had become part of the social calendar far beyond the confines of the university. For some it had become the thing to do rather than the thing to enjoy, as a correspondent to the *Gentleman's Magazine* wrote in 1763: 'In the afternoon, where the company were detained from three to eight, hearing that absurd composition called *Acis and Galatea* . . . I don't doubt but many rosy faces I saw there were of the same opinion, and would have wished for less music and more wine.'[36]

For some there were other interests besides the music, as when at the grand Encaenia of 1793, the new Chancellor was installed, and pickpockets disguised in MA gowns 'did good trade in the area'![37] The undergraduates could also add their special spice of variety, unpleasantly as when a very drunken Mr Woodhouse of University College vomited in the middle of the Theatre and the concert and noisily defied the Proctors,[38] or with greater justification when they felt themselves insulted by the proceedings or the performers. One notable celebrity who aroused their fury was the singer Madam Mara at the Encaenia of 1785. The performances this year, we read, 'were honoured with crowded, brilliant, and polite companyes, and deservedly met with the highest applause'. Part of this audience, however, was not so polite:

> Madam Mara's rude behaviour in leaving the orchestra as soon as she had sung her songs, and refusing to stand up with the other performers during the choruses, gave much offence to the whole audience, and to the young gentlemen of the University in particular, as she was repeatedly hissed for it, but would not comply, saying in her defence, that she had never done it to Majesty, and therefore would not. On the last day of the celebrity she experienced the effects of her obstinacy, a riot ensued, and Madam Mara was hissed and hooted out of the theatre before the conclusion of the performance.[39]

Such behaviour by musical celebrities seems to have been especially infuriating to Oxford audiences, and Thomas Warton reports with obvious relish another such occasion: 'The *Billington* has been here and sung two Nights, but not obeying Encores, occasioned a few excellent Riots.'[40] One suspects such a lively evening would have been more enjoyed by all than the frequent solemn performances of music through a whole afternoon of the academic term to honour visiting dignitaries as, for instance, that extensive consort of music which the Bishop of Durham sat through in 1717.[41]

The colleges, as opposed to the University, made their contribution of song and music, particularly in the day-by-day providing of choral performances of some of the great church music of previous and present composers. The great choral colleges, Christ Church, New College and Magdalen, with their choir schools and masters, were a daily source of beautiful and highly rehearsed choral work, not always with the excitement of the afternoon when the huge and complex wig of one lady in the congregation at New College Evensong caught fire from one of the candles and went up in flames. Luckily the wig was knocked off, the flames extinguished and the devout and ardent lady rescued.[42] In addition the great college halls provided a fine setting for music, as one commentator at such a concert noted: 'Your College Hall isn't half so bad for Musick it seems, as People fancied – Didn't it sound excellently well? – They say there was a deal of good Company.'[43] Magdalen in particular was a regular provider of college concerts, and a performance there received the approval of the not-so-easily-pleased Hearne, who attended 'a very fine Consort of Musick in Magdalen College Hall, at wch were present a vast Number of gentlemen and Ladies'.[44] In another great hall at Christ Church the visitor Uffenbach was not so impressed. He attended the 'usual *collegium musicum* held every Wednesday' which was a much less formal affair than the Magdalen concerts, organized by the gentlemen of the college from among their own musically inclined members, and the audience paying for its entertainment at the end. Uffenbach's visit was in the depths of the Long Vacation, and he was forced to record that

> On this occasion the music was very weak and poor; however these gentlemen assured us that it was much better in winter, when the most distinguished amateurs are not travelling about the country as in summer, but are resident here ... the music lasted until 11 o'clock [from 7 o'clock] when expenses were reckoned up and each paid his share.[45]

Certainly these college concerts, moderate though their musical standards may have been, were popular among the undergraduates for the social and not strictly musical opportunities they provided. One such gentleman revealed in 1750:

> In an University, how much more agreeably is an evening laid out by a select company of friends composing a concert, than in carousing over a bottle, and joining, to say no worse, in an unprofitable conversation? As to the concerts we frequently have in our halls, do they not in some measure contribute, by bringing us into company, to the wearing off of that rust and moroseness which are too often contracted by a long continuance in college? ... If these were abolish'd, what a mortification would many of our smart *fellow-*

commoners undergo, to be deprived of the pleasure of presenting tickets to the ladies, and ushering them into the hall!⁴⁶

How different from a crusty Fellow of Magdalen, to whom the common room joys of the bottle and baccy and talk were supreme, who delivered himself of the opinion 'A Pox Musical Evenings 'em too, I say – We shall ne'er be right, and tight in our Geers again, till we are mery and wise, as we used to be.'⁴⁷

This grumpy college man might, if he had survived until 1748, have welcomed the erection of that small but elegant building, the Holywell Music Room, for here the music-making of Oxford was henceforth centred, away from college halls, a setting where ladies could be introduced with safety and decorum, unlike various taverns where the Oxford Musical Society had previously held its weekly meetings, the Mermaid at Carfax or the King's Head. By the beginning of the century the society, led by the Heather Professor of Music, comprised sixteen performing members and the same number of non-performers. It owned instruments and scores and needed hard work by its elected stewards to organize activities and keep accounts. It was to provide a worthy centre for this lively and flourishing band of enthusiasts that the movement to finance and erect the Music Room sprang, the first purpose-built concert room to be built and where, through prosperous and difficult times, music has been made to this day. The Musical Society provided its permanent resident orchestra and this was frequently reinforced by visiting performers, instrumentalists and singers of high professional standing. The regular Monday evening concerts continued after 1748 as subscription concerts, starting at six or half past six, a convenient time between college dinner, post-prandial rest and supper, and consisting of vocal and instrumental programmes or oratorios.⁴⁸ The annual subscription in 1758 was 10s. 6d., with a payment of 1 shilling at each concert, an accompanied lady being admitted free. By 1762 the subscription had doubled to one guinea and finances became a growing problem as the years went by. By 1789 the Musical Society was in trouble. Too few subscriptions had been received to make a new season viable, and the subscriptions already received were returned. But the faithful supporters were not discouraged. There was a proposal the following year to double the subscription to two guineas, but this was dropped for a new proposal which proved to be successful. The annual subscription remained at one guinea with a 1 shilling payment at each concert, but members of the university were only to be admitted as subscribers. No longer a cheap 1 shilling concert for members of the gown.⁴⁹ So henceforth the new subscription concerts were held each Thursday night, and continued on that same evening of the week for many a year.

But if those non-subscribing undergraduates were banished from the Music Room, their own rooms were often filled with music, perhaps not so finished and note-perfect, but full of the happiness of playing and singing together. We have met John Skinner's account of such an evening at Trinity which started in his own room at the end of the afternoon where, with a moderate amount of wine to enliven them, he and his friends

> Sit and chat till half-past five
> With jest and song are all alive

until other musicians arrive:

> Then Crotch and two musicians more
> And amateurs near half a score
>   To play in concert meet.
> Our chairs to Warren's rooms we move
> And those who strains melodious love
>   Enjoy a real treat.

Warren, Skinner's friend, owned the harpsichord – which was why the move to his room was made – and the visitors brought violins, bass-viol and flute and 'a full piece was played'. After a light supper the music continued, of a rougher but to the young no less enjoyable kind:

> And some sing Catch and Glee.
> For each in turn must something do,
> Attempt old songs or bawl out new
>   By way of harmony.

The music ended, the strangers left college at eleven o'clock, and so to bed.[50]

Music lessons were often a part of these undergraduates' pursuits, especially on the violin. Teachers were readily available and frequently advertised their services, such as Mr Hardy, 'a pupil of Mr. Pinto' who offered violin lessons to the gentlemen of the university for an entrance fee of one guinea, followed by twelve lessons for one guinea.[51] Erasmus Philips, in between hunting and dining with noble friends, 'Began to learn on the violin of Mr. Wheeler, to whom paid 10s. Entrance',[52] and he must have been one of a growing number, large enough to provoke a sour protest from an angry correspondent to *The Student* in 1750:

> ... it would well become the prudence of our wise ALMA-MATER to prevent our young gentry, by some wholesome restrictions, from trifling away their time over *octaves* and *semi-quavers*, and neglecting *logick* for *airs*, or *syllogisms* for *cantatas*. In a word Brother *Student*, if this *scraping Cacoethes*, *this sol-fa-la* Infection be suffered to spread in this place, our *books*, I expect, will be changed into *fiddles*, our *schools* will be turned into *musick-rooms*, and ARISTOTLE kick'd out for CORELLI.[53]

Such a protest inevitably fell on deaf ears in an Oxford which was alive with music, in the Sheldonian, the Music Room and the rooms of undergraduates;

where the inns provided frequent musical evenings of harp recitals, or where, at the King's Head 'Mr. Lambourn performed on the musical glasses . . . to the great satisfaction of members of the University', and Mr Schaftlein played on his pianoforte guitar and offered lessons[54] and where, at the very heart of things, in the senior common room of Christ Church we have seen there could be 'A great day for dancing and singing' costing the students '7s. a piece for the Musick and Entertainment'.[55]

CHAPTER ELEVEN

The Theatre of the Streets

The streets of Oxford were, for town and gown, the setting for a continually varying succession of spectacle and entertainment. For the elderly don, strolling the High between dinner and evening chapel, there were often more exciting encounters than academic acquaintances, more to see than the print shops; for the undergraduates less routine adventures than the taverns and pot-houses, adventures, moreover, not proscribed by statutes and Proctors; for the people of the town a place to celebrate famous victories or to demonstrate anger and frustration as the spirit took them and their politics directed. Don, undergraduate and citizen shared this life and spectacle of the streets, exuberant, unsophisticated and often violent.

Politics and religion, in this city of Jacobite sympathies and High Churchmanship, were the favourite causes which brought the mob on to the streets in demonstrations and riot. Hearne had reason to record many such enlivenings of the city during the early decades of the century. When Henry Sacheverell, that outspoken hammer of Dissenters, was in 1710 found guilty by the Lords of 'malicious, scandalous and seditious libels' but handed down a sentence so lenient that it was considered his triumph, the people of Oxford lit 'Bonfires for Joy at Dr. Sacheverell's being delivered with so gentle a Punishment, and the Mob burnt a tub, with the Image of a tub Preacher, in one of them'.[1] Only a week later the mob, surprisingly well informed or efficiently incited, took revenge on Benjamin Hoadly and his book of satirical essays in support of 'revolution principles', burning him in effigy and burning his book.[2]

Feelings hostile to the Dissenters and the Hanoverians were frequently the motives for the streets breaking into violent life, exciting but often dangerous and destructive. Both combined to excite the citizens when King George's birthday and the commemoration of the Restoration of King Charles fell together in 1715. 'Last night', Hearne noted, a good Part of the Presbyterian meeting House in Oxford was pull'd down. There was such a Concourse of People going up and down & putting a stop to the least Sign of Rejoycing [for King George's birthday] But then the Rejoycing this day [for the commemoration of the Restoration] (not with-standing Sunday) was so very great and publick in Oxford as has not been known hardly since the Restauration. There was not an House next the Street but was illuminated. For if any disrespect was shewn the Windows were certainly broke. The people run up and down crying King James the 3rd., the true King. ... In the Evening they pulled a good part of the Quakers and Anabaptists Meeting Houses down.[3]

On the accession of George II when Oxford displayed no outward sign of rejoicing, an apparently pro-Hanoverian mob roamed the streets threat-ening to break disloyal windows, frightening the citizens to put candles in their windows, and to light bonfires near Merton and All Souls.[4]

More genuine rejoicing erupted when news of the defeat of Walpole's Excise Bill reached Oxford in 1733: 'the bells rung from between ten and eleven Clock that night, till two or three in the morning at most of the Parish Churches, & there were Bonfires also, throwing of Serpents, and other rejoycings in Oxford upon this occasion.'[5] Fire crackers and fireworks became increasingly popular as the century progressed, and the streets were lit with these displays rather than the bonfires of the mob. In 1763, in celebration of the General Peace, a certain Mr Parry organized a grand display on the banks of the Isis below Friar Bacon's Study where among other spectacles 'Sky and Water Rockets, Floroney wheels ... a cascade with Jack in the Box, a Half Moon and Seven Stars' gave 'great satisfaction to a prodigious Concourse of People'.[6]

Along with fireworks the illumination of buildings with candles, lanterns and coloured lights beautified the streets of the city when there was cause to celebrate. The fading of Oxford's antagonism to the Hanoverians was evident in 1789 when, on the King's recovery from his illness, for the first time the colleges along with the houses of the citizens were illuminated, and New College, Queen's, All Souls, University and Trinity Colleges were 'particularly distinguished for their judicious Arrangement of Lights'.[7] When news arrived of Lord Howe's victory over the French fleet in 1794 the streets shone with an exceedingly splendid illumination, while bands played, a wind consort sounded in Queen's, and that same college was particularly successful in its display, the façade and the cupola being *covered* with candles, and everywhere lights behind coloured transparencies in windows and on buildings lit up the night and the streets.[8]

In contrast to this carnival brilliance were the darker and often savage spectacles provided by the public enforcement of the sentences of the law, which never failed to draw great crowds on to the streets and around the scaffold, crowds not only of the low and brutal who at other times formed the mob, but many undergraduates and senior members of the University. Woodforde had a fondness for visiting the prisoners awaiting execution in the Castle and notes these diverting encounters in his diary along with entries on shooting, skating and cricket: 'Went and saw Dumas alias Dorking, a famous Highwayman, in the Castle. Gave a girl there, in for stealing a Shift o.o.2.'[9] and

> Went with Dyer, Russell and Masters after dinner down to the Castle to see the Prisoners; where we drank two Bottles of Port and for Wine etc., paid o.1.6. William Cartwright, a young, good-looking Fellow, who is in the Castle for High Way Robbery, drank with us the last Bottle, and smoaked a Pipe with us, and seemed very sorry for what he had committed. We gave him between us o.2.o.[10]

When the day of execution arrived Woodforde was often a spectator. 'Went to the Castle this morning', he notes, 'and at eleven o'clock saw Shadrach Smith, a Gypsy … executed.'[11] and 'At half past eleven this morning went with Cooke to see George Strap hanged. … I do believe that there were more than six thousand spectators present when he was hanged.'[12] Thomas Warton could also have been in the crowd for he loved exhibitions and public sights. We are told 'that such was his propensity to be present at public exhibitions, as to have induced him at a time, when he was desirous of not being discovered, to attend an execution in the dress of a carter.'[13] No such disguise was needed to witness the punishment of a rogue who had invaded Brasenose senior common room proposing Jacobite toasts to entrap the Fellows into sedition. For such an outrage he was 'whipp'd at the Cart's Tale from Carfax to Eastgate'.[14]

The part the undergraduates played on these hanging days often added further horror, exposing a violence and savagery in them which is sometimes hard to believe. They came not only to witness the hanging, but to obtain the corpse. Hearne describes many such scenes, sometimes quite laconically as run-of-the-mill events, but sometimes with detail which suggests his own outrage. 'On Wednesday night last about six Clock was hanged, at the Castle at Oxford, one Joan Oliver. … After the execution, the body was got off by Scholars and dissected at Exeter College.'[15] An earlier execution had seen the scholars more heartless and violent when

> was hang'd at Oxford … a young Man about 22 Years of Age, for divers Crimes … the Scholars, having combin'd to have him dissected, took the Body away by force, abused the Father and Mother in such a degree that the Woman miscarried, & is since dead, & carried the Body off naked upon their Shoulders, to Exeter College, where one Dr. Furneaux of that College dissected it.[16]

Nine years later a similar struggle for the body produced scenes of horror which Hearne vividly describes:

On Tuesday last ... there was hanged at Oxford one Richard Fuller, of Caversham in Oxfordshire, a young man of 26 years of age, for murdering his Wife, there was sad work on that occasion, the Scholars endeavouring to get the dead body, assisted by some Townsmen, & others on the contrary hindering. The relations had provided a Coffin to have it decently buried at Caversham, but the Scholars broke it all to pieces, the body being in it; after wch those opposite to the Scholars had it again, & so for several times sometimes one side had it & sometimes the other, but the Proctors, favouring the relations the body was at last delivered to them in order again for Caversham, & a second Coffin was made, wch the Scholars also broke, rescued the body, cutt off the Head &c. after wch 'twas again recovered for the relations, and then got from them again & brought to Queen's College, where 'twas made a Skeleton & the Flesh dispersed up and down. ...[17]

Well might Hearne have called this awfulness 'sad work'. Fortunately there was much more to the theatre of the Oxford streets than this bloody *Grand Guignol*.

Considerably less gruesome street life involved the laying of bets and wagers which were not the pursuit only of the senior common rooms, primly recorded in their wager books. The wagers and contests of the citizens were played out on the streets and provided excitement and entertainment for gown as well as town. Challenges to races, both running and walking, offered frequent spectacles around the houses and the fields, as when

two Blacksmiths run a race, for a wager, from the Corner of Buddard's garden, by Wadham College, to the middle of New- Parks, and so round to the said Corner again. The wager was 8s. apiece, and they were to run six times. One gave out after he had run five times, the other continued running 'till he had ended the 6th time. They both ran naked.[18]

Another wager over time rather than endurance brought out 'one Mayne, (a Journey man Cook of St. John's College)'. This man, 'lame and upwards of 50 years of age, but thin and slim, walk'd eleven Times round Magd. Coll. Walk in less than 2 Hrs, for a Wager. He was to perform it in 2 Hours Time. ... He had done it in about 21 minutes sooner than the time.'[19] One June evening in hot fine weather a Mr William Armstrong, a forty-year-old Scot was seen off from Magdalen Bridge, having accepted a considerable wager that he could walk to St Gyles's Pound in London in fifteen hours. He won, completing the marathon in fourteen and three-quarter hours.[20]

Wagers on horses as well as athletes were popular, as when the horse of Mr Underwood, keeper of the Red Lion at Henley, set out on the same route from Magdalen Bridge to London as Armstrong was to run later on foot. Thirty guineas were staked that the journey to London and back could be made in twelve hours. The other party to the wager, a dancing master of Oxford, lost his guineas, for the horse leaving the bridge at four in the

37   Entering Oxford over Magdalen Bridge

morning returned to the waiting and amazed crowd seventeen and a half minutes before four in the afternoon. Underwood won his guineas but lost his horse, for sadly 'the nag (a pretty creature) died in less than an hour after at the Black Nag at St. Clements by Oxford'.[21] The following month a little horse of eleven and a half hands galloped the same course in sixteen hours, won its owner £10 and lived to run another day.[22]

Other and stranger wagers and contests attracted fascinated crowds. Later in the century we read of great crowds turning out to watch a 40 guinea challenge race in single-horse chaises over a 30 mile course,[23] or an equally large concourse assembling on Port Meadow to watch a stone-throwing contest. The challengers were to throw 180 yards at least, but the winner achieved 200 yards and 40 guineas prize money.[24] Hearne had more of an eye for odder and more picturesque contests which entertained equally large and enthusiastic crowds. One such crowd journeyed out of Oxford to see the fun when

> one Brasier, of St. Peter's in the East, Oxon., saying in Company ... that he would lay a guinea he could bowl down a hill 250 yards, and the Bowl would not stop till it came so far, one Plastin ... took him up, saying that himself would venture a Guinea that he would run down the hill, and stop the Bowle before it got 250 yards. The Wager was confirm'd, the Money ... being put in the Mayor's hands.

38   A view of Broad Street, the scene of many wagers

Off they went to Stokenchurch Hill, the chosen place for the contest. Plastin, seeing the steepness of the hill, cried off, but the evening out was not in vain for 'they all dined at Tetsworth, and returned to Oxford like Fools in the evening'.[25] Nearer home, in Broad Street itself, was staged a more curious challenge to all comers, when

at two Clock in the Afternoon, was a smoking Match over against the Theater in Oxford, a scaffold being built up for it just at Finmore's, an Alehouse. The Conditions were that any one (Man or Woman) that could smoak out three Ounces of Tobacco first, without drinking or going off the stage, should have twelve shillings. ... Many try'd, and 'twas thought that a Journeyman Taylour of St. Peter's in the East would have been victor, he smoaking faster than, and being many Pipes before the rest, but at last he was so sick that 'twas thought he would have dy'd, and an old Man that had been a Souldier, & smoaked gently, came off Conqueror.[26]

Sometimes visiting performers provided more startling spectacles than these home-spun diversions. We shall never know exactly what happened, for instance, when Hearne records that 'Last Night between seven and eight Clock a fellow, who goes by the name of Cornish Tom, who was lately a Souldier, pretended to fly from Carfax Tower, but had like to have broke his Neck.'[27] Whether Tom had constructed wings, whether he simply jumped or whether he only made pretend flying gestures on top of the tower, we are not told. Far nearer flying was an amazing performance which Hearne must have witnessed as he stood in the crowd which filled the High Street, so detailed is his description of the occasion:

> Yesterday, at two Clock in the Afternoon, a young man, who had been a good while a seaman, flew the rope from the Battlements of St. Marie's Steeple in Oxford, down to High Street, the Rope being tied or fastened at Bottom on the south side of the way at a House above St. Mary Lane. He performed to the great admiration and satisfaction of all the Spectators. He first with great agility climed up to the top of the Battlement to wch the Rope was fastened, then flew down, his Arms extended, in about half a minute of an hour, then he climed up the Rope again, wch was more strange, quite to the top of the Battlement, hung by his legs upon the Rope, when he was about half way up, pulled off his clothes (nay his very shirt) as he hung upon it, put them on again, undone his breeches & tucked his shirt in, &c. done them up again as he hung, then (when he got to the top of the Pinnacle) he flew down again, and in his descent had a pint of ale (the pint being tied to a Packthread in his hand) drawn up to him, wch he drank upon the Rope. And 'tis withall remarkable that he flew down the second time with two Pistolls in his hands, both wch he let off as he came or flew down. . . .[28]

Even this remarkable feat of earth-anchored flying would have seemed tame when the city and the university, in the 1780s, were seized with what can only be called 'Balloonomania'. The local newspaper reflects the continuous excitement in the city in its unfailing reports on all matters to do with balloons. The earliest notice in the *Jackson's Oxford Journal* of 7 February 1784, informed its readers that Mr Sadler, who was to become the central figure and hero of these aerial expeditions, had constructed his balloon and that it would be exhibited three days later as it was being filled with 4,000 gallons of gas.[29] Weather permitting the launch was to be from Dr Sibthorp's property in St Clement's. From there it duly made a successful ascent 'before a great concourse of people'. '[It rose] Amidst the repeated Shouts and Acclamations of the surrounding multitude' to a great height and moved off to the north-east and appeared to be travelling over Buckinghamshire towards Northamptonshire. It was not until the end of the following week that the balloon was found, having, however, flown south-east to Stansted in Kent. For this achievement 'Mr Sadler received the Approbation of the whole University',[30] and encouraged by this proceeded to solicit subscriptions from friends but especially from the university, towards the construction of an even larger balloon, which he completed towards the end of March. This magnificent machine, with a grand triumphal car, double-gilt and heavily ornamented, was nearly 70 feet in circumference and was exhibited in the town hall, filled with hydrogen and suspended from the roof. Mr Sadler gave explanatory lectures to the crowds who poured in to see this wonder, and announced that the launch would take place on 8 May.[31] Bad weather delayed the launch from the Physic Garden for a week but finally, amidst a large audience and the music of a band, it took off and made a rapid ascent, carrying this time a living passenger, albeit only an animal suspended beneath it. Unfortunately the balloon burst and made an equally rapid descent, but the people were reassured to read that 'the little aerial Traveller. though much affected while in the upper regions, came down without receiving any material injury'.[32]

Encouraged by the animal's survival Sadler announced that he was now constructing a larger aerial machine and that he himself would ascend in it to do experiments.[33] Aided by subscriptions he was able to announce in early September that his new balloon was almost complete. It was 160 feet in circumference and carried a triumphal car equipped with wings and oars, attached to a net covering the upper half of the sphere. With these he hoped to be able to control the balloon horizontally and vertically during his ascent from the Physic Garden on 12 November 1784.[34] It was a grand occasion. Tickets for the event sold at half a guinea, 5 shillings and 2s. 6d. The bells of Magdalen rang from eight until ten and the balloon with its hopeful navigator took off amidst a huge multitude, collected in the meadows, in trees, and perched on buildings and towers. The ascent was rapid and he moved safely over Otmoor and Thame, until a rent appeared in the fabric, forcing him to jettison all his ballast and instruments in a vain attempt to keep height. He landed in a tree, was swept to the ground, bounced again, and finally anchored in a hedge. Despite the damaged balloon, the triumph of a manned flight had been achieved. On his return to Oxford the horses were taken out of his carriage and he was drawn by the populace through the main streets of the city. His portrait was painted by Mr Lunardi and a local poet acclaimed him:

> O happy Sadler! whom the Gods design'd
> To scorn the Terrors of a fearful Mind.[35]

Balloonomania was catching. While Sadler was at work balloons were going up all around. A Mr Rudge launched his own construction from Queen's College, which travelled as far as Watlington; the Marquis of Blandford, an undergraduate at Christ Church, launched one from Mr Broderick's garden in St Giles which covered 40 miles towards Stratford; one went up at Weston Underwood in Buckinghamshire 'To the Astonishment of a surrounding Multitude'; another was launched at Stratford.[36]

After the celebrated ascent at Oxford, Sadler moved his activities away, and his admirers could only read of his further exploits: how he was deprived of being the first to cross the Channel when his balloon was damaged on its sea route to Dover; how he ascended from Hampton Court with four aboard, passing over London to land at the Nore; how he made two ascents from Manchester, the latter coming to rest at Pontefract after a freezing flight and a frightening landing when the balloon escaped and floated upwards without him.[37]

Oxford had one more day of excitement in June 1785 when Sadler's balloon returned to the scene of its first triumph in Christ Church Meadows. Crowds poured into the city to witness Colonel Fitzpatrick pilot its journey, and make another addition to the festivities of Encaenia week.[38] With his flight the balloon craze seems to have died, and the city and the university returned to the unceasing round of entertainments and curiosities of which they appear never to have tired. The banned Terrae Filius of 1763 mocked this fondness of Oxford's academics for quacks, performers and raree shows:

> You, who have shown yourselves willing to afford general Encouragement, who have committed your Eyes to the Care of *Chevalier* TAYLOR, and your Tongues to *Professor* SHERIDAN; you, who have given a hospitable Reception to *Drybuttes* on the Glasses, and *Maddox* on the Wire; you, who have welcomed the Arrival of the Fire-Eater, and the Giant and the Dwarf, and the Hermaphrodite; you, who with infinite Propriety circulated Papers, proposing to honour that accomplished Master of *Legerdemain*, *Highman Palatine*, the HIGH GERMAN ARTIST, with the Degree of MASTER of ARTS. . . .[39]

Whether such proposals were ever made is doubtful, but certainly Woodforde was a great admirer and went four times to see Hyman Palatine in 1762, and loved a puppet show.[40] Warton loved public exhibitions, and even the serious Thomas Hearne took a sufficient interest in a famous ostrich which was shown in Oxford in 1725, to record its death in London: 'What'r kill'd it was cramming of it too much, particularly with Iron, Stones &c. wch (notwithstanding what they say) it could not digest.'[41]

The Ostrich was but one of a procession of exotic creatures which passed through Oxford throughout the century and were exhibited at some hostelry to the astonishment of all. At the Chequers Inn in 1759 was shown 'an amazing Dromedary from Persia and a lofty Camel from Cairo'; the same inn was host to 'a Fish of Prodigious Size' – for a very short stay. An elephant 'a half Reasoning Beast' passed through on his way to London and a year later was followed by a zebra; and at the Crown Inn in Cornmarket a famous electrical eel gave an exhibition of its powers to stun and kill other fish. For an extra 1s. 6d. the visitor was privileged to see the spark. It is sometimes difficult to know what beast was on show at that same Crown Inn from the description of Mr Didcock's 'Grand Cassowar' which had allegedly just arrived live from Java. It had the head of a warrior, the defence of a porcupine, the swiftness of a courser, legs like an elephant, three toes, and stood 6 feet high. On its head and neck it was sky blue, orange and purple, while its sides were crimson. While this feathered creature was at Warwick it had laid an egg, 20 inches by 18 inches, green with white spots. Later in 1787 Mr Hearns informed 'all who are curious in beholding the Eccentric Productions of Nature' that they could examine the 'first living Unicorn' at

39   Sadler's balloon ascending from Merton Field

the Chequers Inn, standing 16 hands with a single horn 42 inches in circumference and long in proportion. One strange find from Captain Cook's voyages of discovery, which had interested Dr Johnson and provoked him to attempt an imitation of the creature in movement, reached Oxford when a 6 foot high 'Kongerrew' from Botany Bay arrived at the Anchor in Cornmarket. Sometimes whole travelling zoos arrived with a variety of caged creatures. In 1790 was exhibited a collection of thirty wild beasts, purchased from the French Assembly who had refused to finance their keep. Their proprietor boasted that his charges now lived on good English beef, in a better style than they had known in France. Four years later came 'A Grand Menagerie of Wild Beasts Alive ... well secured in Iron Dens' to be viewed in the Greyhound yard. For 1 shilling (servants, labouring people and children half price) one could see a lioness, tiger, sea lion, leopard, kangaroo, hyena, zebra etc., as well as 'a whitefaced female Fairy' which might have been some breed of monkey.[42]

40   The Wonderful Pig

41   The Surprising Giant

Immensely popular in this academic city were animals possessing, according to their owners, intellectual powers and accomplishments far beyond those of their less able brethren. Such was 'The amazing Learned English Dog' which performed at the King's Head in the High in 1755. It was claimed that it could read and write and cast accounts, that it could answer questions on Ovid's *Metamorphoses*, geography and history, and that it could tell the time. Here was a true treat for 'All lovers and Admirers of the Sagacity and Docility of the Brute Creation'. The same words as these, some thirty years later, announced the arrival of 'the amazing Pig of Knowledge' which, in a room at the Crown in Cornmarket, told the time, did card tricks, counted, read thoughts and valued pieces of money. It does not sound to have been so accomplished as its canine predecessor, but was reported to have performed with great success, and moved on to further triumphs at Woodstock and Banbury.[43]

Human freaks also drew the curious to the inns and rooms where they were put on show: at the Chequers, Siamese twins born at Witney; at the Bell in Cornmarket a 3 foot male dwarf of great strength; and a year later at the same hostelry, to complement the dwarf, appeared a giant and a giantess, 'twins from the wilds of Sussex'. She was 7 feet 2 inches in height and he 7 feet 3 inches, 'strong, vigorous and of a comely aspect'. Many years later they were outstripped by the arrival of Mr O'Brien, the Irish Giant, 'descended from King Brien Boreau' who displayed his 8 feet 4 inches at the Chequers in the High, expressing his hope that he would reach 9 feet when he was of age. Half-human was the mermaid presented by Mr Jonas at the Dancing Room in Ship Lane. Be she what she may, she 'rowed herself on water, and read thoughts'.[44]

More lively than all these exhibitions, which only invited the audience to stare and wonder, were the many visiting performers and entertainers who provided a constantly changing programme of circus acts and spectacles. Some were musical like Mr Lambourn whom we have met performing on the musical glasses at the King's Head 'to the great satisfaction of members of the University', or when Master Crotch the Musical Child arrived in Town, performing on the harpsichord and violin at Mr Underhill's in the High and in the Music Room itself. Some four years later appeared another provincial Mozart, Master Bryson aged four, who performed on the piano. He was alleged never to have received any benefit of musical instruction and could play 'God Save the King' before he was taken from the breast. Less artistic but more thrilling favourites were the fire-eaters such as Mr Powell who performed for a week at the King's Head in 1757. He made a return visit two years later when his act included eating hot coals, licking red-hot pokers, broiling a slice of beef on a grid-iron held in his mouth and eating boiling lead with a spoon. At the close of the century arrived a performer with a different appetite 'the Original Stone-Eater from Germany ... a prodigy of human nature'. Though we have no detail of his much acclaimed performance, it was no doubt like that of an earlier proponent of the art, Mr Frederick, who ate 150 stones at a go, and added walking on red-hot iron bars to his programme.

More extended and varied acts took over the large rooms of the town, and most popular of these were performances on the wire. In 1755 Matteaux Solomon, the famous wire-walker, took over the dancing school in Ship Lane and there, for an entry fee of 1 shilling, provided an amazing show on the slack wire. With the wire at full swing, he crossed it with a dog in a wheelbarrow, or beating a drum or whilst he juggled with balls and drinking glasses. For good measure he added conjuring and card tricks and fire-eating, besides offering lessons to teach gentlemen his arts. Music and acrobatics combined at another attraction in the same hall for it was between pieces of music that Mr Abriseo and Mynheer Kevenbarlem-Vanbent tumbled, and Mr Saunders performed somersaults on the slack wire, sounding the French horn while in full swing. He returned five years later, now 'the celebrated Equilibrist' and still at full swing, added the drum to the horn, and stood on his head on a pint bottle, all between whirling somersaults. Time does not allow us to tell of the huge variety of entertainers, of the famous Native Hussar with his 'vast variety of uncommon Performances' who returned again and again, of George Stevens with his satirical lectures to 'a very numerous academic audience' which he delivered from 1765 to 1780, or of Woodforde's favourite, the celebrated Highman Palatine the conjuror. One more variety show must suffice, which appears to have managed to include most of the favourite attractions to the immense satisfaction of packed audiences. For a whole fortnight they could witness Signor Crowdenno imitating the violincello, the African Prince Abbobreco on the slack wire, an original learned dog which knew Greek and Hebrew, Jackey Midnight the balancer, and the famous Norfolk dwarf Mr John Coan.[45]

Equestrian shows and exhibitions of trick horsemanship grew in popularity and complexity in the second half of the century. In 1759 in the Bowling Green at the bottom of Holywell, Mr Johnston performed wonderful feats on horseback, standing upright at full gallop on one, then two, then three horses. By 1771 in Brockelby's Yard in St Aldates, Charles and Mrs Hughes not only rode two horses at once, but galloping around blindfolded picked up handkerchiefs. In 1777 there arrived Mr Astley, a name to become famous in the circus world, and he and his pupils exhibited 'feats of activity on Horseback' on Gloucester Green. He held the stage until a rival appeared in 1792, Mr Franklin with his troop of riders. He prepared a far more elaborate performance and setting than the improvised rings on greens or in stable yards. A weatherproof amphitheatre, commodiously fitted out, was built on the grounds of Mr Higgins a horse-dealer, opposite the church of St Mary Magdalen and here, for an entrance fee of 3 shillings, one could witness among other acts 'a child of promise' riding on Mr Franklin's shoulders while playing the violin, trampoline jumps over six horses and, after dances and hornpipes, 'the little Devil Master Smith' and 'the young English Mercury' leaping on horseback through fire, catching balloons and picking up handkerchiefs.

The circus had indeed come to town for at least five weeks, and we know it had come to the gown too. When a drunken blacksmith at one performance dared to hiss 'God save the King', two gownsmen descended into the pit and escorted the offender out. But Mr Astley was still in competition and a war for audiences developed in the 1790s. Astley returned in 1796 and set up his headquarters for equine entertainment in the Manège d'Ozier in Gloucester Green. His attempt at promotion was to send his infant jockeys, who featured in his pony races, riding through the streets of Oxford before each performance. His opponent now was a Mr Jones who, using Franklin's amphitheatre opposite Mary Magdalen's, presented an equestrian variety show with clowns, burlesques and a dancing horse, besides serious feats of horsemanship. The reporter was certain that this amphitheatre with boxes and seats of various prices would prove 'a fashionable evening lounge'. Astley replied by adding to his bill of fare fireworks surrounding the War Horse and an elaborate display of set pieces, rockets and Roman candles. Jones, not to be outdone, replied with his own firework display, with more complex set pieces concluding with a 'Brilliant Fire' on one thousand lights and Astley, approaching desperation, added wire walking to his horses' performance, with Mr Carr standing on his head in a ball of fire and finally ascending to the roof like an air-balloon.[46] As the century drew to its close we leave these rivals in an escalating struggle to provide the greatest excitement in feats of man and horse and vying in the splendour of their fireworks, successors to generations of impressarios, performers, beasts and freaks who through these ten decades provided this unceasing round of entertainment for town and gown, in taverns and tents, in dancing rooms and on the streets, often lit by bonfires, candle-covered buildings and these ever popular displays of fireworks.

Envoy

The anonymous writer of those fascinating articles on 'Oxford in the Last Century' published periodically in *The Oxford Chronicle* of 1859, drew his labours to a close in his sixteenth installment on 5 November of that year. Looking back over those labours, he wrote:

> Sketches of a period, such as those we have endeavoured to produce, must often be constructed from the most heterogeneous materials. The pamphlet, the libel, the broadsheet, must in turn be ransacked by one who would picture the social life of the time. The writer must resemble the alchemist and extract gold from the very vilest materials. ... And so the generations, if they would learn not merely how their forefathers fought and died, but how they walked, were dressed, ate, drank, spoke, laughed or swore, must turn into the bye-ways of literature. ...

One who has followed him along those bye-ways and often found his footsteps in the snow can only agree, except that those multifarious sources seldom proved vile, most often proved amusing and endearing, and the writer's alchemy, such as it may be, not only produced a book, but developed a warm affection for the characters and the doings of this century in Oxford. It was full of colour, exuberance, enjoyment and variety. No one could deny its shortcomings and indulgences, but even they had a fine excess which provokes half-guilty admiration.

This combination of affectionate remembrance of Oxford days and comrades, not unmixed with critical insights, fills many of the nostalgic memories and farewells we find in these years, laments for a lost youth and the life it enjoyed. One of these provides the Envoy and the epigraph of this book, verses by Henry Headley, a Trinity man and a protégé of Thomas Warton, in a volume of *Poems and other Pieces* published in 1786, with the title 'A Parody of Gray's Elegy written in a Country Churchyard: the Author leaving College'. The scene is set:

The sullen Tom proclaims the parting day
In bullying tone congenial to his place,
The Christ-Church misses homeward trip to pray,
And High-Street leave to solitude and space.

The poet too must leave, and asks

For who at Hymen's block in youthful bloom
His scholarship and freedom e'er resign'd,
Left the warm precincts of the common room,
Nor sighing cast one farewell wish behind?

For me who, mindful of the life I loved,
In these weak lines its happiness relate,
And with fair images of past joys moved
Compare my present to my former state; . . .

Even so, his sighs over lost happiness have not been loud enough to repress his strong satirical picture of the possible later state of that youthful scholarship and freedom:

Beneath those domes in Gothic grandeur grey,
Where rears that spire its old fantastic crest,
Snug in their mouldy cells from day to day
Like bottled wasps the Sons of Science rest; . . .

The grey walls of its colleges may well have had their mouldy cells, but their denizens were for the most part snug and content, not realizing that, as the fireworks and illuminations of the end of the century faded, they were doomed to extinction, as a new and more serious age came on, and shoved them from the stage.

Notes

FOREWORD

1. L. Stone, 'The Size and Composition of the Oxford Student Body, 1580 –1910', in *The University in Society* (Princeton, 1975), p. 37.
2. Ibid., p. 5.
3. A. Clark (ed.), *The Life and Times* (Oxford Historical Society, xxvi, 1894), Vol. 3, p. 163.
4. The Abbé Prevost, *Memoires et Aventures d'un Homme de Qualité*, ed. M. Robertson (Paris, 1927), Vol. 5, p. 124.
5. L. G. Mitchell, *The History of the University of Oxford*, Vol. V: *The Eighteenth Century* (Oxford 1986); Introduction, pp. 7–8.
6. For greater detail on these scholarly achievements see *The History of the University of Oxford*, Vol. V, Ch. 9 'Oriental Studies' by P. J. Marshall; Ch. 27 'Antiquarian Studies' by S. Piggott; Ch. 18 'Oxford and the Literary World' by David Fairer, and Ch. 29 'Anglo-Saxon Studies' by David Fairer.
7. For more detailed statistics on admission numbers, class and geographical distribution of undergraduates, see Stone, 'Oxford Student Body', and V. H. H. Green in *The History of the University of Oxford* (Oxford, 1986), Vol. V, pp. 309–16.
8. Vicesimus Knox, *Works* (7 vols, London, 1824), *Liberal Education* (1781), Vol. 4, p. 163.

CHAPTER ONE: *Hierarchy and Rank: the Social Structure*

1. *Gentleman's Magazine*, 1772, xlii, p. 401.
2. Ibid., 1758, xxviii, p. 176.
3. Thomas Hearne, *Collections*, ed. C. E. Doble and H. E. Salter (Oxford Historical Society, 1885–1918), 11 vols, 15 Dec. 1722, Vol. 8, p. 24; hereafter 'Hearne'.
4. Ibid., 26 Aug. 1730, Vol. 10, p. 322.
5. James Harris, 1st Earl of Malmesbury, *Diaries and Correspondence* (1844), Vol. 1, p. ix.
6. E. Gibbon, *The Memoirs of the Life of Edward Gibbon*, ed. G. B. Hill (Oxford, 1900), p. 59.
7. R. Polewhele, *The Follies of Oxford* (London, 1785), pp. 131 and 142.
8. *Brasenose Quatercentenary Monographs* (Oxford Historical Society, liii, 1909), Vol. II, pt i, Monograph xiii.
9. *Gentleman's Magazine*, 1798, lxviii, pt 1, pp. 14–16.
10. Polewhele, *The Follies of Oxford*, p. 160.
11. Ibid., pp. 237–44.
12. *An Order of the Vice Chancellor and Heads of Houses*, 30 Sept. 1723.
13. W. N. Mawdsley (ed.), *Woodforde at Oxford* (Oxford Historical Society, NS Vol. xxi, 1969), 15 Nov. 1759; (hereafter 'Woodforde').
14. *Memoirs of an Oxford Scholar, written by himself* (London, 1756), p. 40.

15. R. Mant (ed.), *The Poetical Works of the late Thomas Warton* (Oxford, 1802), Vol. II, p. 181, T. Warton, *A Panegyric on Oxford Ale.*

16. Alicia D'Anvers, *Academia: or the Humours of the University of Oxford* (London, 1691), p. 40.

17. A. Allardyce (ed.), *Letters from and to Charles Kirkpatrick Sharpe Esq.* (Edinburgh and London, 1888), to his father, 1799 and 1801, Vol. I, pp. 89 and 107.

18. D'Anvers, *Academia*, pp. 59 and 64.

19. J. Austen (ed.), *The Loiterer* (2 vols, 1790), no. 4.

20. D'Anvers, *Academia*, p. 59.

21. C. Thornton and G. Colman (eds), *The Student, or the Oxford Monthly Miscellany* (Oxford, 1750), Vol. I, pp. 114–15; hereafter *The Student.*

22. C. Thornton and F. McLaughlin (eds), *The Fothergills of Ravenstonedale* (London, 1905); letter of 11 July 1724, p. 88.

23. J. Hawkins, *The Life of Dr. Samuel Johnson* (London, 1787), pp. 12–13.

24. G. Whitefield, *A Short Account of God's Dealings with the Rev. George Whitefield* (London, 1740), pp. 38 and 24.

25. R. Graves, *Recollections of some particulars in the Life of the late William Shenstone Esq.* (London, 1788), p. 30.

26. R. Newton, *A Scheme of Discipline with Statutes intended to be established by a Royal Charter for the education of Youth in Hart-Hall in the University of Oxford* (Oxford, 1720), p. 30; hereafter *A Scheme of Discipline.*

27. Samuel Johnson, *The Letters of Samuel Johnson*, ed. R. W. Chapman (Oxford, 1952), Vol. I, p. 170.

28. Tom Baker, *An Act at Oxford* (London, 1704), I. i. p. 10.

29. James Boswell, *A Journal of a Tour to the Hebrides*, eds Pottle, F. A. and Bennett, C. H. (London, 1963), p. 89 and note.

30. Hawkins, *The Life of Dr. Samuel Johnson*, p. 18.

31. *Gentleman's Magazine*, 1787, lvii, pt 2, pp. 1146–7.

32. Graves, *Recollections of some partic-*

ulars in the Life of the late William Shenstone, Esq., p. 27.

33. Newton, *A Scheme of Discipline*, p. 24.

34. D. E. Jenkins (ed.), *The Life of the Rev. Thomas Charles, B.A. of Bala* (Denbigh, 1908), Vol. I, pp. 74–5.

35. Hearne, 5 Oct. 1725, Vol. IX, p. 36.

36. Whitefield, *God's Dealings with Whitefield*, p. 39.

37. *The Servitour: a Poem written by a Servitour of the University of Oxford* (London, 1709), pp. 6, 8.

38. Ibid., pp. 14, 15.

39. Polewhele, *The Follies of Oxford*, pp. 105–18.

40. Manuscript journal of John Skinner (BL MS Add. 33634), p. 11.

41. Allardyce, *Letters of Charles Kirkpatrick Sharpe*, *The New Oxford Guide* printed in the Introduction, Vol. I.

42. N. Amhurst, *Strephon's Revenge* (London, 1718), p. 4.

43. Austen, *The Loiterer*, no. 11.

44. Thornton and Coleman, *The Student*, Vol. II, p. 107.

45. Allardyce, *Letters of Charles Kirkpatrick Sharpe*, Vol. I, p. 121.

46. MS journal of John Skinner, p. 10.

47. Hearne, 4 May 1730, Vol. X, p. 275.

48. Tom Baker, *An Act at Oxford*, (London, 1704) Act I, sc. i, p. 6.

49. Hearne, 14 May 1730, Vol. X, p. 275.

50. *A Letter to a Young Gentleman of Fortune, just entered at University* (Oxford, 1784), p. 19.

51. *Remarks on some Strictures lately published, entitled Observations upon Statute Tit. XIV De Vestitu et Habitu Scholastico* (Oxford, 1770), p. 1.

52. Ibid., p. 7.

53. *Gentleman's Magazine*, 1798, lxviii, pt 1, note p. 282.

54. Hawkins, *The Life of Dr. Samuel Johnson*, p. 18.

55. Shakespeare, *Troilus and Cressida*, I. iii. ll. 100–110.

CHAPTER TWO: *Arriving and Settling In*

1. G. Sherburn (ed.), *The Correspondence of Alexander Pope* (Oxford, 1956), Vol. I, p. 430.

2. Lord Cockburn, *The Life of Lord Jeffrey* (Edinburgh, 1852), Vol. I, p. 34.
3. J. Boswell, *The Life of Samuel Johnson DD* (Oxford, 1904), Vol. I, p. 41.
4. *The Oxonian, A Poem* (Oxford, 1778).
5. Boswell, *The Life of Samuel Johnson*, Vol. I, pp. 41, 42, 180.
6. MS journal of John Skinner (BL MS Add. 33634), p. 105.
7. *Memoirs of an Oxford Scholar* (London, 1756), pp. 39 and 46–7.
8. Austen, *The Loiterer*, no. 58.
9. Newton, *A Scheme of Discipline*, p. 19.
10. M. Evans (ed.), *The Letters of Richard Radcliffe and John James* (Oxford Historical Society, 1888), p. 44.
11. *A Few General Directions for the Conduct of Young Gentlemen in the University of Oxford* (1705), p. 5.
12. Letter (Aug. 1790), HMC Carlisle MSS vi. 689.
13. Cockburn, *Life of Lord Jeffrey*, Vol. II, p. 3.
14. Boswell, *The Life of Samuel Johnson*, Vol. I, p. 231.
15. D'Anvers, *Academia*, pp. 34, 35, and 39.
16. Knox, *Liberal Education*, Vol. IV, p. 142.
17. Hill, *Memoirs of the Life of Edward Gibbon*, p. 48.
18. Allardyce, *Letters of Charles Kirkpatrick Sharpe*, Vol. I, p. 91.
19. G. Colman, *Random Records* (London, 1830), pp. 274 and 295–6.
20. *The New Oxford Guide*; Letter I in Allardyce, *Letters of Charles Kirkpatrick Sharpe*, Introduction.
21. MS journal of John Skinner, Vol. II, p. 132.
22. Ibid., p. 9.
23. Johnson, *Letters of Samuel Johnson*, letter to William Strahan, 24 Oct. 1764, Vol. I, p. 170.
24. Evans, *Letters of Richard Radcliffe and John James*, p. 45.
25. Newton, *A Scheme of Discipline*, p. 29.
26. V. Green, *Lincoln* (Oxford, 1979), pp. 405 and 407.

27. *A Few General Directions, etc.*, p. 8.
28. Colman, *Random Records*, p. 299.
29. *The New Oxford Guide*, Letter I; see note 20 above.
30. *Memoirs of an Oxford Scholar* (1756), p. 76.
31. T. F. Dibdin, *Reminiscences of a Literary Life* (London, 1836), Vol. I, p. 82.
32. Evans, *Letters of Richard Radcliffe and John James*, pp. 44–6.
33. Cockburn, *Life of Lord Jeffrey*, Vol. I, p. 36.
34. Woodforde, 25 Dec. 1759.
35. Hearne, 13 Dec. 1709, Vol. II, p. 327.
36. Ibid., 6 Nov. 1727, Vol. IX, p. 307.
37. Evans, *Letters of Richard Radcliffe and John James*, p. 3.

CHAPTER THREE: *Eating:
Undergraduates in Hall and Out*

1. Newton, *A Scheme of Discipline*, p. 30, note 1.
2. Austen, *The Loiterer*, Vol. I, p. 9.
3. Ibid., 'Diary of an Oxford Man', Vol. I, no. 4.
4. MS journal of John Skinner, Vol. II, p. 31.
5. Cockburn, *Life of Lord Jeffrey*, Vol. II, p. 3.
6. George Colman the Younger, *Random Records* (London, 1830), p. 302.
7. Evans, *Letters of Richard Radcliffe and John James*, pp. 47 and 60.
8. MS journal of John Skinner, Vol. II, p. 31.
9. Austen, *The Loiterer*, no. 8.
10. Hearne, 10 Feb. 1722, Vol. VII, p. 327.
11. Ibid., 23 Feb. 1723, Vol. VIII, p. 48.
12. Ibid., 27 Feb. 1723, Vol. VIII, p. 50.
13. *Brasenose Quartercentenary Monographs*, Vol. II, Pt. 1, Monograph XIII.
14. Woodforde, 16 Dec. 1760 and 21 Aug. 1768.
15. Thomas Mozley, *Reminiscences chiefly of Oriel College and the Oxford Movement* (London, 1882), p. 203.

16. H. E. D. Blakiston, *Trinity College* (Oxford, 1898) and Newton, *A Scheme of Discipline*, p. 70.
17. Colman, *Random Records*, p. 263.
18. C. C. Southey (ed.), *The Life and Correspondence of Robert Southey* (London, 1849), Vol. I, pp. 170–1.
19. J. Bowring, *Memoirs of Jeremy Bentham* in *The Works of Jeremy Bentham* (1843), Vol. X, p. 39.
20. MS journal of John Skinner, Vol. II, p. 34.
21. Hearne, 2 July 1723; Vol. VIII, p. 94.
22. *An Address to the Worshipful Company of Barbers in Oxford* (Oxford, 1749), p. 8.
23. *Advice to the Universities of Oxford and Cambridge* (London, 1783), pp. 55–6.
24. MS journal of John Skinner, Vol. II, p. 12.
25. Ibid., pp. 35–6.
26. Allardyce, *Letters of Charles Kirkpatrick Sharpe*, Vol. I, pp. 80–81.
27. W. H. Quarrell and W. J. C. Quarrell (eds), *Oxford in 1710 from The Travels of Z. C. von Uffenbach* (1928), pp. 35–6; hereafter *Uffenbach*.
28. Ibid., p. 60.
29. Thomas Fowler, *The History of Corpus Christi College* (Oxford Historical Society 1893), p. 309.
30. Cockburn, *Life of Lord Jeffrey*, Vol. II, p. 3.
31. Evans, *Letters of Richard Radcliffe and John James*, 3 March 1779 and 17 May 1779.
32. Newton, *A Scheme of Discipline*, p. 27.
33. Raff. See *OED* sb. 5.
34. *Advice to the Universities of Oxford and Cambridge*, p. 49.
35. Bodleian Don. B. 12. 56.
36. Orders of 30 Sept., 30 March 1763, 5 June 1766.
37. Order of 11 April 1748. Bodleian GA Oxon. b. 19 (60).
38. Order of 5 June 1766.
39. 5 April 1791. Fowler, *The History of Corpus Christi College*, p. 296.
40. Newton, *A Scheme of Discipline*, p. 27.

41. *Jackson's Oxford Journal*, 5 Dec. 1764; hereafter *JOJ*.
42. Ibid., 16 July 1785.
43. William Puddle, *The Rival Shoe-Black*, Bodleian Gough. Oxf. 90 (39).
44. E. Philips, 'Extracts from the Diary of Erasmus Philips', *Notes and Queries*, 2nd Ser. X, pp. 366 and 443.
45. Colman, *Random Records*, p. 299.
46. *Advice to the Universities of Oxford and Cambridge*, p. 58.
47. Allardyce, *Letters of Charles Kirkpatrick Sharpe*, Introduction, Letter II.
48. MS journal of John Skinner, Vol. II, p. 41.
49. *JOJ*, 24 Oct. 1761.
50. Ibid., 13 Jan. 1759.
51. Ibid., 25 Nov. 1758.
52. Ibid., 1 March 1760.
53. Ibid., 3 Nov. 1759.
54. L.G.W.L. (ed.), *A little book of Recipes of New College* (Oxford, 1922) fo. 3v.
55. *JOJ*, 11 Oct. 1777.
56. Ibid., 7 Oct. 1797.
57. Ibid., 6 Oct. 1792.
58. Ibid., 9 Nov. 1782.
59. Ibid., 6 Oct. 1787.
60. Ibid., 28 Sept. 1793.
61. Woodforde, 9 Dec. 1760.

CHAPTER FOUR: *Eating: the Dons on the Dais*

1. A custom at New College; see J. Walker, *Oxoniana* (London, 1809), Vol. I, p. 61.
2. *The Humours of Oxford, a Comedy* (Dublin, 1730), I. i.
3. *An Evening Contemplation in a College* in Warton, *The Oxford Sausage*, p. 37.
4. Thomas Warton, *A Panegyric on Oxford Ale*.
5. Woodforde, 30 Nov. 1759; 24 April 1761; 26 Feb. 1763.
6. *The Terrae Filius Speech as it was to have been Spoken at the Publick Act* (London, 1733), pp. 5–6.
7. MS journal of John Skinner, Vol. II, p. 35.

8. T. Campbell, *Diary of a Visit to England in 1775 by an Irishman*, ed. S. Raymond (Sydney, 1824), pp. 19–20.

9. Hearne, 25 Jan. 1724, Vol. VIII, p. 161.

10. E. M. Thompson (ed.), *The Letters of Humphrey Prideaux to John Ellis* (Camden Society, NS xv, Westminster, 1874), p. 116.

11. N. Amhurst, *Oculus Britanniae: an Heroic-Panegyrical Poem on the University of Oxford* (London, 1724), p. 24.

12. Hearne, 25 Dec. 1733, Vol. XI, p. 287, footnote.

13. Ibid., 6 Jan. 1706, Vol. I, p. 59.

14. Woodforde, 25 Dec. 1733.

15. Ibid., 6 April 1774; 22 June 1774.

16. Ibid., 5 Dec. 1774.

17. Ibid., 27 July 1774.

18. Ibid., 17 Aug. 1763; 3 Sept. 1763; 28 Feb. 1775.

19. Ibid., 20 April 1774.

20. Ibid., 9 April 1774.

21. Ibid., 11 April 1774.

22. Ibid., 18 April 1774.

23. *Brasenose Quatercentenary Monographs*, Vol. II, pt i, Monograph XIII.

24. Woodforde, 26 Jan. 1775.

25. L.G.W.L. (ed.), *A little book of Recipes of New College*, fol. 15.

26. Ibid., fol. 20.

27. Ibid., fol. 7.

28. Hearne, 15 Aug. 1715, Vol. V, p. 90.

29. Ibid., 2 Nov. 1719, Vol. VII, p. 62.

30. C. L. S. Linnell (ed.), *The Diaries of Thomas Wilson, D.D., 1731-7 and 1750* (London, 1964); 8 June 1732.

31. Hearne, 12 Oct. 1715, Vol. V, p. 126.

32. Ibid., 28 Sept. 1711, Vol. III, p. 238.

33. Ibid., 11 July 1718, Vol. VI, p. 378.

34. Woodforde, 25 Dec. 1773.

35. *The Idler*, no. 33; *Journal of a Fellow of a College*.

36. Woodforde, 20 Dec. 1762; 14 July 1774; 27 July 1774; 24 Aug. 1774; 17 Nov. 1774.

37. A. Pope, *Imitations of Horace*, Sat. II. ii. ll. 69–72.

38. *The Idler*, no. 33.

CHAPTER FIVE: *The Society of the Senior Common Room*

1. Charles P. Moritz, *Travels, chiefly on foot, through several parts of England in 1782* (London, 1795), p. 176.

2. A. Wood, *The History & Antiquities of the Colleges and Halls in the University of Oxford*, ed. J. Gutch (Oxford, 1786), p. 528.

3. Mr. Salmon, *The Foreigner's Companion through the Universities of Cambridge and Oxford* (London, 1748), p. 42.

4. *The New Oxford Guide* (Oxford, 1759), pp. 48 and 54.

5. *The Oriel Record*, Dec. 1925, p. 304: 'Antiquities of Oriel Common Room'.

6. See Chapter VI.

7. Mozley, *Reminiscences chiefly of Oriel College*, Vol. I, pp. 69–70.

8. Woodforde, 4 Nov. 1762.

9. Colman, *Terrae Filius*, no. 3, p. 45.

10. *JOJ*, 7 June 1788; 11 April 1789.

11. Amhurst, *Oculus Brittaniae*, pp. 17–19.

12. Mant, *The Poetical Works of Thomas Warton*, p. xxiii.

13. *The Idler*, no. 33.

14. Mant, *The Poetical Works of Thomas Warton*, p. xcii.

15. Woodforde, 26 Jan. 1762.

16. Linnell, *The Diaries of Thomas Wilson*, 2 Feb. 1731.

17. *The Oriel Record*, Dec. 1925, p. 304.

18. *Oxford during the Last Century*, published in *The Oxford Chronicle*, 1859, NST No. V, 18 Aug. 1859.

19. Philips, 'The Diary of Erasmus Philips', pp. 366 and 443.

20. C. Welsh, *A Bookseller of the Last Century* (London, 1885), pp. 67–9.

21. C. Wordsworth, *Social Life at the English Universities in the Eighteenth Century* (Cambridge, 1874), p. 150.

22. Corpus Christi College wager book.

23. V. Knox, *Essays Moral and Literary* (1782), Vol. I, no. lxxv, p. 325.

24. Austen, *The Loiterer*, no. 18.

25. Warton, *The Oxford Sausage*, pp. 37–41.

26. Amhurst, *Oculus Britanniae*, pp. 34–5.
27. *Terrae Filius*, no. 1, pp. 14–15.
28. Evans, *Letters of Richard Radcliffe and John James*, 3 Feb. 1733, p. 33.
29. J. Hurdis, *The Village Curate, a Poem* (London, 1788), pp. 4–5.
30. T. Warton, *The Progress of Discontent* (London, 1746), ll. 33–40 and 111–22.
31. *Magdalen-Grove, or a Dialogue between the Doctor and the Devil* (London, 1713), p. 17.
32. *Terrae Filius*, no. 43, 7 June 1721.
33. Thornton and Coleman, *The Student*, Vol. II, pp. 301–2.
34. *Alma Mater: a Satirical Poem* (Oxford, 1733), pp. 17 and 21.
35. E. Gibbon, *The Memoirs of the Life of Edward Gibbon*, ed. G. B. Hill (London, 1900) pp. 57–9.
36. *The Humours of Oxford*, II. i.
37. Evans, *Letters of Richard Radcliffe and John James*, 7 Oct. 1779, p. 85.
38. Austen, *The Loiterer*, no. 18.
39. Hearne, 9 Nov. 1721, Vol. VII, p. 293.
40. Ibid., 11 Nov. 1721, Vol. VII, p. 296.
41. Ibid., 16 Aug. 1726, Vol. IX, p. 181.

CHAPTER SIX: *Drinking and Riot*

1. C. C. Southey (ed.), *The Life and Correspondence of Robert Southey* (London, 1849), Vol. I, p. 177.
2. *The Diaries and Correspondence of James Harris* (1844), Vol. I, p. ix.
3. L. Holberg, *Memories of Lewis Holberg written by himself in Latin, and now first translated into English* (London, 1829), p. 20.
4. *The Terrae Filius's Speech as it was to have been Spoken etc.*, p. 7.
5. *A Step to Oxford* (London, 1704), p. 8.
6. A. Pope, *The Dunciad* (B), Book III, ll. 337–8.
7. *Advice to the Universities of Oxford and Cambridge*, p. 26.
8. Woodforde, 11 March 1761.

9. Ibid., 1 June 1763.
10. Ibid., 7 Sept. 1763.
11. Ibid., 4 Aug. 1774.
12. Ibid., 15 Dec. 1774.
13. Ibid., 4 Nov. 1761.
14. Ibid., 16 July 1763.
15. Ibid., 28 Jan. 1762.
16. Ibid., 16 Jan. 1762; 'looking glass': a chamber pot.
17. R. H. Hodgkin, *Six Centuries of an Oxford College* (Oxford, 1949), p. 165 note.
18. A. H. Crosse (ed.), *Memorials ... of Andrew Crosse* (London, 1857), Vol. I, p. 33.
19. Hearne, 15 Dec. 1722, Vol. VIII, p. 24.
20. *Magdalen-Grove etc.*, pp. 5–6.
21. Fowler, *The History of Corpus Christi College*; 24 Jan. 1757 and 22 Jan. 1787.
22. Hearne, 2 Jan. 1712, Vol. III, p. 287.
23. Ibid., 8 June 1716, Vol. V, p. 236.
24. Ibid., 3 April 1706, Vol. I, p. 215.
25. H. Twiss, *The Public and Private Life of Lord Eldon* (London, 1844), Vol. I, p. 53.
26. Boswell, *The Life of Samuel Johnson*, Vol. II, p. 187.
27. F. Madan, *A Century of the Phoenix Common Room* (Oxford, 1888).
28. *Advice to the Universities of Oxford and Cambridge*, pp. 22–3.
29. Evans, *Letters of Richard Radcliffe and John James*, 26 Jan. 1786, p. 265.
30. Knox, *Liberal Education*, p. 325.
31. Evans, *Letters of Richard Radcliffe and John James*, July 1783, p. 258.
32. Knox, *Liberal Education*, p. 321.
33. *Terrae Filius*, no. 34, 6 May 1721.
34. *The Oxonian: A Poem. In Imitation of The Splendid Shilling* (Oxford, 1778), p. 10.
35. Graves, *Recollections of some particulars in the Life of the late William Shenstone Esq.*, pp. 14–16.
36. Ibid., p. 20.
37. MS journal of John Skinner, Vol. II, p. 49.
38. *Memoirs of an Oxford Scholar*, p. 44.
39. *The Oxford Magazine*, lxvi (1947–8), p. 90.
40. Woodforde, 14 June 1761.

41. Ibid., 19 June 1775; 28 Nov. 1775.
42. Ibid., 21 May 1761.
43. Routh, quoted in Wordsworth, *Social Life of the Universities etc.*, p. 145.
44. J. R. Green, *Oxford Studies* (London, 1901), p. 34 note.
45. Campbell, *Diary of a visit to England in 1775 by an Irishman*, p. 19.
46. *A Plea against an order to inhibit Wine-Cellars* (Oxford, 1734), (Bod. G.A. Oxon. 4 6 (11)).
47. Green, *Oxford Studies*, p. 72 note 4.
48. Thornton and Coleman, *The Student* (1751), Vol. 2, p. 373.
49. Warton, *A Panegyric on Oxford Ale*, ll. 20–39.
50. Thompson, *Letters of Humphrey Prideaux to John Ellis*, p. 9.
51. Moritz, *Travels etc.*, pp. 166–71.
52. Holberg, *Memoirs of Lewis Holberg*, p. 21.
53. Warton, *A Panegyric on Oxford Ale*, ll. 55–64.
54. *A Step to Oxford*, p. 4.
55. Holberg, *Memoirs of Lewis Holberg*, p. 20.
56. *Magdalen-Grove etc.*, p. 5.
57. Woodforde, April 21 1774.
58. Austen, *The Loiterer*, no. 4.
59. *The Oxonian, a Poem etc.*, p. 14.
60. Bodleian Don. B. 12. 58b.
61. Woodforde, 5 July 1774.
62. *Gentleman's Magazine* (1798) lxviii, pt 1, pp. 14–16.
63. Hearne, 18 May 1711, Vol. III, p. 163; 2 Nov. 1715, Vol. V, p. 126; 7 Nov. 1716, Vol. V, p. 335; 17 Nov. 1716, Vol. V, p. 338.
64. Thompson, *Letters of Humphrey Prideaux to John Ellis*, p. 26.
65. P. Toynbee and L. Whitley (eds), *The Correspondence of Thomas Gray* (Oxford, 1935), Vol. I, p. 318.

CHAPTER SEVEN: *Women and Love*

1. G. Colman, *The Oxonian in Town* (Dublin, 1769), I. ii.
2. *The University Miscellany, or, More Burning Work for the Ox–f——d Convocation* (London, 1713), p. 17.
3. Thornton and Coleman, *The Student*, Vol. I, p. 240: 'Of writing on Celebrated Toasts'.
4. *A Letter to a Young Gentleman of Fortune, just entered at the University* (Oxford, 1784), pp. 20–21.
5. J. Philips, *The Splendid Shilling*, ll. 5–10.
6. Amhurst, *Strephon's Revenge*, pp. v and ii.
7. *The Oxonian in Town*, the Prologue.
8. Ibid., I. ii.
9. *The Oxford Toast's Answer to the Terrae Filius Speech* (1723), p. 20.
10. Thornton and Coleman, *The Student*, Vol. II, p. 187.
11. *The Oxford Act: a Poem* (1693), p. 18.
12. Amhurst, *Oculus Britanniae*, p. 25.
13. *The Cruelty, Injustice, and Impolicy of the present mode of Information and Punishment relative to Prostitution Established in the University* (1779), p. iv.
14. Amhurst, *Strephon's Revenge*, p. 3.
15. Ibid., p. 43.
16. Amhurst, *Terrae Filius*, no. 25, 5 April 1721.
17. Amhurst, *Oculus Britanniae*, p. 48.
18. D'Anvers, *Academia*, p. 40.
19. Hearne, 8 Jan. 1728, Vol. IX, p. 390
20. *An Act at Oxford*, I. i, p. 2.
21. Colman, *The Oxonian in Town*, I. ii.
22. Hearne, 24 Aug. 1725, Vol. IX, p. 9.
23. Ibid., 7 Sept. 1730, Vol. X, p. 327.
24. Ibid., 3 Feb. 1731, Vol. X, p. 381.
25. *Jeremiah Miles's Diary*, 14 and 16 March, 15 May 1702.
26. Hearne, 5 Jan. 1726, Vol. IX, p. 77.
27. *JOJ*, 28 July 1781 and 6 July 1765.
28. Amhurst, *Strephon's Revenge*, p. 3.
29. Ibid., p. 9.
30. *Merton Walks, or the Oxford Beauties* (London, 1717), pp. 11, 30.
31. Amhurst, *Strephon's Revenge*, p. 29.
32. Hearne, 30 July 1723, Vol. VIII, p. 102.
33. Corpus Christ College B14/1/1 16 Jan. 1769.
34. Hearne, 5 Dec. 1726, Vol. IX, p. 232.
35. *JOJ*, 26 Jan. 1760.

36. Hearne, 19 Sept. 1707, Vol. II, p. 47.
37. Ibid., 25 May 1716, Vol. V, p. 228.
38. Ibid., 14 June 1723, Vol. VIII, p. 87.
39. Ibid., 25 May 1716, Vol. V, p. 228.
40. Colman, *Terrae Filius*, no. 1, p. 14.
41. Thornton and Coleman, *The Student*, Vol. II, pp. 257.
42. Amhurst, *Terrae Filius*, no. 32, 29 April 1721.
43. *The New Oxford Guide*, Letter I, Intro. to Vol. I of Allardyce, *Letters of Charles Kilpatrick Sharpe, Esq.*
44. Amhurst, *Terrae Filius*, no. 37, 17 May 1721.
45. Ibid., no. 1, 11 Jan. 1721 and no. 5, 25 Jan. 1721.
46. Hearne, 19 Feb. 1706, Vol. I, p. 188.
47. Ibid., 16 May 1732, Vol. XI, p. 59.
48. Ibid., 24 Feb. 1728, Vol. IX, p. 403.
49. Ibid., 10 Sept. 1725, Vol. VIII, p. 266.
50. Ibid., 29 Nov. 1727, Vol. IX, p. 376.
51. D'Anvers, *Academia*, p. 64.
52. Hearne, 15 Dec. 1717, Vol. VI, p. 119.
53. Ibid., 11 Oct. 1720, Vol. VII, p. 176.
54. *The Terrae Filius's Speech as it was to have been Spoken etc.* (1773), pp. 13 and 25–6.
55. Amhurst, *Oculus Britanniae*, pp. 48–9.
56. Hearne, 5 March 1711, Vol. III, p. 126.
57. Ibid., 29 June 1714, Vol. IV, p. 371.
58. Ibid., 26 July 1717, Vol. VI, p. 75.
59. Ibid., 16 May 1732, Vol. XI, p. 59.
60. *The Terrae Filius's Speech etc.*, p. 26.
61. Hearne, 10 Dec. 1725, Vol. IX, p. 68.
62. Ibid., 20 Nov. 1717, Vol. VI, p. 109.
63. Ibid., 4 Dec. 1732, Vol. XI, p. 133.
64. Linnell, *The Diaries of Thomas Wilson D.D.*, 30 Nov. 1732.
65. After the publication of the Recantation, Baker's friends published a pamphlet intended to give the true facts and thereby defend Baker's probity: *A Faithful Narrative of the Proceedings in the late Affair between the Rev. Mr. John Swinton and Mr. George Baker, Both of Wadham College, Oxford . . . To which is prefix'd a Particular Account of the Proceedings against Robert Thistlethwayte, Late Doctor of Divinity, and Warden of Wadham College, for a Sodomitical Attempt upon Mr. W. French, Commoner of the same College* (London, 1739). The above account is based on this pamphlet.
66. *College-Wit Sharpen'd: or, The Head of a House with a Sting in the Tail . . . Address'd to the Two Famous Universities of S–d–m and G–m–rr–h*, subtitled *The Wadhamites* (1739), p. 17.
67. Ibid., pp. 3–4.

CHAPTER EIGHT: *Walking and Sauntering*

1. MS journal of John Skinner, Vol. II, p. 237.
2. *An Address to the Freemen and the Inhabitants of the City of Oxford* (Oxford, 1764), pp. 3, 5, 6, 9, 10.
3. *Oxford during the Last Century* in *The Oxford Chronicle* (1859), 2 April.
4. Mr Salmon, *The Foreigner's Companion through the Universities of Cambridge and Oxford* (London, 1748), p. 21.
5. *An Act to amend and enlarge The Powers of the Act passed in the Eleventh Year of His Present Majesty's Reign . . . for making improvements within the University and City of Oxford* (1705), 21 Geo. III. 1781.
6. Mozley, *Reminiscences chiefly of Oriel College*, Vol. I, p. 69.
7. *A Few General Directions etc.* (Oxford, 1795), p. 6.
8. See Chapter XI.
9. *Uffenbach*, pp. 2 and 38.
10. Salmon, *The Foreigner's Companion etc.*, p. 80.
11. MS journal of John Skinner, Vol. II, p. 113.
12. *Uffenbach*, p. 60.
13. Salmon, *The Foreigner's Companion etc.*, p. 26.
14. Woodforde, 12 July 1762.
15. A. Pope, *Epistle IV, To Burlington. Of the Use of Riches*, ll. 117–20.

16. J. G. Jackson, *Wadham College* (Oxford, 1893), p. 216.
17. *Uffenbach*, p. 32.
18. Wadham College Convention Book, 1719–1828.
19. *Uffenbach*, p. 24.
20. Salmon, *The Foreigner's Companion etc.*, p. 62.
21. *A Pocket Companion for Oxford* (1761), pp. 67–8.
22. Ibid., p. 55.
23. *Uffenbach*, p. 8.
24. Woodforde, 22 May 1760.
25. Hearne, 25 Oct. 1727, Vol. IX, p. 361. A print after J. M. W. Turner shows this barren turfed quad and the 'Silly Statue' on a large square plinth.
26. Hearne, 12 April 1706, Vol. I, p. 224.
27. *The Gentleman and Lady's Pocket Companion for Oxford* (Oxford, 1747), p. 46.
28. See Chapter VII.
29. Amhurst, *Strephon's Revenge*, pp. 6–7.
30. *The Oxford Toast's Answer to the Terrae Filius Speech*, p. 11.
31. *Memoirs of an Oxford Scholar*, p. 75.
32. Salmon, *The Foreigner's Companion*, p. 67.
33. Thornton and Coleman, *The Student*, Vol. II, p. 51.
34. Evans, *Letters of Richard Radcliffe and John James*, Feb. 1779.
35. MS journal of John Skinner, Vol. II, p. 51.
36. *A Few General Directions etc.*, p. 5.
37. Gibbon, *Memoirs of the Life of Edward Gibbon*, p. 61.
38. T. Warton, *A Companion to the Guide, and a Guide to the Companion* (London, 1760), p. 40.
39. MS journal of John Skinner, Vol. II, p. 237. Josiah Pullen (1631–1714) was Vice-Principal of Magdalen Hall and from 1675 vicar of St Peter-in-the-East. He was a great walker. The elm tree which he planted at the head of the footpath to Headington grew to great proportions, and survived until 1894 when it was felled.

40. Philips, 'The Diary of Erasmus Philips', 19 Sept. 1721.
41. Woodforde, 9, 10, 12, 18 April 1763.
42. Dibdin, *Reminiscences of a Literary Life*, Vol. I, p. 82.
43. Hearne, 10 June 1715, Vol. V, p. 65.
44. Ibid., 28 March 1716, Vol. V, p. 188.
45. Ibid., 26 March 1716, Vol. V, p. 186.
46. Ibid., 11 March 1718, Vol. VI, p. 154.
47. Ibid., 7 June 1718, Vol. VI, p. 182.

CHAPTER NINE: *Sports and Pastimes*

1. Stephen Penton, *The Guardian's Instruction* (London, 1688), p. 56.
2. *A Few General Directions etc.* (1795), p. 9.
3. *Advice to the Universities of Oxford and Cambridge* (1783), pp. 56–7.
4. Statute 11 July 1772.
5. *An Act to amend and enlarge the Powers of the Act etc.* (1781).
6. Evans, *Letters of Richard Radcliffe and John James*; James jr to Boucher, 16 Sept. 1781, p. 155.
7. Hearne, 29 Nov. 1730, Vol. X, p. 358.
8. *JOJ*, 14 July 1753.
9. Warton, *The Oxford Sausage*, p. 43.
10. Letter dated 13 July 1733 (Bodleian MS Don. c. 152).
11. Green, *Lincoln*, p. 409.
12. Woodforde, 20 April 1763.
13. Philips, 'The Diary of Erasmus Philips', 5 Aug. 1722.
14. Woodforde, 18 May 1763.
15. Ibid., 7 July; 20, 22, 25 April 1763.
16. Philips, 'The Diary of Erasmus Philips', 21 April, 26 Aug., 9 Sept., 14 Sept. 1721; 16 May, 4 and 5 July 1722.
17. BL Landsdowne MS 841, f. 177.
18. Philips, 'The Diary of Erasmus Philips', 18 Sept. 1722.
19. Hearne, 6 Sept. 1706, Vol. I, p. 287.
20. Philips, 'The Diary of Erasmus Philips', 12 Sept. 1722.
21. *JOJ*, 27 Aug. 1768.

22. *Uffenbach*, pp. 50 and 52.
23. *JOJ*, 13 Sept. 1755; 22 Aug. 1767.
24. Hearne, 24 Aug. 1725, Vol. IX, p. 9; 8 Sept. 1729, Vol. X, p. 174; 3 Sept. 1730, Vol. X, p. 327; 31 Aug. 1732, Vol. XI, p. 103.
25. *JOJ*, 7 Aug. 1790; 31 July 1790; 25 Aug. 1753; 12 Sept. 1767; 18 June 1768; 7 Aug. 1790; 30 July 1774.
26. Philips, 'The Diary of Erasmus Philips', 28 March 1721.
27. Hearne, 3 Sept. 1735, Vol. IX, p. 16; 15 Oct. 1719, Vol. VII, p. 56.
28. *JOJ*, 20 Nov. 1762.
29. Austen, *The Loiterer*, no. 21.
30. Ibid., no. 58.
31. Thompson, *Letters of Humphrey Prideaux to John Ellis*, 28 July 1674.
32. Statutum de reprimendis sumptibus non Academicis, 1772.
33. Newton, *A Scheme of Discipline*, p. 25.
34. Trinity Liber Decani 1, 15 April 1778; Worcester Book no. 10, 29 Oct. 1785.
35. Woodforde, 4 Nov. 1760.
36. Ibid., 10 July 1761; 24 July 1761; 14 Oct. 1761; 26 Oct. 1761; 16 Nov. 1761; 28 Jan. 1762.
37. *JOJ*, (to note but a few): 21 May 1763; 3 Feb. 1770; 1 Jan. 1771; 24 Dec. 1774; 2 Aug. 1777; 15 Nov. 1777; 29 May 1779; 5 June 1779; 12 June 1779; 11 Aug. 1781; 15 Sept. 1781; 13 July 1782; 9 Nov. 1782; 12 March 1785; 7 July 1787; 13 Oct. 1787; 10 Oct. 1789; 21 Nov. 1789; 13 March 1790; 5 Feb. 1791.
38. D'Anvers, *Academia*, p. 51.
39. John Bowring (ed.), *Memoirs of Jeremy Bentham* in *The Works* (Edinburgh, 1838–43), Vol. X, p. 39.
40. *JOJ*, 30 June 1787.
41. Ibid., 3 Oct. 1772; 30 Jan. 1773.
42. Hearne, 3 May 1716, Vol. V, p. 215.
43. Ibid., 5 Oct. 1705, Vol. I, p. 52.
44. Order of 16 April 1739.
45. *JOJ*, passim!
46. BL Landsdowne MS 841 f. 177.
47. Philips, 'The Diary of Erasmus Philips', 13 Feb. 1722.
48. Penton, *The Guardian's Instruction*, p. 81.
49. Warton, *A Companion to the Guide etc.*, p. 11.
50. P. Manning, *Sport and Pastime in Stuart Oxford* (Oxford Historical Society, Vol. LXXV, 1923). Today the court in Merton Street is still in use; the court in Oriel Street is now in the midst of extensive college development; the third court has disappeared although the former teashop at the corner of Blue Boar Lane and St Aldates was called The Rackett.
51. Woodforde, 29 April 1760; 4 June 1761.
52. Ibid., 9 June 1763.
53. *JOJ*, 26 May 1770; 6 June 1767; 18 July 1772; 21 May 1774; 16 July 1774; 6 Aug. 1774; 25 July 1778; 15 Sept. 1781; 16 May 1789; 17 July 1790; 30 July 1796.
54. G. Bolton, *The History of the O.U.C.C.* (Oxford, 1962), pp. 1–3.
55. R. L. Edgeworth, *The Memoirs of Richard Lowell Edgeworth* (London, 1820), Vol. I, p. 91; and *JOJ*, 16 March 1793.
56. Woodforde, 9 Dec. 1760.
57. *JOJ*, 25 Oct. 1755; 15 Oct. 1768; 15 Oct. 1791; 18 May 1793; 20 Jan. 1798; 3 Aug. 1799.
58. Woodforde, 7 May 1761.
59. Samuel Johnson, *The Letters of Samuel Johnson*, ed. R. W. Chapman (Oxford, 1952), Vol. II, p. 115; Vol. III, p. 263.
60. Colman, *Terrae Filius*, no. 4, p. 60.
61. Southey, *The Life and Correspondence of Robert Southey*, Vol. I, p. 176.
62. *The Village Curate*, pp. 81 and 94.
63. Polewhele, *The Follies of Oxford*, pp. 201–4 and 211–16.
64. *Epistle to a College friend, written in the Country*, n.pl. (1775), II. 97–112.
65. MS journal of John Skinner, Vol. II, p. 112.
66. F. Sidgwick (ed.), *The Poems of George Wither* (London, 1902), Vol. I, p. 148.
67. *The Oxonian* (1778), p. 12.
68. Southey, *The Life and Correspondence of Robert Southey*, Vol. I, p. 176.

69. Hearne, 10 June, 1718, Vol. VI, p. 186.
70. Warton, *A Companion to the Guide etc.*, p. 34.
71. D'Anvers, *Academia*, p. 48.
72. Woodforde, 20 July 1761; 27 June 1763.
73. Hearne, 31 Oct. 1718, Vol. VI, p. 404; 19 July 1730, Vol. X, p. 309.
74. Philips, 'The Diary of Erasmus Philips', 3 July 1722.
75. Ibid., 19 Sept. 1721.
76. Woodforde, 26 May 1760.
77. MS journal of John Skinner, Vol. II, pp. 98–9.
78. Philips, 'The Diary of Erasmus Philips', 4 July 1721.
79. Woodforde, 25 Aug. 1774.
80. See Chapter VI, page 77.
81. *JOJ*, 14 July 1759; 14 May 1763; 25 March 1769; 15 July 1769; 13 April 1776; 28 May 1796; 27 May 1797.
82. Ibid., 26 March 1785.
83. Ibid., Jan. 1798.
84. MS journal of John Skinner; Letter III to Wm. P — Esq., Vol. II, p. 33.
85. *The Anecdote Book of John Scott, Lord Eldon* in Twiss, *The Life of Lord Eldon*, Vol. I, p. 54.
86. Woodforde, 24 Jan. 1762.
87. Ibid., 3, 4, 5, 6, 10, 11, 12, 13, 14, 18, 19, 21, 22, 24, 25, 27 Jan. 1763.
88. *JOJ*, 22 Jan. 1763; 8 Jan. 1763; 29 Jan. 1763.

CHAPTER TEN: *The Theatre and Music*

1. Thompson, *Letters of Humphrey Prideaux etc.*, 28 July 1774, p. 5.
2. A. D'Anvers, *The Oxford Act* (London, 1693), pp. 14–15.
3. Hearne, Vol. II, p. 411, note 26.
4. R. W. Lowe (ed.) *An Apology for the Life of Mr. Colley Cibber* (London, 1889), Vol. II, p. 133; Vol. II, pp. 134–5; Vol. II, p. 138; Vol. II, pp. 138–9; Vol. II, p. 137.
5. *The University Miscellany*, The Players' Epilogue, p. 25.
6. Hist. MSS Commission Duke of Portland, Vol. III, p. 154.
7. Hearne, 6 July 1733, Vol. XI, p. 225.
8. Woodforde, 3 June 1774.
9. Amhurst, *Terrae Filius*, no. 30, 22 April 1721.
10. *JOJ*, 16 Dec. 1786.
11. Ibid., 6 Jan. 1787.
12. Ibid., 12 Jan. 1754; 30 March 1754; 17 Jan. 1756; 13 March 1756; 1 Sept. 1759; 6 July 1765; 12 Oct. 1765; 12 Dec. 1767; 25 June 1768; 4 Feb. 1769; 11 March 1769; 23 May 1769; 27 May 1769; 28 Oct. 1769; 12 Jan. 1771; 29 June 1776; 17 Oct. 1778; 22 July 1780.
13. Ibid., 12 Jan. 1754.
14. Ibid., 12 Jan. 1754 to 20 Aug. 1774; 17 Jan. 1756; 29 Jan. 1763; 6 July 1765; 12 Oct. 1765; 27 Nov. 1773; 23 July 1774; 29 June 1776; 22 July 1780; 28 June 1783; 4 March 1786; 6 May 1786; 13 Jan. 1787; 10 March 1798; 4 May 1799.
15. Ibid., 8 Oct. 1757; 17 Jan. 1756; 12 Oct. 1765; 27 Nov. 1773; 12 Feb. 1774; 1 July 1780; 28 June 1783; 13 Jan. 1787; 14 June 1788.
16. Ibid, 6 Feb. 1773.
17. Ibid., 15 Jan. and 5 Feb. 1774.
18. Ibid., 7 Jan. 1775.
19. Ibid., 9 Nov. 1776.
20. Ibid., 25 Oct., 15 Nov., 29 Nov. 1777.
21. Ibid., 25 Dec. 1779; 12 Aug. 1780; 2 Feb. 1782.
22. Ibid., 3 Nov. 1787.
23. W. F. Mavor, *A New Description of Blenheim* (London, 1789), pp. 41–2 and *JOJ*, 19 Jan. 1788.
24. David Fairer (ed.), *The Correspondence of Thomas Warton* (Oxford, 1995); Leter 556 to Charlotte Warton, 14 Nov. 1788.
25. *JOJ*, 18 Oct. 1788; 28 Nov. 1789.
26. *Reading Mercury*, 25 June 1792.
27. *JOJ*, 9 Jan. 1790; 18 Sept. 1790; 10 Dec. 1791; 24 Dec. 1791; 23 June 1792; 7 July 1792; 13 Oct. 1792.
28. For a fuller account of the Blenheim and Walgrave theatres, see S. Rosenfeld, *Temples of Thespis* (London, 1978), Chapters II and VII.
29. Colman, *Terrae Filius*, no. 2, p. 28.
30. Possibly the company and its manager being great favourites of the

King at Windsor helped to overcome Vice-Chancellarian opposition.

31. *Monthly Mirror*, Sept. 1802.
32. *JOJ*, 17 Aug. 1799; 31 Aug. 1799; 14 Sept. 1799. For a fuller account of these performances see *Review of English Studies*, Oct. 1943, p. 366, S. Rosenfeld, 'Some Notes on the players in Oxford'.
33. *The Oxford Act A.D. 1733* (London, 1734), p. 44.
34. Hearne, 5 July 1733, Vol. XI, p. 224; 6 July 1733, Vol. XI, p. 225; 28 April 1734, Vol. XI, p. 331.
35. *The Oxford Act*, p. 44.
36. *Gentleman's Magazine*, no. xxxiii (1763), p. 349.
37. *JOJ*, 6 July 1793.
38. Woodforde, 5 July 1774.
39. Bodleian G.A. Oxon. b 19.254 a. 6.
40. Faircr, *The Correspondence of Thomas Warton*; Letter 556 to Charlotte Warton, 14 Nov. 1788.
41. Hearne, 29 Aug. 1717, Vol. VI, p. 84.
42. *JOJ*, 24 Oct. 1778.
43. *The Oxford Act*, p. 45.
44. Hearne, 10 April 1725, Vol. VIII, p. 355.
45. *Uffenbach*, p. 36.
46. Thornton and Coleman, *The Student*, Vol. I, p. 131.
47. *The Oxford Act*, p. 56.
48. For more detail on the Music Room and its activities see Susan Wollenberg's chapter, 'Music and Musicians', in *The History of the University of Oxford*, Vol. V, p. 865.
49. *JOJ*, 18 March 1758; 20 March 1762; 9 May 1789; 23 Jan. 1790; 17 Dec. 1791; 28 Jan. 1792.
50. MS journal of John Skinner, Vol. II, pp. 45–9.
51. *JOJ*, 24 Feb. 1781.
52. Philips, 'The Diary of Erasmus Philips', Vol. X, p. 443.
53. Thornton and Coleman, *The Student*, no. 3, 31 March 1750.
54. *JOJ*, 8 May 1756; 22 Nov. 1760; 17 March 1764; 8 March 1766; 19 May 1770; 1 Dec. 1764; 5 July 1793.
55. Linnell, *The Diaries of Thomas Wilson*, 2 Feb. 1732.

CHAPTER ELEVEN: *The Theatre of the Streets*

1. Hearne, 23 March 1710, Vol. II, p. 365.
2. Ibid., 1 April 1710, Vol. II, p. 365.
3. Ibid., 19 May 1715, Vol. V, p. 62.
4. Ibid., 18 June 1727, Vol. IX, p. 317.
5. Ibid., 14 April 1733, Vol. XI, p. 185. 'Serpents' are firecrackers, rip-raps.
6. *JOJ*, 7 May 1763.
7. Ibid., 14 March 1789.
8. Ibid., 14 June 1794.
9. Woodforde, 2 Feb. 1761.
10. Ibid., 28 Feb. 1763.
11. Ibid., 22 March 1762.
12. Ibid., 13 March 1775.
13. Mant, *The Poetical Works of Thomas Warton*, introductory memoir, p. ciii.
14. Hearne, 31 March 1721, Vol. VII, p. 228.
15. Ibid., 4 Aug. 1727, Vol. IX, p. 335.
16. Ibid., 31 March 1721, Vol. VII, p. 228.
17. Ibid., 30 July 1730, Vol. X, p. 314.
18. Ibid., 20 Oct. 1721, Vol. VII, p. 287.
19. Ibid., 13 Jan. 1727, Vol. IX, p. 257.
20. Ibid., 17 June, 1731, Vol. X, p. 428.
21. Ibid., 11 Aug. 1730, Vol. X, p. 316.
22. Ibid., 8 Sept. 1730, Vol. X, p. 316.
23. *JOJ*, 16 Nov. 1793.
24. Ibid., 2 March 1799.
25. Hearne, 13 Aug. 1725, Vol. IX, p. 2.
26. Ibid., 5 Sept. 1723, Vol. VIII, p. 113.
27. Ibid., 21 July 1715, Vol. V, p. 79.
28. Ibid., 26 Oct. 1728, Vol. X, p. 60.
29. *JOJ*, 7 Feb. 1784.
30. Ibid., 14 Feb. 1784; 21 Feb. 1784.
31. Ibid., 20 March 1784; 1 May 1784.
32. Ibid., 15, 20 May 1784.
33. Ibid., 24 July 1784.
34. Ibid., 4, 11 Sept. 1784.
35. Ibid., 6, 13, 20 Nov. 1784.
36. Ibid., 21 Feb. 1784; 5 June 1784; 28 Aug. 1784; 27 Nov. 1784.
37. Ibid., 15 Jan. 1785; 7 May 1785; 21, 28 May 1785.
38. Ibid., 25 June 1785.
39. Colman, *Terrae Filius*, no. 1, p. 12.
40. Woodforde, 12 July 1762.
41. Hearne, 30 Sept. 1725, Vol. IX, p. 34.

42. *JOJ*, 25 June 1757; 13 Feb. 1762; 16 Nov. 1771; 11 April 1772; 10 May 1777; Jan. 1779; 10 Nov. 1787; 13 Nov. 1790; 25 Sept. 1790; 6 Dec. 1794.

43. Ibid., 6 Dec. 1755; 6 May 1786.

44. Ibid., 1 April 1758; 18 Feb. 1764; 16 March 1765; 14 Nov. 1789.

45. Ibid., 1 Dec. 1764; 24 May 1783; 7 April 1787; 28 May 1757; 6 May 1769; 25 Oct. 1794; 19 April 1755; 12 May 1759; 26 May 1764; 12 June 1756; 16 Feb. 1765; 23 April 1757.

46. Ibid., 8 Dec. 1759; 26 Oct. 1771; 22 March 1777; 3, 10 Nov., 1 Dec. 1792; 23 April 1796; 30 April 1796; 7 May 1796.

Bibliography

Allardyce, A. (ed.), *Letters from and to Charles Kirkpatrick Sharpe, Esq.* (Edinburgh and London, 1888).

Amhurst, N., *Strephon's Revenge: A Satire on the Oxford Toasts* inscribed to the author of *Merton Walks* (London, 1718).

Amhurst, N., *Terrae Filius* (London, 1721; the collected edn, 1726).

Amhurst, N., *Oculus Britanniae: an Heroic-Panegyrical Poem on the University of Oxford* (London, 1724).

An Act to amend and enlarge The Powers of an Act passed in the Eleventh Year of His Present Majesty's Reign . . . for making improvements within the University and City of Oxford (1705), 21 George III, 1781.

Anon., *A Letter of Advice to a Young Gentleman at the University and Directions for Young Students* (London, 1701).

Anon., *A Step to Oxford* (London, 1704).

Anon., *The Servitour: a Poem. Written by a Servitour of the University of Oxford, and faithfully taken from his Own original Copy* (London, 1709).

Anon., *Magdalen-Grove: or, A Dialogue between the Doctor and the Devil* (London, 1713).

Anon., *The Miscellany, or, More Burning Work for the Ox---fo-d Convocation* (London, 1713).

Anon., *Merton Walks, or the Oxford Beauties, a Poem* (London, 1717).

Anon., *The Oxford Toast's Answer to the Terrae Filius Speech* (Oxford, 1723).

Anon., *The Humours of Oxford, a Comedy* by a gentleman of Wadham College (Dublin, 1730).

Anon., *Alma Mater, a Satirical Poem* by a gentleman of New Inn Hall (Oxford, 1733).

Anon., *The Terrae Filius's Speech as it was to have been Spoken at the Publick Act, 1733* (London, 1733).

Anon., *A plea against an order to inhibit Wine-Cellars lately opened in Oxford* (Oxford, 1734) (Bod. G.A. Oxon. 4 6 (11)).

Anon., *The Oxford Act A.D. 1733* (London, 1734).

Anon., *A Faithful Narrative of the Proceedings in a Late Affair between The Rev. Mr. John Swinton and Mr. George Baker, Both of Wadham College, Oxford . . . To which is* prefix'd a Particular Account of the Proceedings against Robert Thistlethwayte, late Doctor of Divinity, and Warden of Wadham College, for a Sodomitical Attempt upon Mr. W. French, Commoner of the same College (London, 1739).

Anon., College-Wit Sharpen'd: or, The Head of a House with a Sting in the Tail . . . Address'd to the Two Famous Universities of S–d–m and G–m–rr–h, subtitled The Wadhamites (London, 1739).

Anon., An Address to the worshipful Company of Barbers in Oxford (Oxford, 1749).

Anon., Memoirs of an Oxford Scholar written by himself (London, 1756).

Anon., The New Oxford Guide (Oxford, 1759).

Anon., An Address to the Freemen and other Inhabitants of the City of Oxford (Oxford, 1764).

Anon., Remarks on some Strictures lately published, entitled Observations upon the Statute Tit. XIV, De Vestitu et Habitu Scholastico (Oxford, 1770).

Anon., Epistle to a College Friend, written in the Country, n.pl. (1775).

Anon., The Oxonian, a Poem. In Imitation of The Splendid Shilling (Oxford, 1778).

Anon., The Cruelty, Injustice, and Impolicy of the present mode of Information and Punishment relative to Prostitution Established in the University (Oxford, 1779).

Anon., Advice to the Universities of Oxford and Cambridge (London, 1783).

Anon., A Letter to a Young Gentleman of Fortune, just entered at the University (Oxford, 1784).

Anon., A Few General Directions for the Conduct of Young Gentlemen in the University of Oxford (Oxford, 1795).

Anon., Oxford during the Last Century in The Oxford Chronicle for 1859, Jan.–April, July–Nov. 1859.

Anon., Antiquities of Oriel Common Room in The Oriel Record, Dec. 1925.

Austen, J. (ed.), The Loiterer (Oxford, 1790).

Baker, T., An Act at Oxford, a Comedy, by the author of the Yeoman o' Kent (London, 1704).

Beresford, J. (ed.), The Diary of a Country Parson, the Reverend James Woodforde (Oxford, 1931).

Blakiston, H. E. D., Trinity College (Oxford, 1898).

Bolton, G., The History of the O.U.C.C. (Oxford, 1962).

Boswell, J., The Life of Samuel Johnson, D.D. (Oxford Standard Authors, 2 vols, 1904).

Boswell, J., A Journal of a Tour to the Hebrides, ed. F. A. Pottle and C. H. Bennett (London, 1963).

Bowring, J. (ed.), Memoirs of Jeremy Bentham in Vol. X of The Works of Jeremy Bentham (Edinburgh, 1838–43).

Brasenose Quatercentenary Monographs, Vol. II, Pt. i, Monograph XIII (Oxford Historical Society, liii, 1909).

Burnet, G., A History of my own Time, ed. G. Burnet and T. Burnet (London, 1724–34).

Campbell, T., Diary of a visit to England in 1775 by an Irishman, ed. S. Raymond (Sydney, 1854).

Cockburn, Lord, The Life of Lord Jeffrey (Edinburgh, 1852).

Colman, G., Terrae Filius nos 1–4 (Oxford, 1763).

Colman, G., The Oxonian in Town, A Comedy (Dublin, 1769; London, 1770).

Corpus Christi Wager Book, 1745–1808, in the college archives.

Crosse, A. H. (ed.), *Memorials, Scientific and Literary, of Andrew Crosse, the Electrician* (London, 1857).

D'Anvers, A., *Academia: or the Humours of the University of Oxford* (London, 1691).

D'Anvers, A., *The Oxford Act: A Poem* (London, 1693).

Dibden, T. F., *Reminiscences of a Literary Life* (London, 1836).

Edgeworth, R. L., *The memoirs of Richard Lovell Edgeworth Esq.* (London, 1820).

Evans, M. (ed.), *The Letters of Richard Radcliffe and John James* (Oxford Historical Society, 1888).

Fairer, D. (ed.), *The Correspondence of Thomas Warton* (Oxford, 1995).

Fowler, T., *The History of Corpus Christi College* (Oxford Historical Society, Vol. XXV, 1893).

Gentleman's Magazine, 1758, xxviii, p. 176; 1763, xxxiii, p. 348; 1772, xlii, p. 401; 1787, lvii, pp. 1146–7; 1798, lxviii, pt I, pp. 14–16, 282–5.

Gibbon, E., *The Memoirs of the Life of Edward Gibbon*, ed. G. B. Hill (London, 1900).

Graves, R., *Recollections of some particulars in the Life of the late William Shenstone Esq.* (London, 1788).

Green, J. R., *Oxford Studies* (London, 1901).

Green, V. H. H., *Lincoln* (Oxford, 1979).

Green, V. H. H., 'The University and Social Life' in *The History of the University of Oxford*, Vol. V: *The Eighteenth Century* (Oxford, 1986).

Gray, Thomas, *The Correspondence of Thomas Gray*, ed. P. Toynbee and L. Whitley (Oxford, 1935).

Harris, James, 1st Earl of Malmesbury, *Diaries and Correspondence* (London, 1844).

Hawkins, J., *The Life of Dr. Samuel Johnson* (London, 1787).

Heany, J., *Oxford, The Seat of the Muses* (Oxford, 1738).

Hearne, T., *Collections*, ed. C. E. Doble and H. E. Salter (Oxford Historical Society, 1885–1918).

Hodgkin, R. H., *Six Centuries of an Oxford College* (Oxford, 1949).

Holberg, L., *Memoirs of Lewis Holberg written by himself in Latin, and now first translated into English* (London, 1829).

Hurdis, J., *The Village Curate, a Poem* (London, 1788).

Hurdis, J., *A Word or two in vindication of the University of Oxford and of Magdalen College in Particular from the Posthumous Aspersions of Mr. Gibbon* (Bishopstone, c. 1800).

Jackson, J. G., *Wadham College* (Oxford, 1893).

Jackson's Oxford Journal, 5 May 1753, and through the eighteenth century.

Jenkins, D. B. (ed.), *The Life of the Rev. Thomas Charles, B.A., of Bala* (Denbigh, 1908).

Johnson, Samuel, *The Letters of Samuel Johnson*, ed. R. W. Chapman (Oxford, 1952).

Knox, V., *Liberal Education* (London, 1781).

L.G.W.L. (ed.), *A little book of Recipes of New College, two hundred years ago* (Oxford; privately printed, 1922).

Linnell, C. L. S. (ed.), *The Diaries of Thomas Wilson, D.D., 1731–7 and 1750* (London, 1964).

Loggan, D., *Oxonia Illustrata* (Oxford, 1675).

Lowe, R. W. (ed.), *An Apology for the Life of Mr. Colley Cibber* (London, 1889).

Madan, F., *A Century of the Phoenix Common Room* (Oxford, 1888).

Manning, P., *Some notes on the early history of Boating in Oxford* (Oxford, 1904).

Manning, P., *Sport and Pastime in Stuart Oxford* (Oxford Historical Society, Vol. LXXV, 1923).

Mant, R. (ed.), *The Poetical Works of the late Thomas Warton* (Oxford, 1802), Introduction.

Mavor, W. F., *A New Description of Blenheim* (London, 1789).

Mawdsley, W. N. (ed.), *Woodforde at Oxford* (Oxford Historical Society, NS Vol. XXI, 1969).

Milles, Jeremiah, his Diary, Balliol College Library.

Mitchell, L. G., *The History of the University of Oxford. Vol. V: The Eighteenth Century* (Oxford, 1986).

Moritz, C. P., *Travels, chiefly on foot, through several parts of England, in 1782* (London, 1795).

Mozley, T., *Reminiscences chiefly of Oriel College and the Oxford Movement* (London, 1882).

Newton, R., *A Scheme of Discipline with Statutes intended to be established by a Royal Charter for the Education of Youth in Hart-Hall in the University of Oxford* (Oxford, 1720).

Oxford Magazine; or, University Museum (London, 1768–74), various contributors.

Parker, S. et al., *The Booksellers of Oxford on the inconvenience of allowing Students unlimited credit* (Bodleian MS Top. Oxon. d.247, 1779).

Penton, Stephen, *The Guardian's Instruction* (London, 1688).

Philips, E., 'Extracts from the Diary of Erasmus Philips, Fellow Commoner of Pembroke', in *Notes and Queries*, 2nd ser., Vol. X, pp. 366 and 443.

Philips, J., *The Splendid Shilling* (London, 1705).

Polewhele, R., *The Follies of Oxford, or, Cursory Sketches on a University Education to his Friend in the Country* (London, 1785).

Pope, A., *The Correspondence of Alexander Pope*, ed. G. Sherburn (Oxford, 1956).

Pope, A., *The Poems of Alexander Pope*, Twickenham edition (London, 1939–61).

Prevost, the Abbé, *Memoires et Aventures d'un Homme de Qualité*, ed. M. Robertson (Paris, 1927).

Programmes of music in the theatre at Encaenia, 2, 4, 6, 7, 8 July 1793 (Bodleian, Gough, Oxf. 90 (29).

Puddle, W., *The Rival Shoe-Black* (Oxford, *c.* 1800), (Bodleian, Gough, Oxf. 90 (39).

Quarrell, W. H. and Quarrell, W. J. C. (eds), *Oxford in 1710, from the Travels of C. Z. von Uffenbach* (Oxford, 1928).

Quiller-Couch, A. T., *Reminiscences of Oxford* (Oxford, 1892).

Salmon, Mr, *The Foreigner's Companion through the Universities of Cambridge and Oxford* (London, 1748).

Skinner, J., his MS journal containing 'Sketches at Oxford' (BL MS. Add. 33634).

Southey, C. C. (ed.), *The Life and Correspondence of Robert Southey* (London, 1849).

Stone, L., 'The Size and Composition of the Oxford Student Body, 1580–1910', in *The University in Society* (Princeton, 1975).

Thompson, E. M. (ed.), *The Letters of Humphrey Prideaux to John Ellis* (Camden Society, NS XV, Westminster, 1874).

Thornton, C. and Coleman (eds), *The Student, or the Oxford Monthly Miscellany* (Oxford, 1750).

Thornton, C. and McLaughlin, F. (eds), *The Fothergills of Ravenstone Dale* (London, 1905).

Twiss, H., *The Public and Private Life of Lord Eldon, with selections from his correspondence* (London, 1844).

Walker, J., *Oxoniana* (London, 1809).

Warton, T., *Journal of a Fellow of a College* (London, *Idler*, no. 33, 1758).

Warton, T., *A Companion to the Guide, and a Guide to the Companion* (London, 1760).

Warton, T. (ed.), *The Oxford Sausage: or Select Poetical Pieces, written by the most celebrated Wits of the University of Oxford* (London, 1764).

Welsh, C., *A Bookseller of the Last century* (London, 1885).

Whitfield, G. A., *Short Account of God's Dealings with the Revd. George Whitfield* (London, 1740).

Williams, W., *Oxonia Depicta* (Oxford, 1733).

Wither, G., *The Poems of George Wither*, ed. F. Sidgwick (London, 1902).

Wollenberg, S. L. F., 'Music and Musicians', in *The History of the University of Oxford*, Vol. V: *The Eighteenth Century* (Oxford, 1986).

Wood, A., *The History and Antiquities of the Colleges and Halls in the University of Oxford*, ed. J. Gutch (Oxford, 1786–90).

Wood, A., *The Life and Times of*, ed. A. Clark (Oxford, 1894).

Wordsworth, C., *Social Life at the English Universities in the Eighteenth Century* (Cambridge, 1874).

Index

Page numbers in *italic* refer to illustrations